DATA STRUCTURES

An Advanced Approach
Using C

Jeffrey Esakov

Tom Weiss

PRENTICE HALL SOFTWARE SERIES
Brian W. Kernighan, Series Editor

PRENTICE HALL, Englewood Cliffs, New Jersey 07632

Library of Congress Cataloging-in-Publication Data

ESAKOV, JEFFREY.
    Data structures : and advanced approach using C / Jeffrey Esakov,
Tom Weiss.

      p.   cm.
    Includes index.
    ISBN 0-13-198847-6 :
    1. C (Computer program language)   2. Data structures (Computer
science) I. Weiss, Tom. II. Title.
QA76.73.C15E83 1989
005.13'3—dc19   88-28856
               CIP

Editorial/production supervision: John Fleming
Cover design: Lundgren Graphics, Ltd.
Manufacturing buyer: Mary Noonan

The author and publisher of this book have used their best efforts in preparing this book. These efforts include development, research, and testing of the theories and programs to determine their effectiveness. The author and publisher make no warranty of any kind, expressed or implied, with regard to these programs or the documentation contained in this book. The author and publisher shall not be liable in any event for incidental or consequential damages in connection with, or arising out of, the furnishing, performance, or use of these programs.

 © 1989 by Prentice-Hall, Inc.
A Division of Simon & Schuster
Englewood Cliffs, New Jersey 07632

Printed in the United States of America

10 9 8 7 6 5 4 3

ISBN 0-13-198847-6

Prentice-Hall International (UK) Limited, *London*
Prentice-Hall of Australia Pty. Limited, *Sydney*
Prentice-Hall Canada Inc., *Toronto*
Prentice-Hall Hispanoamericana, S.A., *Mexico*
Prentice-Hall of India Private Limited, *New Delhi*
Prentice-Hall of Japan, Inc., *Tokyo*
Simon & Schuster Asia Pte. Ltd., *Singapore*
Editora Prentice-Hall do Brasil, Ltda., *Rio de Janeiro*

CONTENTS

PREFACE

This is a text for a one-semester college course in data structures. It provides both a strong theoretical basis in data structures and an advanced approach to their representation in C. It should prove useful to C programmers as well as computer science students.

The organization we have chosen is somewhat different from most other books on this subject. Early programming languages had neither pointers nor dynamic memory allocation, so most data structures, including linked lists, were based on arrays. In such a situation, it is logical to start the presentation with stacks and queues as they are easily coded using arrays. In this book, array representations are deemphasized. Dynamic linked lists are presented first, as they provide a natural tool for building subsequent data structures. Although an array implementation of stacks is provided (this technique is straightforward and widely used), array-based simulation of linked lists is omitted.

Another important difference is that the data structures are presented within the context of complete working programs that have been tested both on a UNIX™ system and a personal computer (using Borland's Turbo C™ compiler). The code is developed in a top-down fashion, typically with the low-level data structure implementation following the high-level application code. This approach helps foster good programming habits and makes the subject matter more interesting. Applications vary from a simple parenthesis checker to a sophisticated LISP interpreter.

This book has three goals: to develop a consistent programming methodology, to develop data structure access techniques, and to introduce algorithms. The bulk of the text is devoted to data structures. Programming style and development methodology are introduced as the applications are presented. This has the advantage of allowing the reader to concentrate on the data structures, while showing how good practices can make programming easier.

We chose C from a desire to present polymorphic data structures which can store data of any type without requiring modification of the code. There are not many programming languages that support this concept. Strongly typed languages such as Pascal clearly do not. LISP was a possibility, however, we chose C for several reasons. Although LISP is a good language for programming data structures, C is more efficient and better standardized. Furthermore, since C is becoming the language of choice at many universities, a text combining both C and data structures provides an easy way of gaining proficiency in both.

We assume the reader has a basic knowledge of C or some other high-level language. Since this book employs sophisticated programming techniques, Chapter 1 presents a variety of advanced C concepts, including structures, pointers, typedef, unions, enumerated types, and parameter passing.

Chapter 2 introduces recursion. Proper and improper use of recursion is distinguished with a variety of examples. Divide and conquer algorithms and tail recursion are also discussed.

Chapter 3 contains an overview of data abstraction, polymorphism, and the software engineering principles used throughout the book.

The study of data structures begins with lists in Chapter 4. The basic technique for dynamic memory allocation used throughout the book is described. Linear linked lists are presented in the context of a polynomial addition program and a graphical display list program.

Stacks and queues are covered in Chapter 5. Static array, dynamic array, and list implementations of stacks are used in a parenthesis checker, graphical fill routine, and infix-to-postfix translator. Queues are used in an operating system simulation.

Chapter 6 presents advanced list applications. A LISP interpreter uses circular linked lists, a text editor uses doubly-linked lists, and sparse matrix routines are implemented using lists with header nodes.

Chapter 7 covers binary trees. Dynamically allocated trees are presented in the context of an expression evaluator. Heaps are used to represent priority queues in a continuation of the operating system simulation presented in Chapter 5. N-ary trees used to implement a small game.

The book concludes with sets and sorting in chapter 8. Since the focus of this chapter is algorithms, there are no complete applications. O notation is introduced as a basis for analyzing algorithms. This technique is used to compare a variety of sorting algorithms and set implementations.

The material adheres very closely to ACM CS2. Knowledgeable readers may wish to skip Chapters 1 and 2. All subsequent chapters use linked lists developed in Chapter 4; it is therefore important that the topics in that chapter be fully understood. Section 5.5, Chapter 6, and Chapter 8, may be omitted if desired. A fast-moving course should be able to cover the entire book.

The text was typeset using LATEX. Apple Computer courteously provided a Macintosh computer to draw the figures. Camera-ready copy was generated using an Apple Laserwriter™.

We would like to thank the reviewers, Dr. Peter Allen (Columbia University), Dr. Alan Filipski, and Dr. Robert McCoard (California State University), and Marcia Horton and the editorial staff of Prentice Hall.

We would like to thank the following people from the University of Pennsylvania's Department of Computer and Information Science: Norm Badler, Jean Gallier, Craig Meyer, Richard Paul, and Ira Winston. We would also like to thank Sharon Camins, Veronique Weiss, David Branner, Scott Mandelker, and Peters B. South for their comments and support.

Jeffrey Esakov

Tom Weiss

CHAPTER ONE

ADVANCED C CONSTRUCTS

The implementation of the data structures that are described in this book requires a clear understanding of certain high-level programming constructs. In this chapter, these constructs are discussed with respect to the C language.

1.1 Structures

A structure is a "compound" type that contains an arbitrary group of related data. In some other programming languages (e.g., Pascal), the comparable type is called a record. Any kind of data can be contained within a structure, including another structure or an array. A structure is defined using the following syntax:

struct *tag* {
    member declarations
};

where **struct** is a keyword, *tag* is an optional structure tag, and *member declarations* are standard variable declarations. Note that defining a structure does not declare a variable. When a variable is declared, space is allocated, whereas when a structure is defined, the compiler records information about the new type for use when variables of that type are declared and used. To declare a structure variable the following syntax is used:

struct *tag variablename*;

where *variablename* is the name of the variable being declared.

    For example, consider the declarations that would be needed to maintain data about the frequency of words within some text. One implementation would require declarations to hold the word (a string) and the frequency.

    The statement

```
struct wordcount {
    char word[WORDLENGTH];
    int frequency;
};
```

defines a single structure containing two fields. The declaration

```
struct wordcount wordfrequency[WORDCOUNT];
```

then declares an array of such structures.

    It is also possible to declare variables in the same statement as the structure definition. For example, the two previous statements can be combined:

```
struct wordcount {
    char word[WORDLENGTH];
    int frequency;
} wordfrequency[WORDCOUNT];
```

If no further use of the structure definition will be made, the tag can be omitted. This usage is most common when defining nested structures. For example,

```
struct employee_data {
    struct {
        char street[16];
        char city[8];
        char state[2];
        int zipcode;
    } address;
    struct {
```

```
        int salary;
        int yearsemployed;
    } misc;
};
```

1.1.1   Operations on Structures

The primary operation on a structure is member reference. This is done using the member reference operator "." (period) as in

```
varname.member
```

Therefore, to get the frequency of the first word in the **wordfrequency** array, one would write **wordfrequency[0].frequency**. The first character of the first word is **wordfrequency[0].word[0]**. Similarly, with the declaration

```
struct employee_data d;
```

one would write **d.address.zipcode** to access the zip code field.[1]

It is not possible to perform formatted input or output on an entire structure. Instead, one must read the data individually into the structure members. For example, to read a line of input containing a single word and a frequency, the following statement would be used:

```
scanf("%s %d", wordfrequency[0].word, &wordfrequency[0].frequency);
```

On the other hand, in most modern implementations of C, it *is* possible to copy a structure without copying the members individually, as in

```
wordfrequency[1] = wordfrequency[0];
```

1.2   Unions

Unions are similar to structures, except that a variable can hold data for only a single member at any given time. For example, the statement

```
union symbol {
    char name[4];
    int value;
};
```

---

[1]The other member reference operator "->" is discussed later.

defines a type that can hold either an array of four **char**'s or an **int**. Unions are implemented by allocating enough space for the largest possible member, and overlaying the members. Assuming **sizeof(char)** is 1 and **sizeof(int)** is 2, the previous **union** can be shown as

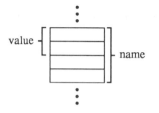

Unions are most practical when the members use about the same amount of space, or when larger members are stored most of the time. Otherwise, they are wasteful, and more sophisticated methods should be employed.

It is up to the programmer to ensure that the same member is used to retrieve the data as was used to store the data. A convenient way of doing this is to make a structure containing two fields: the union and a "type" field to specify which union member is currently stored.

1.3   Enumerated Types

Modern implementations of C contain a facility for allowing the user to define enumerated types. In an enumerated type, the user lists (enumerates) all the data tokens (items) that are part of that type. This is done using the following syntax:

enum tag { *tokens* };

where **enum** is a keyword, *tag* is the name of the enumerated type, and the *tokens* are separated by commas. For example, to make a special type field for the **union** discussed in the previous section, the following could be used:

```
enum member_type {name, value};
```

A structure could then be written:

```
struct symbol {
    enum member_type type;
    union {
        char name[4];
        int value;
```

```
      } symbol;
};
```

Assuming the declaration

```
struct symbol sym;
```

the programmer could then make assignments using the statements

```
sym.type = value;
sym.symbol.value = 6;
```

Note that the **type** and **symbol** fields are syntactically independent; it is up to the programmer to maintain their semantic relationship.

Enumerated types can be used for any purpose where a fixed set of values is desired. The main problem with enumerated types is that formatted input and output may not be as one would expect. When reading or writing enumerated types, it is not possible to directly enter the string corresponding to the token name (as in "var1" for the enumerated value **name**). Instead, enumerated values are defined in the C language to be integer values. The first token in the list of values is 0, with each succeeding token having succeeding integer values. It is also possible to give explicit values to the token names by listing the name followed by an equal sign and the value. Token values for names that follow the specified value follow in an integer sequence:

```
enum numbers { zero, two=2, three, ten=10, eleven };
```

This method of implementation makes enumerated types seem equivalent to using preprocessor #**define**'s, but in fact, they are not. As the compiler performs syntax checking, it will recognize when an enumerated type is being used incorrectly more often than the equivalent #**define**. Since the preprocessor does "blind" substitution, by the time the compiler sees the code, only the integer value appears, and hence error messages will be more cryptic.

1.4   Function Invocation

All meaningful C programs contain function calls. Since nearly every function included in this book has parameters, it is very important to understand how argument passing works.

To begin, some terminology should be clarified. Refer to the following code segment as necessary.

```
/* 1 */ main()
           {
/* 2 */        int X = 0;    /* simple data type */
/* 3 */        int *pX;      /* pointer data type */
/* 4 */        f(X, pX);
                  /* ... */
           }

/* 5 */ f(L, pL)
/* 6 */ int L;
/* 7 */ int *pL;
           {
/* 8 */        int Y;
/* 9 */        int *pY;
                  /* ... */
           }
```

Pointer. A pointer is an address. A pointer variable is a variable that holds an address. To get the address in C, the address & operator is used. Lines 3, 7, and 9 contain declarations for pointer variables. The use of pointers is discussed later.

Local Variable. A local variable is one declared inside the open brace that starts a function. The variables declared on lines 2, 3, 8 and 9 are local variables. A local variable may be referenced only from within the function in which it was declared.

Argument. Often called an *actual parameter*, this is the data passed when the function is invoked. In line 4, **X** and **pX** are the arguments to the function **f()**.

Parameter. Often called a *formal parameter* or *dummy parameter*, this is the identifier used inside the called function. Parameters must be declared after the function name and before the left brace that starts the function. The parameters for function **f()** are declared on lines 6 and 7. In this book, there should always be a one-to-one correspondence between arguments and parameters.

1.4.1 "Simple" Variables as Function Arguments

When a function is called, memory space for the declared parameters is allocated, and the values of the arguments are copied into that space.[2] Memory

---

[2]This parameter-passing technique is called "call by value."

space is then allocated for the variables local to the function and execution of the function begins.

Program **Noswap** provides an example of how memory is allocated:

```
main ()
{
    int x, y;
    x = 0;
    y = 1;
    printf("In main before noswap: x = %d, y = %d\n", x, y);
    noswap(x, y);
    printf("In main after noswap: x = %d, y = %d\n", x, y);
    exit(0);
}

void noswap(x, y)
int x, y;
{
    int temp;

    printf("In noswap at start, x = %d and y = %d\n", x, y);
    temp = x;
    x = y;
    y = temp;
    printf("In noswap at end, x = %d and y = %d\n", x, y);
}
```

The intended function of this program is to swap the values of **x** and **y** in **main()**. Unfortunately, this program does not work. A program trace shows why.

Although **main()** has no parameters, it contains two local variables. Therefore, when the function is invoked (by running the program), two memory spaces for **x** and **y** are allocated.

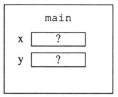

Subsequent use of **x** and **y** refer to the contents of the memory spaces that were allocated. The variable names **x** and **y** are symbolic labels for those spaces. When the assignment operations x = 0 and y = 1 are executed, the values 0 and 1 are copied into the memory locations that correspond to **x** and **y**.

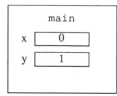

When **noswap()** is called, memory space for the parameters is allocated. That is, a new pair of integer variables are created. The names that were chosen for those parameters were **x** and **y**, but any names could have been used. It is important to realize that when **noswap()** refers to **x** and **y**, it is referencing its own local variables. After space for **noswap()**'s **x** and **y** are created, the values of the arguments **x** and **y** are copied into the corresponding parameter. Space for **temp** is created as well. The state when **noswap()** begins execution is

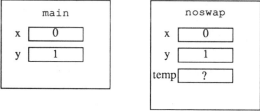

Noswap() then swaps the value of its own copies of **x** and **y**. At the second **printf()** function call in **noswap()**, the state is

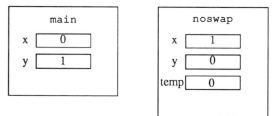

When **noswap()** finishes execution, all its variables are destroyed and their memory space returned to the available memory pool. Therefore, when **main()** reaches its second **printf()** function call, it is referring to its own variables **x** and **y**, which were never altered.

1.4.2   Structures as Function Arguments

Modern implementations of C allow structures to be passed as arguments in the same manner as "simple" variables. The contents of the entire structure are copied to the corresponding parameter. If values of the members are changed within the function, the change will *not* have any effect on the actual parameter. So, for example, the function **noswapstruct()** yields results similar to **noswap()**; it doesn't work!

```
#define NAMELENGTH 52

struct student {
    char name[NAMELENGTH];
    int  idno;
};

void noswapstruct(s, t)
struct student s, t;
{
    struct student temp;

    temp = s;
    s = t;
    t = temp;
}
```

1.4.3   Arrays as Function Arguments

When arrays are passed as arguments to functions, the semantics are slightly different. In particular, when a function changes the value of an element of an array, the corresponding element will be changed in the actual parameter.[3] This type of argument passing can be visualized by assuming the dummy parameter refers to the same memory location as the actual parameter.

```
main()
{
    int x[4];

    f(x);
}

f(y)
int y[];
{
    /* ... */
}
```

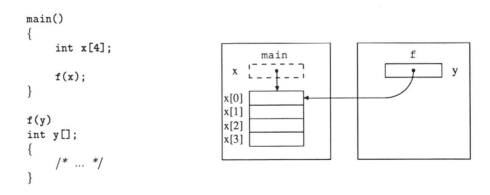

A complete discussion of this topic is deferred until Section 1.5.2.

---

[3]This parameter-passing technique is called "call by reference."

1.5   Pointers

In Sections 1.4.1 and 1.4.2, it was shown that functions cannot change the contents of actual parameters that are "simple" variables or structure variables. There are three solutions to this problem. One solution is to make all variables arrays and to pass the arrays to the functions. Clearly, this approach is far from ideal.

Another solution is to use global variables. By declaring variables outside of any function body, they become directly accessible to all subsequently defined functions. At times, global variables may be appropriate, but in this case, they are not. In general, the use of global variables is poor programming practice because they open a "Pandora's box" of possible errors and accidental modifications. Therefore, another method is preferred. This alternative uses the pointer data type.

A pointer variable contains the address of another variable (it "points" to another variable). Since an address is machine-dependent, the contents of a pointer variable are shown graphically using an arrow:

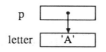

In this example, **p** is a pointer variable that "points" to the variable **letter** (which contains the character value 'A'). The C statements that correspond to this figure are

```
/* 1 */   char letter, *p;
/* 2 */   p = &letter;
/* 3 */   letter = 'A';
```

Line 1 contains the variable declarations: **letter** is a variable of type **char**, and **p** is a pointer to a **char**. Line 2 modifies the contents of **p**, and line 3 modifies the contents of **letter**. In particular, **p** is set to "point" to **letter** (the "arrow" is drawn) by setting the contents of **p** to the address of **letter**.

The address of **letter** is determined using the & operator, which returns a pointer value that can be assigned to a pointer variable or used as a parameter. It has been used all along with **scanf()**, and now it can be understood why. In the statement

```
scanf("%d", &x);
```

scanf() is told the address of **x**, because that is where it will place the value it reads.

To access the memory location to which a pointer variable "points," the *variablename* construct is used. Continuing with the previous example, the following figure shows the results of executing the statement:

/* 4 */   *p = 'B';

A convenient way to think of the dereferencing operator ("*") is "follow the arrow." So "**p**" can be thought of as "follow the arrow stored in **p**."

Note that in this case, **p** and **letter** refer to the contents of the same memory location, and are therefore completely equivalent. That is, they are not merely equal, but refer to the same physical object in the computer's memory. Changing the value of **p** changes the value of **letter**.

It is for this reason that it is necessary to declare pointer variables as a pointer to a particular type. When a reference to **p** is made, the computer will know what kind of data to expect. It also follows that a pointer to one type of data should not be set to point to a variable of a different type.

A short program will illustrate these concepts:

```
main ()
{
    char letter, *p;
    char character;

    p = &letter;
    letter = 'A';
    printf("letter = %c, *p = %c\n", letter, *p);
    *p = 'B';
    printf("letter = %c, *p = %c\n", letter, *p);
    p = &character;
    *p = 'Z';
    printf("letter = %c, *p = %c, character = %c\n",
        letter, *p, character);
}
```

The output of this program is

```
letter = A, *p = A
letter = B, *p = B
letter = B, *p = Z, character = Z
```

It is now possible to write a swap program that will work. Instead of passing **x** and **y**, the pointer values **&x** and **&y** are passed. These are copied into the parameters **p_x** and **p_y** used by **swap()**. Using this parameter-passing technique, ***p_x** and ***p_y** are equivalent to **x** and **y** and hence the values of **x** and **y** can be modified in the called function. In this book, parameter variables receiving pointer values will usually be prefixed with a "p_" to signify that they are pointers.

```
main ()
{
    int x, y;

    x = 0;
    y = 1;
    printf("In main before swap: x=%d, y=%d\n",x,y);
    swap(&x, &y);
    printf("In main after swap: x=%d, y=%d\n",x,y);
    exit(0);
}

void swap(p_x, p_y)
int *p_x, *p_y;
{
    int temp;

    temp = *p_x;
    *p_x = *p_y;
    *p_y = temp;
}
```

The execution trace of this program follows. The output of the program is shown in boldface.

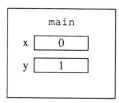

In main before swap: x = 0, y = 1

Swap() is then called and the formal parameters are set to point to **x** and **y**:

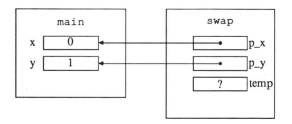

A statement-by-statement trace of function **swap**() shows how variable **temp** is used to interchange the values:

```
temp = *p_x;
```

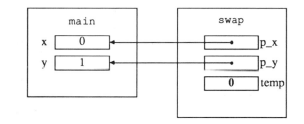

```
*p_x = *p_y;
```

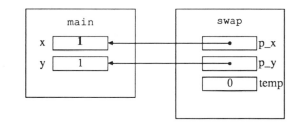

```
*p_y = temp;
```

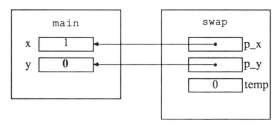

In main after swap: x =1, y = 0

1.5.1   Using Pointers to Return Values

Since the **return** statement can only return one value, pointers as parameters can be used when a function computes two or more values. The following program, which computes the equation of a line given two points on the line, is an example of this technique. An equation for a line is given by the function:

$$y = Mx + b$$

where M is the slope of the line, and b is the Y intercept.

The key function in the program is **line()**, which has four parameters. The first two parameters represent two points on the line and the last two parameters represent the slope and Y intercept of the line. The points on the line are represented using a structure and are used to calculate the slope and Y intercept that are returned via pointer parameters.

The slope of a line can be determined from two points on the line by dividing the change in Y coordinates by the change in the X coordinates. Given the slope, computing the Y intercept is straightforward. The only problem with this technique is that the slope of a vertical line is undefined. This case occurs when the change in the X coordinates is 0. Therefore, this condition is checked before the actual computations are made.

```
struct point {
    float x, y;
};

int line(pt1, pt2, p_M, p_B)
float *p_M, *p_B;
struct point pt1, pt2;
{
    if (pt1.x == pt2.x)
        return -1;
    else {
        *p_M = (pt2.y - pt1.y) / (pt2.x - pt1.x);
        *p_B = pt1.y - *p_M * pt1.x;
        return 0;
    }
}

main()
{
    struct point pt1, pt2;
    float M, B;

    printf("Input x, y for point 1: ");
```

```
    scanf("%f , %f", &pt1.x, &pt1.y);
    printf("Input x, y for point 2: ");
    scanf("%f , %f", &pt2.x, &pt2.y);
    printf("pt1(%g,%g) pt2(%g,%g)\n", pt1.x, pt1.y, pt2.x, pt2.y);
    if (line(pt1, pt2, &M, &B) == -1) {
        printf("Error in computing equation.  Exiting program\n");
        exit(-1);
    } else {
        printf("Y = %gX + %g\n", M, B);
        exit(0);
    }
}
```

Function **line()** has a return value that indicates success (0) or failure (−1). Any function that could potentially fail should return some status indicator. Most standard C library functions follow this convention (return error flags), although in practice, the returned error status of some functions is not always checked (e.g., **scanf()** returns an error flag that is usually ignored).

Some stylistic points are in order. In particular, functions that return error flags should perform error checking before modifying any of the calling function's variables. That way, the calling function will have the best chance to salvage the situation. For simplicity, the functions that have previously been presented used the assumption that the calling routine would perform error checking. In reality, it is a better practice to have error checking take place within the called function to guarantee that no illegal operations are ever attempted.

Furthermore, library routines such as data structure code should have no *side effects* (changes to the operating environment). For example, there should be no input or output. Some programmers have functions print an error message and terminate execution if an error is encountered. This is undesirable if the library function may be used in many contexts because (1) the calling function may want to continue execution in spite of the error, possibly following a different path of execution, and (2) it is better to let the calling routine print an error message (if it desires) because it is at a higher level and therefore more likely to say something meaningful to the user.

1.5.2   Pointers and Arrays

Recall that when an array is passed as an argument to a function, the function is able to modify the contents of the array. The reason for this is when an array is referenced by its name alone (not using [] to get an element), it is in fact a pointer to the start of the array. It can be pictorially represented as

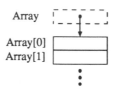

The memory location representing the array name value is shown as a dashed box because, in general, C compilers do not actually generate a separate variable to hold that value. Instead, the address of the first element is substituted whenever the array name is used.

Since array names are pointers, when an array is passed as an argument, a pointer is passed. Pragmatically, this saves the time and space of making a new copy of the array. It also means that when the called function references array elements using [], it is referencing the same elements used by the calling function. It is this aspect of parameter passing that allows a function in C to operate on arrays of any size. For example, the following program uses the same function to swap the first and last elements of two different arrays.

```
void arrayswap(X, size)
char X[];
int size;
{
    char temp;

    temp = X[0];
    X[0] = X[size−1];
    X[size−1] = temp;
}

main ()
{
    char A[2];
    char B[4];

    A[0] = 'a';
    A[1] = 'b';
    printf("Before call, A[0] = %c, A[1] = %c\n", A[0], A[1]);
    arrayswap(A, 2);
    printf("After call, A[0] = %c, A[1] = %c\n", A[0], A[1]);
    B[0] = 'c';
    B[3] = 'd';
    printf("Before call, B[0] = %c, B[3] = %c\n", B[0], B[3]);
    arrayswap(B, 4);
    printf("After call, B[0] = %c, B[3] = %c\n", B[0], B[3]);
}
```

The execution trace of this program follows. The output of the program is shown in boldface.

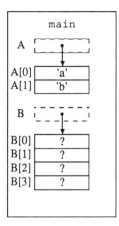

Arrayswap() is then called and the formal parameters are set to correspond the **A** array.

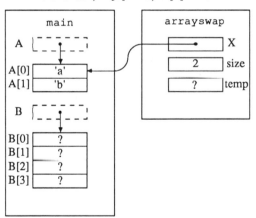

A statement-by-statement trace of function **arrayswap()** shows how variable **temp** is used to interchange the values of the first and last elements in array **A**.

```
temp = X[0];
```

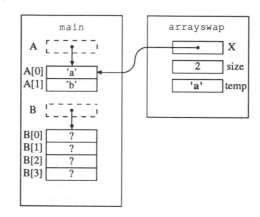

```
X[0] = X[size-1];
```

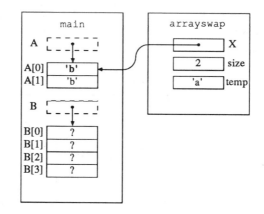

```
X[size-1] = temp;
```

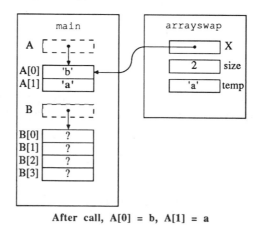

After call, A[0] = b, A[1] = a

When **arrayswap()** is called the second time, the formal parameters are set to correspond to the **B** array.

Before call, B[0] = c, B[3] = d

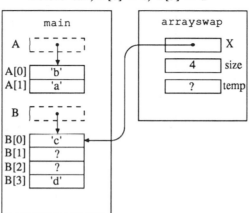

Since **B** was passed as an argument, when the formal parameter **X** is accessed using the array notation, the contents of **B** will be used:

```
temp = x[0];
```

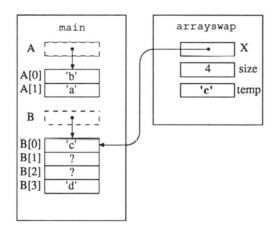

```
X[0] = X[size-1];
```

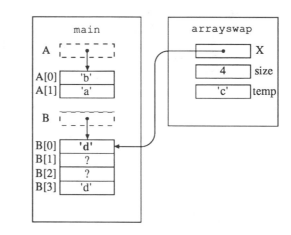

X[size-1] = temp;

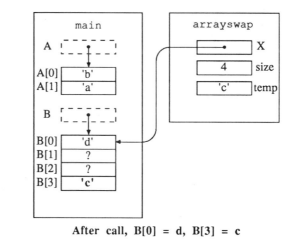

After call, B[0] = d, B[3] = c

Note also, that although the parameter **X** was declared as an array (**char X[];**), it could equivalently have been declared as a pointer (**char *X**). The choice of the style of declaration is up to the programmer. In general, the code is easier to read if the parameter is declared in the same style as it is used.

1.5.3   Pointers and Structures

A pointer to a structure is no different from a pointer to the basic types. In the following example, the arrow is shown pointing to the first member of the structure, although that may not necessarily be the case.[4]

```
main()
{
    struct {
        int i;
        float f;
    } s, *p_s;

    p_s = &s;
    p_s->i = 5;
    p_s->f = 1.1;
}
```

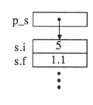

Note the use of the member reference operator "->." The construct **p_S->i** is a more convenient way to write **(*p_S).i**. Pointers to structures are often used as parameters for efficiency. If a large structure is passed as a parameter, the memory allocation and copying may cause considerable overhead. Pointers, on the other hand, are usually quite small. When using this technique, one must be careful to avoid unintended modifications to the structure.

1.5.4   Pointer Arithmetic

Two common operations that are performed on pointers are integer addition and pointer subtraction. The operation of adding integer values to pointers is implicitly performed in programs using arrays. Consider an example consisting of the array **Array** with five elements. As was stated in Section 1.5.2, when the name of the array is used, it is in fact an implicitly defined pointer to the first element.

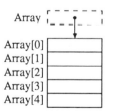

When the ith element is accessed via **Array[i]**, the compiler automatically performs pointer addition. For example, accessing **Array[0]** is equivalent to writing ***(Array + 0)**; accessing **Array[3]** is equivalent to writing ***(Array + 3)**. The compiler takes the address stored in **Array** and modifies it so that

---

[4]For compilers that conform to the draft ANSI proposal for the C language, the pointer does point to the first member. For other compilers, it is undefined.

it will reference to the address **i** units away. An important thing to realize, however, is that the "unit" is not necessarily the same for all arrays. Consider two arrays, one of **ints** and one of structures containing an **int** and a **float**.

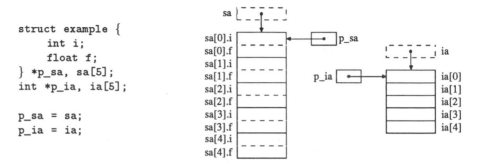

```
struct example {
    int i;
    float f;
} *p_sa, sa[5];
int *p_ia, ia[5];

p_sa = sa;
p_ia = ia;
```

Clearly an element in **sa** will require more physical memory than an element in **ia**. Therefore, pointers must be declared to point to a particular type. By adding 1 to **p_sa**, **&sa[1]** will be correctly referenced; and by adding 1 to **p_ia**, **&ia[1]** will be referenced. The determination of the "units" is done by the compiler and is completely transparent to the programmer. The programmer can confidently add integers to pointers knowing that the address that will be referenced will be the appropriate distance from the pointer value.

A similar transformation occurs when subtracting one pointer from another. Consider two pointers to **sa**:

```
struct example *p_base, *p_tmp;

p_base = sa;
p_tmp = &sa[4]; /* alternatively: p_tmp = sa + 4; */
```

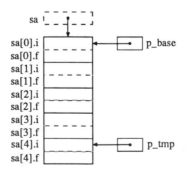

By subtracting **p_base** from **p_tmp**, the appropriate integer value **4** is returned. Note that it is a syntax error to subtract pointers of different types (as in **p_sa** and **p_si**).

1.6 Pointers to Functions

A very powerful aspect of the C language is the ability to take the address of a function and store that address in a pointer. When the pointer is subsequently dereferenced, it is equivalent to calling the function. This construct is essential in the development of abstract data types and polymorphic (type-independent) data structures[5] because it allows the calling of a programmer-defined function (to operate on programmer-defined data) from within the context of application-independent functions.

Every C programmer is familiar with the function call syntax:

```
f(arg1, ...);
```

which indicates that function **f()** should be called with arguments **arg1,**.... It is the parentheses that indicate that this is a function call. By writing the function name alone, without the parentheses or the arguments, one takes the address of the function. By declaring a variable to be a pointer to a function, that address can be stored:

```
extern int f();
int (*p_f)();
```

The first line is a simple function declaration indicating that **f** is a function that returns an **int** and is defined elsewhere. The second line indicates that the variable **p_f** is a pointer to a function that returns an **int**.

```
p_f = f;
(*p_f)();
f();
```

Once **p_f** has been assigned the address of **f()**, when it is dereferenced (using the required parentheses), it is entirely equivalent to calling **f()** directly. The parentheses around ***p_f** are required due to operator precedence, and the empty parentheses following that is where function arguments would appear (if there were any).

1.7 Typedef

C provides a facility to make new type names using the **typedef** statement. Unlike preprocessor **#define**'s, the C compiler recognizes the names created

---

[5]See Chapter 3 for a discussion of polymorphism.

with **typedef** and can perform more complex substitutions. **Typedef** is used to provide a single type name to represent structures, arrays of a predetermined size, or descriptive aliases for general-purpose types.

For example, suppose there is a structure that represents student data:

```
struct student {
    char name[80];
    int id;
};
```

A **typedef** statement could be added so that **student_data** can be used in declarations instead of **struct student**:

```
typedef struct student student_data;
```

The new name appears where a variable name would appear in a declaration, not after the keyword **typedef**. The new name can be the same as the structure tag. The statement

```
typedef struct student student;
```

lets **student** substitute for **struct student**. **Typedef** statements can also be combined with structure definitions:

```
typedef struct {
    char name[80];
    int id;
} student;
```

Note that **student** is the new type name, not a variable. It is not possible to declare variables within a **typedef** statement.

Another more slightly complicated example defines the type **string** to be another name for a character array holding 80 characters:

```
typedef char string[80];
```

Declaring variables of this type is straightforward

```
string buffer, name;
```

and is entirely equivalent to

```
char buffer[80], name[80];
```

1.8 Dynamic Memory Allocation

Another important use of pointers is in conjunction with dynamic memory allocation, which allows a program to request memory for storing data during execution. It is used when it is not known in advance how much space will be needed.

The general approach to dynamic memory allocation in C is to call a function that returns the address of some "new" space. This address can then be stored in a pointer variable and accessed using standard pointer operations. In C, this is done by using the library function **malloc()**. Malloc() returns a pointer to a character (**char ***), which should be cast to the appropriate pointer type. It has one argument, the amount of space to allocate.

Each data type (e.g., **int**, **float**, structures) may require a different amount of space. Furthermore, that amount of space is machine-dependent. To handle this problem, C includes an operator that determines the amount of space required to store its operand (in bytes). The operand may be either a type or an expression. The **sizeof** operator has a single operand enclosed in parentheses.[6]

For most applications, the exact integer value determined by **sizeof** is unimportant. That is, except for low-level code (e.g., in operating systems), it should not be necessary to examine the result of a **sizeof** operation. The use of **sizeof** is important in situations where the actual bytes of a data type are to be manipulated, as with **malloc()**.

In the following example, **malloc()** is used to allocate space for an array of **int**'s. The number of elements in the array is entered by the user, and that value is multiplied by the **sizeof(int)** to determine the actual number of bytes to allocate. The result is cast to a pointer to an **int**.

```
main()
{
    int *p_Array;
    int i, count;

    printf("How many integers? ");
    scanf("%d", &count);
    p_Array = (int *) malloc(count * sizeof(int));
    if (p_Array == NULL) {
        printf("Couldn't allocate the space.");
        exit(1);
    }
    printf("Enter %d integers.\n", count);
```

---

[6]Note, however, **sizeof** is not a function — it is an operator built in to the C language (just as **+** is an operator).

```
      for (i = 0; i < count; i++) {
          scanf("%d", &p_Array[i]);
      }
      /* ... */
      free(p_Array);
  }
```

Since space is allocated in consecutive bytes, the pointer can be treated as
though it were the base of an array and array subscripting can be used. Note
that through the use of pointer math, the loop that reads the integers could
be written as

```
      for (i = 0; i < count; i++) {
          scanf("%d", p_Array + i);
      }
```

or, alternatively, using another pointer:

```
      /* assume the declaration: int *p_tmp; */
      for (p_tmp = p_Array; p_tmp - p_Array < count; p_tmp++) {
          scanf("%d", p_tmp);
      }
```

When the space that was allocated is no longer needed, it can be returned
to the operating system for use during the next dynamic memory allocation.
This is done by using the library function **free()**, which has one argument:
the pointer to the space to be freed. Note that once space is freed, it should
not be accessed even though the pointer variable may seem to point to a valid
location. It is good practice to assign such pointers the value **NULL** (defined
in the standard C include file **stdio.h**), which is guaranteed not to correspond
to any real pointer value.

   *Note: The C functions available for dynamic storage allocation vary on dif-
ferent systems. If* **malloc()** *and* **free()** *do not work on your computer, perform
the following substitutions:*

Replace	*With*
extern char *malloc();	extern char *calloc();
malloc(sizeof(node));	calloc(1, sizeof(node));
extern void free();	extern int cfree();
free(P);	cfree(P);

1.9 Exercises

1. A binomial is of the form $y = ax^2 + bx + c$ where a, b, and c are constants. The roots of a binomial are the values of x for which $y = 0$ and are given by the quadratic equation,

$$y = \frac{-b \pm \sqrt{b^2 - 4ac}}{2a}$$

   Write a function that computes the roots of a binomial that is passed as a parameter giving careful thought to the following.

   (a) Under what conditions will that function fail?

   (b) How should the failure be reported to the calling function?

   (c) How should the results be reported to the calling function?

2. Describe a structure definition for a student-grading program. Associated with each student is his name, student number, and homework and test grades.

   (a) Can your structure handle a student name with 35 characters? Can your structure handle 13 homework assignments and 10 quiz grades?

   (b) Rework your structure so that any number of homework assignments and test grades can be entered.

3. Write a student-grading program using the structure in Exercise 2b. The student should be organized into classes. There should be options for adding new classes, students, and grades. It should also be possible to print a report for each class. There should be a menu displayed showing the user the commands available and functions should be called depending upon the menu item chosen. If it is feasible, organize your program to use pointers to functions.

4. Write a program that, given a structure definition, will generate a C function that allocates and initializes the structure (such a function is called a "constructor"). For example, given the input

```
struct complex {
    double real;
    double imaginary;
};
```

function **create_complex()** will be created having two arguments of type **double**.

5. Write a program that, given a C enumerated type definition, will generate a C function that, when called with a single argument, will return a string corresponding to the enumerated type token name. For example, given the input

```
enum numbers { one=1, two, three, four, fifty=50, fiftyone };
```

function **numbers_to_string()** will be created which will have a single argument of type **enum numbers** and will return the string "one" if the enumerated value **one** is passed, the string "two" if the enumerated value **two** is passed, etc.

6. Write a program that, given a C **union** definition, will generate a C structure and set of C functions that will insure that the type of data extracted from the **union** is the same as the type that was stored.

7. Write a program that, given a C **typedef** statement and a variable declaration using the using the type just defined, will output the corresponding variable declaration without the use of a **typedef**. For example, given the input

```
typedef struct A *Aptr;
Aptr p_a;
```

the program should output

```
struct A *p_a;
```

Be sure to test the program with complex **typedef** statements such as

```
typedef int (*PF)();
typedef PF *PPF;
PPF pp_cmp;
```

CHAPTER TWO

RECURSIVE FUNCTIONS

A powerful concept in the development of algorithms and programs is the ability for a function to refer to itself to solve a problem. This control technique, called *recursion*, is convenient for a variety of problems that would be difficult to solve using iterative constructs such as **for**, **while** and **do** loops. Recursion is used extensively in many of the data structures and algorithms that are discussed in this book.

2.1 What Is Recursion?

In mathematics and computer science, recursion means self-reference. A recursive function, therefore, is a function whose definition is based upon itself. For example, the factorial function can be recursively defined as in Equation (2.1).

$$n! = \begin{cases} 1 & \text{if } n = 0 \\ n \times (n-1)! & \text{if } n > 0 \end{cases} \qquad (2.1)$$

Note that $n!$ is defined in terms of $(n-1)!$. Using this formula, the calculation of 3! proceeds as in Equation (2.2).

$$
\begin{aligned}
3! &= 3 * (2!) = 3 * (2 * (1!)) = 3 * (2 * (1 * (0!))) \\
&= 3 * (2 * (1 * (1))) = 3 * 2 * 1 * 1 \\
&= 6
\end{aligned}
\tag{2.2}
$$

It now becomes clear why the definition of factorial is not circular:

1. When the function refers to itself, it uses an argument smaller than the one it was given.

2. The value of the function for the minimal case(s) is defined without self-reference, so that the chain of recursion terminates.

Recursive functions can be implemented directly in C. A recursive function computing factorials can be written based upon the recursive definition.

```
int factorial(n)
int n;
{
    if (n == 0)
        return 1;
    else
        return n * factorial(n-1);
}
```

The factorial function uses *tail recursion*. That is, the last statement contains a single recursive call. Because of this structure, tail recursive functions always have direct iterative equivalents. For example, the factorial function can be rewritten as

```
int factorial(n)
int n;
{
    if (n == 0)
        return 1;
    else {
        int i, fact = 1;

        for (i = 2; i <= n; i++)
            fact *= i;
        return fact;
    }
}
```

Iteration is slightly more efficient,[1] but the choice of tail recursion or iteration is largely a question of style, and depends on how the problem is viewed.

---

[1]Some well-written compilers can convert tail recursion to iteration.

For example, the iterative factorial function is based on an iterative definition of the problem:

$$0! = 1 \qquad (2.3)$$
$$n! = \prod_{i=1}^{n} i$$

Similarly, recursive and iterative definitions (and corresponding C functions) exist for computing the positive exponential power of a number. The recursive definition is

$$x^n = \begin{cases} 1 & \text{if } n = 0 \\ x \times x^{n-1} & \text{if } n > 0 \end{cases} \qquad (2.4)$$

The recursive function **power()** based upon Equation (2.4) is

```
double power(x, n)
double x
int n;
{
    if (n == 0)
        return(1);
    else
        return(x * power(x, n−1));
}
```

The iterative definition is

$$x^0 = 1 \qquad (2.5)$$
$$x^n = \prod_{i=1}^{n} x$$

The iterative function **power()** is left as an exercise.

2.1.1 Divide And Conquer

Recursive algorithms are based on the principle of solving problems by decomposing them into discrete subproblems of smaller size. Tail recursion generates the solution for the nth case from the complete solution for the $n^{th} - 1$ case. More generally, recursive functions may recombine several subproblems (making several recursive calls) before generating the solution. This technique, called *divide and conquer*, often leads to more efficient solutions than a naive iterative approach.

For example, consider the problem of simultaneously finding the maximum and the minimum of an array of integers. What follows is a naive iterative function:

```
minmax(a, n, p_max, p_min)
int a[], n, *p_max, *p_min;
{
    int i;

    *p_max = *p_min = a[0];

    for (i = 1; i < n; i++) {
        if (a[i] > *p_max)
            *p_max = a[i];
        if (a[i] < *p_min)
            *p_min = a[i];
    }
}
```

This function makes $2 * (n - 1) = 2n - 2$ comparisons, because at each of the $n - 1$ iterations of the **for** loop, 2 comparisons are made. Now consider the following recursive algorithm:

```
if n = 1
    min = max = a[0];
if n = 2
    compare a[0] and a[1] and assign min the smaller and max the
    larger.
else
    Divide the array in two, and recursively find the min
    and max of each half.
    Assign min the smaller of the two min's, and max the larger
    of the two max's.
```

Using techniques presented in Chapter 8, it can be shown that this algorithm makes only $1.5 \times n - 2$ comparisons. Although these two algorithms differ only by a constant, there are algorithms where the technique of divide and conquer can be used to realize more significant improvements. The C implementation of the function follows:

```
void minmax(numberlist, n, p_min, p_max)
int numberlist[], n, *p_min, *p_max;
```

```
{
    int min2, max2;

    if (n == 1)
        *p_min = *p_max = numberlist[0];
    else if (n == 2) {
        if (numberlist[0] < numberlist[1]) {
            *p_min = numberlist[0];
            *p_max = numberlist[1];
        } else {
            *p_min = numberlist[1];
            *p_max = numberlist[0];
        }
    } else {
        minmax(numberlist, n / 2, p_min, p_max);
        minmax(numberlist + n / 2, n - (n / 2), &min2, &max2);
        if (min2 < *p_min)
            *p_min = min2;
        if (max2 > *p_max)
            *p_max = max2;
    }
}
```

2.2   The Towers of Hanoi

Another famous recursive problem is the Towers of Hanoi, which is based on
a game consisting of three pins and a set of disks of graduated size. The game
starts with the disks stacked in decreasing size on the first pin. The object
is to move the disks to the third pin subject to the constraints that (1) only
one disk can be moved at a time, and (2) at no time may a disk be placed on
top of a smaller disk. All three pins may be used, and a disk may be moved
directly from any pin to any other.

To determine a general algorithm for solving this problem of moving n
disks from pin C, it is helpful to look at some examples with only a
few disks. The base case is when there is only one disk. In this case, the disk
should be moved directly from pin A to pin C.

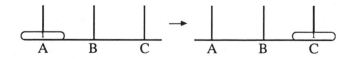

The two-disk case is also simple. First, disk 1 is moved to pin B, then disk
2 is moved to pin C. The last step places disk 1 on top of disk 2.

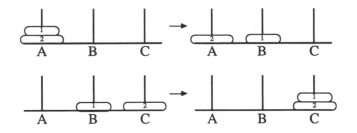

With three disks, the problem becomes more complex. To solve the problem, it is necessary to find a pattern in the solution.

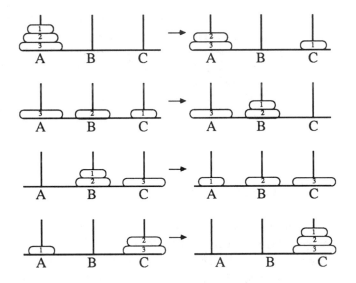

Examining the cases with two and three disks, the following is seen: in order to move the the largest disk from A to C, we must move the smaller disks that are on top to pin B. Once the largest disk has been moved, we must move all the smaller disks to pin C. We can now recursively describe the steps needed to move n disks from pin A to pin C using pin B.

```
if n = 1 then
    Move the disk from A to C
if n > 1 then
    Move the n-1 smallest disks from A to B
    Move the largest disk from pin A to pin C
    Move the n-1 smallest disks from pin B to pin C
```

Analyzing the solution in the three-disk case shows that the first step was to place the two smallest disks on B. Then the largest disk was moved to C.

Lastly, the two disks on B were moved to C. The first and last phases can themselves be recursively decomposed: to move two disks from A to B, first the smaller disk must be moved to C, then the larger disk to B, and, finally, the smaller to B.

The implementation of this algorithm is surprisingly short:

```
main()
{
    int n;

    printf("Input the number of disks: ");
    scanf("%d", &n);
    if (n <= 0) {
        printf("Illegal number\n");
        exit(-1);
    }
    else {
        hanoi('a', 'c', 'b', n);
        exit(0);
    }
}

void hanoi(from, to, other, n)
char from, to, other, n;
{
    if (n == 1)
        printf("Move disk from %c to %c\n", from, to);
    else {
        hanoi(from, other, to, n-1);
        hanoi(from, to, other, 1);
        hanoi(other, to, from, n-1);
    }
}
```

2.3   Fibonacci Numbers

Another problem that is easily solved using recursion is generation of the Fibonacci numbers: $0, 1, 1, 2, 3, 5, 8, 13, 21, \ldots$. In general:

$$fib(n) = \begin{cases} 0 & \text{if } n = 1 \\ 1 & \text{if } n = 2 \\ fib(n-1) + fib(n-2) & \text{if } n > 2 \end{cases} \qquad (2.6)$$

From this definition, the recursive function **fib()** can be written.

```
int fib(n)
int n;
{
    if (n == 1)
        return(0);
    else if (n == 2)
        return(1);
    else
        return(fib(n-1) + fib(n-2));
}
```

Note how this problem has two minimal cases: both $fib(1)$ and $fib(2)$ must be explicitly defined because an attempt to calculate them recursively would involve a reference to the nonexistent $fib(0)$.

The problem with this implementation is that the recursive subproblems overlap, causing many redundant computations. For example, the top-level recursive call **fib(n−1)** causes a recursive call of **fib(n−2)** in the next layer of recursion, but **fib(n−2)** is then recalculated from scratch in the top level. The time required to compute **fib(n)** thus grows exponentially.

An iterative function **fib()**, left as an exercise, has a running time that grows in linear proportion with n. Better still, in this and many other cases, techniques from discrete mathematics can reveal an analytical solution to recursive formulas. For $n >= 5$,

$$fib(n) = \frac{1}{\sqrt{5}} \times \left(\left(\frac{1 + \sqrt{5}}{2} \right)^{n-1} - \left(\frac{1 - \sqrt{5}}{2} \right)^{n-1} \right)$$

Thus, three methods for implementing recursive algorithms may exist: (1) a recursive function, (2) an iterative function, and (3) an analytical solution.

2.4   Exercises

1. Write an iterative program to compute x^n.

2. Write an iterative program to compute $fib(n)$. Compare your iterative program with the recursive version listed in the previous section. Which program is more straightforward based on the definition? Can you think of a nonrecursive definition of $fib(n)$?

3. **(a)** Suppose that C did not contain a built-in multiply function (*), but only addition (+). Write a recursive function **mult** that takes as arguments two nonnegative integers m and n, and returns the product $m \times n$ computed using recursive addition.

(b) Suppose that C did not contain a built-in addition function, but only increment. Write a recursive function **add** that takes as arguments two nonnegative integers m and n, and returns the sum $m + n$ computed using recursive increment.

4. Write a C program to recursively compute the greatest common divisor of two numbers using this algorithm:

$$gcd(n,m) = \begin{cases} gcd(m,n) & \text{if } n < m \\ m & \text{if } n \geq m \text{ and } n \bmod m = 0 \\ gcd(m,n \bmod m) & \text{otherwise} \end{cases}$$

5. The combination function $C(n,r)$ can be expressed be defined recursively as $C(n-1,r) + C(n-1,r-1)$. Write a recursive program to compute $C(n,r)$. What is the base case?

6. Implement Strassen's Matrix Multiplication algorithm for arbitrary 64 × 64 matrices. For large matrices, this algorithm is superior to the conventional technique.

The algorithm states: Given the problem of computing $\mathbf{C} = \mathbf{A} \times \mathbf{B}$, where $\mathbf{A}$ and $\mathbf{B}$ are $n \times n$ matrices and n is a power of 2, it is possible to compute $\mathbf{C}$ as follows:

```
If n is not equal to 2
      divide A, B and C into four n/2 × n/2 submatrices
      and recursively apply this algorithm to
      each of the four submatrices.
otherwise
      Compute the following subproducts:
```

$$\begin{aligned}
M_1 &= (A_{1,2} - A_{2,2}) \times (B_{2,1} + B_{2,2}) \\
M_2 &= (A_{1,1} + A_{2,2}) \times (B_{1,1} + B_{2,2}) \\
M_3 &= (A_{1,1} + A_{2,1}) \times (B_{1,1} + B_{1,2}) \\
M_4 &= (A_{1,1} + A_{1,2}) \times B_{2,2} \\
M_5 &= A_{1,1} \times (B_{1,2} - B_{2,2}) \\
M_6 &= A_{2,2} \times (B_{2,1} - B_{1,1}) \\
M_7 &= (A_{2,1} \times A_{2,2}) \times B_{1,1}
\end{aligned}$$

```
Form the product matrix C:
```

$$
\begin{aligned}
C_{1,1} &= M_1 + M_2 - M_4 + M_6 \\
C_{1,2} &= M_4 + M_5 \\
C_{2,1} &= M_6 + M_7 \\
C_{2,2} &= M_2 - M_3 + M_5 - M_7
\end{aligned}
$$

Use arrays of random numbers to test your program. How can you verify the output?

CHAPTER
THREE

DATA STRUCTURES
AND SOFTWARE
DEVELOPMENT

One of the most important aspects of computer programming is the creation of new data types that are appropriate for a particular problem. Data structures are constructs used to represent these new types. The data types developed in this book conform to the abstract data type model, and many of them are polymorphic.

3.1 Abstract Data Types

An *abstract data type* is a set with associated operators (sometimes called primitive operators, or primops). For example, the integers with addition, subtraction, multiplication, and division constitute an abstract data type. C's built-in **int** type is a software model of the integer abstract data type.

The most important aspect of software models of abstract data types is that they are defined by their functional properties, with no concern for the details of their computer representation. Their internal structure, which is implementation-dependent, is irrelevant to those who use them. Abstract data types provide modularity: as long as their properties remain the same, their underlying data structures can be altered with no effect on code that uses them. Moreover, abstract data types improve portability: hardware and system software-dependent factors influencing the way data is stored and handled only affect the low-level code implementing the abstract data types, not the high-level code using them.

A **data structure** is a particular method of representing an abstract data type. Often several methods are possible. For example, rational numbers could be represented as **float** variables, or as structures containing a pair of **int** variables forming a quotient.

There are three main classes of data types:

Atomic Data Types. These store single indivisible data values. Usually, built-in types exist that are adequate for this kind of data, but it is sometimes necessary to write one's own. For example, one may have to represent integers containing several thousand digits, which is well beyond the capacity of C's built-in integer types.

Fixed-Aggregate Data Types. With these, values can be viewed as containing a fixed number of atomic components. For example, the abstract data type "complex number" can be viewed as a pair of real components: one for the magnitude of the real part, and the other for the magnitude of the imaginary part (this example is elaborated later). Structures or arrays are often used to represent such types.

Variable-Aggregate Data Types. Values of these types contain a varying number of subcomponents. For example, the abstract data type "ordered integer list" contains an arbitrarily long ordered sequence of integers. Though arrays are sometimes satisfactory in this case, it is often appropriate to use data structures containing dynamically allocated memory linked together with pointers. This book deals primarily with this class of data type.

A software model of an abstract data type consists of a set of operators for creating, manipulating, and destroying a particular kind of data object. For example, integers in C are created by declaring **int** variables or using integer constants. They are manipulated using operators such as +, —, *, and /. Their destruction is handled automatically. Since the **int** type is a model of an abstract data type, it is possible to use **int** variables without concern for how they are stored, or how their operators work. The built-in types can be manipulated directly with corresponding built-in abstract data type operators. However, no built-in abstract data type operators exist for variables of user-defined types. Instead, they must be accessed with user-defined functions.

Software models of abstract data types are often imperfect; it is impossible, for example, to represent infinite sets. Note that C provides alternate representations for both integers (**int**, **short**, **long**) and reals (**float**, **double**), allowing the programmer to choose between space and precision. When creating imperfect software models, it is often desirable to provide some mechanism to indicate failure (e.g., overflow, underflow). One way of doing this in C is to use the return values of the primitive operations.

```
typedef enum { OK, ERROR } status;
typedef enum { FALSE=0, TRUE=1 } bool;  /*consistent w/C's notion of T/F*/
```

Functions that can detect success or failure will be declared as type **status**, and return the values **OK** and **ERROR**, whereas those that do not perform error checking will be declared as type **void**, and those returning boolean values (true or false) will be declared to be type **bool**. Note the explicit setting of **FALSE** to zero. Although these values will be chosen automatically by the compiler, it is included here to stress the fact that the boolean type is consistent with the C language notion of true and false.

It is better practice for primitive operators to respond to errors with a return value rather than through an explicit action (such as printing an error message, or aborting the program). This way the calling function, which is at a higher level of abstraction and thus more likely to be able to handle the error intelligently, has the most flexibility.

It is sometimes possible to apply improper operators to variables that appear to be representing abstract data types. For example, if C ints are known to be stored as binary machine words on a particular computer, a programmer might directly apply bit-wise shift operators to **int** variables, rather than using * or / when multiplying or dividing by powers of 2. However, variables that are manipulated with operators that do not belong to an abstract data type can no longer be said to belong to that type. Such methods destroy the abstraction of the implementation, and lose the previously described benefits of abstract data types. In essence, the type of a variable depends not only on its definition, but also on the operations to which it is subjected. Note that although it is not appropriate to apply shift operators to **int** variables being used to represent integers, it may be appropriate to use shift operators on **int** variables being used to represent other abstract data types.

Consider the implementation of the abstract data type "complex number." Although there is more than one way in which complex numbers can be implemented, the functional interface to an abstract data type need not change. Therefore, before writing the actual code, the functional interface to the abstract data type model can be chosen. This consists of function prototypes for the functions used to access variables and any necessary type declarations. A function prototype is an enhanced function declaration that contains type information.[1]

Variables will be declared as instances of the complex number abstract data type using the declaration:

```
complex variablename;
```

The functions that will be implemented for this abstract data type are store a complex number, retrieve the "parts" of a complex number, addition, and multiplication. Functions for subtraction, division and testing for equality of complex numbers will be left as exercises.

There are several methods for representing complex numbers. For example, Cartesian coordinates can be used, as in $z = \alpha + i\beta$, where α and β are real numbers, and α represents the real part and β represents the imaginary part. Alternatively, polar coordinates can be used: $z = re^{i\theta}$, where $r = \sqrt{\alpha^2 + \beta^2}$ and $\theta = \tan^{-1}(\beta/\alpha)$. Since one can easily convert between the two representations, choosing one over the other as an interface is largely a matter of taste. In this example, Cartesian coordinates will be used:

```
void load_complex(complex *p_complex, double real, double imaginary);
void retrieve_complex(complex *p_complex, double *p_real,
                      double *p_imaginary);
void add_complex(complex *p_sum, complex *p_complex1,
                 complex *p_complex2);
void multiply_complex(complex *p_product, complex *p_complex1,
                      complex *p_complex2);
typedef struct {
    double real;
    double imaginary;
} complex;
```

Even though Cartesian coordinates were chosen as the interface between the atomic data types and the complex number data type, it was not necessary for the internal representation to be identical. If it had been more desirable to store complex numbers in polar form, a simple conversion could have been done in the "load" and "retrieve" functions.

The implementation of the complex number functions is straightforward. **Multiply_complex()** makes use of the fact that $i = \sqrt{-1}$ and hence $i^2 = -1$.

---

[1]Although this feature is not available in all implementations of C, the proposed ANSI standardization of C allows it.

```
void load_complex(p_complex, real, imaginary)
complex *p_complex;
double real, imaginary;
{
    p_complex->real = real;
    p_complex->imaginary = imaginary;
}

void retrieve_complex(p_complex, p_real, p_imaginary)
complex *p_complex;
double *p_real, *p_imaginary;
{
    *p_real = p_complex->real;
    *p_imaginary = p_complex->imaginary;
}

void add_complex(p_sum, p_complex1, p_complex2)
complex *p_sum, *p_complex1, *p_complex2;
{
    /*
     *   p_sum  =  p_complex1  +  p_complex2;
     *          =  (a + bi)    +  (c + di)
     *          =  (a + c) + (b + d)i
     */
    p_sum->real = p_complex1->real + p_complex2->real;
    p_sum->imaginary = p_complex1->imaginary + p_complex2->imaginary;
}

void multiply_complex(p_product, p_complex1, p_complex2)
complex *p_product, *p_complex1, *p_complex2;
{
    /*
     *   p_product  =  p_complex1  *  p_complex2;
     *              =  (a + bi)    *  (c + di)
     *              =  (ac    bd)  +  (ad + bc)i
     */
    p_product->real = p_complex1->real * p_complex2->real
        - p_complex1->imaginary * p_complex2->imaginary;

    p_product->imaginary = p_complex1->real * p_complex2->imaginary
        + p_complex1->imaginary * p_complex2->real;
}
```

In practice, function prototypes and **typedef** statements should be placed in header files. The header files should then be referenced by the files that use the new types using the **#include** preprocessor statement.[2] Also, in general,

---

[2]In the code in this book, **#include** statements are not shown in the source code. It

pointers to variables of new types rather than variables themselves should be passed as function parameters. This ensures there will be no portability problems when using compilers that do not support structures as parameters and can also improve efficiency by reducing the overhead associates with passing large structures as parameters.

3.2   Polymorphic Data Types

Consider the abstract data type *list*. A list is an ordered sequence of elements. Primitive operations include adding new elements, deleting elements, determining the number of elements in the list, and applying a particular function to each element in a list. Certainly, it would be annoying if the list abstract data type were specific to a particular type of atomic element. This would require creating new incompatible list types (and sets of primitive operators) for "list of **ints**," "list of **floats**," etc. Indeed, it would even be impossible to make a list of a particular kind of abstract data type (e.g., list of complex numbers), because that would require the list code to be dependent on the specific data structure used to represent the abstract data type. Moreover, there would be no way to make a heterogeneous list (one containing data of a variety of types). It is desirable, therefore, to create *polymorphic* data types, that is, data types that are type-independent. In order to create polymorphic data types, it is necessary to understand a little more about types in general.

Data typing is important because it supplies two essential pieces of information: how much memory a variable uses, and how the data is to be interpreted. Polymorphic types, therefore, must be able to function independently of both the size and the exact nature of the data they store. To attain the first goal, polymorphic data structures never access data elements directly. Instead, pointers are used. Pointers provide a fixed-size reference to elements of any size. In C, pointers to characters (**char ***) can be used to store pointers of any type.[3] The type **generic_ptr** will be used to indicate a pointer specifically used to achieve polymorphism.

```
typedef char *generic_ptr;
```

To achieve the second goal, one must abide by the following principle: data structures used to represent polymorphic data types can make no assumptions about the data being stored. Pragmatically, this means that all type-specific

---

is assumed, however, the include files are created and included in the source code where necessary.

[3]In ANSI C, **void *** serves this purpose.

information must be passed as parameters to the primitive operators. Often these parameters will include pointers to type-specific functions.

3.3 Software Development and Life Cycle

Software development can be divided into five stages:

1. Specification
2. Design
3. Implementation
4. Testing/debugging
5. Maintenance

The first stage, specification, consists of a formal definition of the problem to be solved as well as the criteria that will be used to indicate that the problem has been solved correctly. The input and the expected output of the system must be clearly described. In some respects, this is the most difficult stage; with large programming projects, the person who describes the problem is seldom the person (or among the group of people) who designs and implements the solution. One type of problem encountered in the specification stage is simple miscommunication between the parties involved because requirements are often unstructured or imprecise. When developing requirements, it may be helpful to make a prototype. A prototype is a program (or set of programs) that is used to implement a subset of the overall requirements. It is used to test the feasibility of the requirements as well as to help demonstrate certain functions unambiguously. For example, in programs where user interface is important, a prototype can be developed that does nothing but demonstrate the desired user interface.

Designing a system involves determining how the requirements are to be met. In particular, the enumeration of the various programs that will make up the system and the flow of data between them is decided. Program design consists of determining the types of functions or modules required and the data flow among them. Included in the overall program design should be the types of data structures that will be used and the algorithms that will be applied.

It is at the implementation stage that a design is cast into an actual programming language. Programming is made considerably easier by a clear well-thought design. More importantly, if design decisions are delayed until the implementation stage, the overall development time of the program can suffer, as well as leaving an uncertainty as to whether the requirements will actually be satisfied.

When a design has been implemented, it must then be tested to ensure that the requirements have been met. Function testing ensures that individual functions work as specified. Module testing ensures that subprograms (sets of related functions) work as they should. The programmer who implements a function or a module should perform the appropriate testing. Program testing ensures that all the modules communicate and work together correctly.

When testing a program (or a module or function), careful thought should be given to the test cases. It is rarely possible to perform exhaustive tests. Therefore, the input should be divided into classes and at least one case should be taken from each class. As a minimum, the program should be tested using typical cases, extreme cases, and illegal cases. When possible, it is also desirable to formulate a set of test cases that pass through each of the major internal components of the program.

Once the program has been tested, it can be released to a user. It is at this point that much of the time invested in the previous phases will pay off. Undoubtedly, the program will require some kind of maintenance. Either the user will find a case in which the program does not work as was originally specified, or will discover an error in the original specifications. It is difficult to plan for errors in the original specification. Errors in a program that was supposedly designed according to the original specification, however, can be found by first ensuring that the design allowed for such a case. If it did, then the error is in the implementation and the approximate location of the error should be easy to find given the design.

The design and coding practices used throughout the software development process can make a big difference in productivity and maintainability. The later errors are found, the more costly it is to repair them. It is important then to do the design and implementation carefully. Some general software development guidelines follows:

- *Efforts should be concentrated in the design; never design while coding.* Time spent producing a careful, thorough design will be more than made up for with savings in the later phases of a project. The program design should accurately address the needs of the problem. Pseudo-code should be used to create high-level outlines of the algorithms. Whenever possible, the algorithms should be proven logically and mathematically correct.

- *Programs should be divided into reasonably small modules. The modules should first be tested individually and then their interactions should be tested.* One of the greatest difficulties of writing large programs is that their reliability tends to degrade with their length. For example, one might think that if it takes a programmer one hour to develop 50 lines of code with a 99.95% assurance of correctness, it could then be inferred that in 2000 hours, the same programmer could write a 100,000-line program that would also have a 99.95% chance of being correct. Unfortunately, for the 100,000-line program to be correct, each and every 50-line segment must be correct. This has a probability of $(0.9995)^{2000} = 36.78\%$. For the programmer to be 99.95% sure of the 100,000-line program, the development procedure would have to be made more rigorous (and presumably more time-consuming) to the extent that each 50-line segment is 99.999975% certain of being correct.

Although the implications of this phenomenon are very serious, good programming measures can help one cope with the situation. It is easier to debug a function when it is clear and short, and the functions it calls have already been separately debugged. It is also easier to debug several simple modules, each containing few bugs, than one large module containing many.

- *Programming should be done in a top-down fashion. Large tasks should be divided into manageable subtasks.* Starting with a broad abstract outline of the components of a task should lead to a specification of the highest-level functions and control flow. Always begin with the highest levels of abstraction and work toward the lowest.

- *Let the program "grow" from an initial skeleton of dummy functions.* Once the design is completed, the **main()** function can be written. It should be clear and concise, with calls to lower-level functions. Dummy versions of the secondary functions that do nothing but return can then be written. Such dummy functions are called **stubs**. One by one, the lower-level functions can be written (replacing the stubs), which in turn should call stubs of even lower-level functions. In this way, the program grows naturally in a top-down fashion.

- *Do not duplicate code; use functions.* Very often, the same task is performed in several places. When coding, it can be appear quicker to simply copy a few lines into several places than write a function. The problem is that the program then becomes far more difficult to maintain, because any changes later made to those lines must be made in every place they were copied. It is better to have a bothersome number of small functions than a bothersome number of duplicate lines.

- *Close attention should be paid to communication between functions.* Parameters that are being passed should be appropriate for the role of the subfunction. Sometimes it is appropriate to pass more information than appears to be needed if that information might be necessary for an alternate implementation of the subfunction, or if it is being used to make the subfunction more universal. This enables the same function to be called in many places and in many different modules.

- *Reuse good code; rewrite bad code.* Whenever possible, existing functions should be used to solve parts of the problem, provided that the functions perform the job well. In particular, one should be familiar with standard library functions. However, it is not necessary to use bad code just because it already exists. This may cost more time than it initially saves.

- *Invest time now for a long-term payoff.* Take the time to do things right the first time. Do not be afraid to code several alternatives and then choose. Do not be afraid to rewrite code that works, but works poorly or is unclear.

- *Take comments and documentation seriously.* Without them, programs are impossible to read, use, or maintain.

- *Do not work in a vacuum.* Discuss design and coding issues with others. It is very helpful to read code written by others and have others read yours.

- *Isolate input and output in modules specialized for that purpose.* Do not make them side effects of modules that do other tasks.

- *Do not translate one language into another.* When using a new language, use coding practices that are accepted for that language. Although a programmer trained in an early dialect of FORTRAN might be tempted to use **goto**'s to write simple loops in C, that would be a grave mistake.

- *Above all else, clarity.* Don't be afraid to violate any general principle for the sake of clarity.

- *Avoid global variables. Use functions with parameters instead.* When a program contains no global variables, one knows that each function manipulates only the data that is passed in the form of parameters. Global variables make code unclear because they obscure these data dependencies: when reading a high-level function, one can never be sure which of the functions it calls use or modify the global variables. Furthermore, since functions that use global variables have these variable names "hard coded" in, they are difficult to reuse. If several functions have to share some "private" global data, consider placing them in the same file and using a **static** external variable.[4]

- *Avoid using* **goto***'s.* The **goto** construct disrupts orderly program flow, making programs hard to read. C contains a rich set of control structures, so **goto**s are never needed to build control structures like loops. Moreover, C contains a number of other constructs (**break, continue, return,** and the ability to call termination functions like **exit()**) that can be used in many of the situations where one might think of using a **goto**. Although these other constructs disrupt structure as well (and hence should be used with care), they each fulfill a specific role, so their use is clearer than that of the all-purpose **goto**. Legitimate uses of **goto**'s, such as jumping directly out of a deeply nested control structure, are rare.

- *Use abstract data types.*

- *Write generic/polymorphic functions.* Although they often take slightly longer to write, they are far more likely to be reusable. This way, a "tool box" of routines can be developed over time.

- *Avoid environment-specific language features.* In the interest of writing portable code, stick to the standard features of the language being used.

- *Programs should be crash-proof.* A well-written program should never crash. In particular, it should be able to cope with illegal input.

- *Use all available tools.* Source-level debuggers, interpreters, and code analyzers (such as **lint** for C) are valuable time-savers.

- *Use assertions.* Assertions are statements placed in a program to test that conditions that logically should be met have indeed been met. They help to track logic errors during development.

- *Avoid explicit literals.* Explicit literals (character, numeric, and string values) make programs hard to modify. Use **#define**'d symbolic names instead.

---

[4]Object-oriented programming languages have specific mechanisms for dealing with this situation.

- *C provides great freedom. Use it responsibly.* Avoid side effects in logical tests. Avoid being overly compact at the expense of clarity. Avoid following the "convention" of using truncated cryptic names.

- *Think twice before optimizing.* Programming time is a precious resource. It may be easier to get faster hardware or a better compiler than to "optimize" a program. First consider using a different algorithm altogether. If the program must be optimized, profile the code to find out where it is spending its time. Remember it is always better to improve an algorithm than tune the clarity out of code.

3.4   Summary

Data abstraction and polymorphism are two of the key aspects of data representation. Data abstraction is the specification of types by their function rather than by their implementation. This provides both modularity and portability. Polymorphic data types are independent of the data elements that they store. This independence provides flexibility, abstraction, and heterogeneity.

Good software development practices are increasingly important as programs become large and complex. The illustration of these practices is an important theme throughout this book.

3.5   Exercises

1. Write the following functions for the complex number abstract data type:

   (a) **subtract_complex()**, which takes the difference of two complex numbers.

   ```
   void subtract_complex(complex *p_difference, complex *p_complex1,
                         complex *p_complex2);
   ```

   (b) **equal_complex()**, which returns **TRUE** if two complex numbers are equal and **FALSE** otherwise.

   ```
   bool equal_complex(complex *p_complex1, complex *p_complex2);
   ```

   (c) **divide_complex()**, which determines the quotient of two complex numbers.

```
void divide_complex(complex *p_quotient, complex *p_complex1,
                    complex *p_complex2);
```

(d) Suppose one attempted to divide $10 + 2i$ by $0 + 0i$. The result cannot be computed due to division by 0. However, the way **divide_complex()** is prototyped, there is no allowing for this case. Rewrite the function to return an error indicator.

(e) When doing division with double-precision numbers, division by a very small number is as much a problem as division by 0. Modify the function to return an error when attempting to divide by a very small number. How small should the number be before an error is signaled?

(f) Often when dealing with double-precision numbers, strict equality is impossible to achieve (due to number representation). Modify **equal_complex()** so that it returns **TRUE** if the two complex numbers differ by no more than a small amount. How is this related to the problem in the previous part?

2. What happens when you deliberately overflow or underflow an **int** variable in C? How about divide by zero?

3. Write C code to implement a rational number abstract data type using a structure containing a pair of **int** variables. Write the following functions:

```
void load_rational(rational *p_rational, int numerator,
                   int denominator);
void retrieve_rational(rational *p_rational, int *p_numerator,
                       int *p_denominator);
void add_rational(rational *p_result, rational *p_rational1,
                  rational *p_rational2);
void subtract_rational(rational *p_result, rational *p_rational1,
                       rational *p_rational2);
void multiply_rational(rational *p_result, rational *p_rational1,
                       rational *p_rational2);
status divide_rational(rational *p_result, rational *p_rational1,
                       rational *p_rational2);
bool equal_rational(rational *p_rational1, rational *p_rational2);
```

4. One data structure that can be used to represent large positive integers is an array of digits. For each of the following data structures, write a four-function calculator that can handle integers containing up to 100

digits. In addition to the mathematical operators, write operators to read and write large integers. *Hint:* For input and output, you may want to convert the arrays of digits to and from strings. Be sure to convert from characters to integers in a machine-independent manner (i.e., do not use the fact that you know the collating sequence, ASCII or EBCDIC).

(a) Use the following data structure to represent integers.

```
typedef struct {
    int digits[100], number_of_digits;
} integer;
```

where **digits[0]** contains the leftmost digit, and **number_of_digits** is the number of digits stored.

(b) Use the above type, but have **digits[0]** store the rightmost digit.

(c) Use the following data structure to represent integers.

```
typedef struct {
    int digits[101];
} integer;
```

where **digits[0]** contains the leftmost digit, and the rightmost digit is followed by -1 (a dummy digit).

(d) Use the same type as in part 4c, but have **digits[0]** contain the rightmost digit.

(e) What are the relative merits of the previous four data structures in terms of ease of mathematical manipulation? Input/output?

(f) Extend your calculator to handle large integers that can be either positive or negative. Justify your choice of data structure.

5. Use the complex number routines to develop a small four-function calculator for complex numbers.

6. Write a set of routines to represent integers. Start with **typedef int integer;**, but write your own functions:

```
status add_integer(integer *p_result, integer *p_integer1,
                    integer *p_integer2);
status subtract_integer(integer *p_result, integer *p_integer1,
                        integer *p_integer2);
status multiply_integer(integer *p_result, integer *p_integer1,
```

```
                                integer *p_integer2);
          status divide_integer(integer *p_result, integer *p_integer1,
                                integer *p_integer2);
```

Your functions should check for overflow, underflow, and divide by zero.

CHAPTER
FOUR

LISTS

In this chapter, the list data structure is presented. This structure is of such a general nature that it can be used as the basis for the implementation of other data structures.

4.1   List Concepts

Lists are *ordered* collections of objects. This does not mean that lists are sorted, but rather that as items are added, one can predict their relative positions. For example, one can define an operator that adds items at the front (i.e., the new item will always be the first in the list, with the rest of the items shifting over one position), or at the end, or at any arbitrary position.

Lists have the following properties:

- A list can have 0 or more items.

- A new item can be added to the list at any point.

- Any item in the list can be deleted.

- Any item in the list can be accessed.

- Each item in the list can be visited in turn (i.e., the list can be traversed).

The last property provides for much of the generality of lists.

There is a difficulty in implementing lists as abstract data types, due to the large variety of operations that may be performed on a list. In particular, although it is clear one has to insert items into lists and delete items from them, there are many variations possible on these functions.

For example, it may be desirable simply to insert an item at the beginning of a list. Alternatively, one may want to insert an item at a particular position (*insert_atposition*), or before or after a particular node (*insert_before*, *insert_after*, respectively). Another alternative is to *append* the item (insert at the end). A similar set of operations can be defined for deleting an item from a list.

Nevertheless, lists can be implemented as abstract data types so long as the interface is clearly defined. C function prototypes describe the arguments for a small subset of the possible primitive operations. Additional primitive operations will be defined as applications are developed.

Init_list() has one argument, a pointer to the list to be initialized. Since this function could potentially involve dynamic space allocation, it returns an error indicator. **Empty_list()** also has one argument and returns **TRUE** if the list is not empty. If the list is empty, it returns **FALSE**. The function **append()**, which adds an item to the end of a list, has two arguments, the data to be inserted and a pointer to the list to which it should be added. Similarly, the function **insert()**, which inserts at the front of the list, has two arguments. **Delete()**, the dual of **insert()**, removes the first item from the list passed and places the data from the deleted node in its parameter.

```
status init_list(list *p_L);
bool empty_list(list L);
status append(list *p_L, generic_ptr data);
status insert(list *p_L, generic_ptr data);
status delete(list *p_L, generic_ptr *p_data);
```

Note that these function prototypes are implementation-independent. The type **generic_ptr** is used to represent data of any type. This concept is clarified later.

Most programmers are familiar with one type of implementation of lists, arrays. In general, arrays can provide excellent implementation of lists if few items will be deleted. Note that with an array implementation, it is necessary to shift down all the elements to fill in the hole left by deleting an element in the middle of the array. This can be a very expensive operation.

Another shortcoming with arrays is that they have a fixed size. In many applications, the number of elements needed may vary greatly, depending on the input, so it cannot be known in advance how many array elements will be needed.[1] Also, memory requirements may change *during* execution.

4.2   Linked Lists

What is desired is a way to allocate memory for new items only when necessary and to destroy that memory when it is no longer needed. Furthermore, this newly allocated memory must be logically combined into a single entity (representing the list). A linked list provides this capability. It is comprised of a set of nodes, where each node has two fields: one that points to the information, and one that points to the next node in the list. Unlike the elements of an array, the nodes in a linked list are not necessarily stored contiguously. Therefore, to find an arbitrary node in the list, one must start at the beginning of the list and by using the information that is stored in each node, locate the next node in the list. This procedure must be repeated until the desired node is located.

Formally, a linear linked list and a node are defined as follows:

- A linear linked list is a pointer to a node.

- A linear list node has two fields:

    1. a **datapointer** field, which points to a data element
    2. a **next** field, which is a linked list

The definition of a linked list is recursive, a linked list is a pointer to a node, which in turn points to a linked list. The base case of the recursion is the null list.

Graphically, the list **L** of three integers is represented as

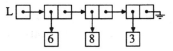

A null list is represented by the value **NULL**. The empty list **N** is represented as

$$N$$

---

[1]This problem can be solved with dynamic arrays, discussed in Chapter 5, but that technique also poses problems.

4.2.1   C Representation of Nodes

To ensure that the list is implemented as a polymorphic data structure, the nodes contain pointers to data, rather than the data itself.

```
typedef struct node node, *list;

struct node {
    generic_ptr datapointer;
    list next;
};
```

By making the **datapointer** field a **generic_ptr**, the low-level routines that manipulate the linked list do not need to know anything about the particular data type. The only difficulty in using this technique is that storage for the data elements will have to be managed by the programmer. This will be handled by developing a layer of routines on top of low-level list routines. The secondary routines will be type-specific and will dynamically allocate space as necessary. For example, if one were going to be storing integers in a linked list, one might create a function called **insert_int()**, which would have two parameters. The first parameter would be the list in which to insert a new node and the second would be the integer value to insert. **Insert_int()** could then allocate space for an **int** variable and call **insert()** to put the newly allocated space in the list.

4.2.2   Using Preprocessor Macros

Two goals in developing list functions are to make the interfaces as clean as possible and to make the source code as readable as possible. To do the latter, preprocessor macros simplify the access of node fields.

```
#define DATA(L) ((L)->datapointer)
#define NEXT(L) ((L)->next)
```

A preprocessor macro is a template that abbreviates another piece of code. Macros can have arguments and thus are similar to functions. The difference is that the code to which a macro expands is actually copied into place before the program is compiled. In applications where speed is critical, macros are used instead of functions. Another advantage of macros (in this case) is that if the implementation of the node were changed (e.g., using arrays for lists instead of linked nodes), only the macros will have to be redefined. By convention, macro names are in uppercase.

4.2.3 An Interface for Allocating Nodes

In general, whenever a variable is declared, it should also be initialized. This also holds true for dynamically allocated space. Therefore, the function to allocate a new node, **allocate_node()** will use **malloc()** to obtain the actual memory, and then will initialize the data fields. The **NEXT** field will always be initialized to **NULL**. The **DATAPOINTER** field, however, will be initialized to a passed parameter. It was deliberately chosen not to initialize the **NEXT** field from a passed parameter because higher-level functions are more readable when the **NEXT** is set "locally."

Since it is possible for memory allocation to fail, it is important for **allocate_node()** to return an error code as necessary. There can be no error freeing a node using **free_node()** (except for passing an invalid address, which is very difficult to catch). This yields the following functions:

```
status allocate_node(p_L, data)
list *p_L;
generic_ptr data;
{
    list L = (list) malloc(sizeof(node));

    if (L == NULL)
        return ERROR;

    *p_L = L;
    DATA(L) = data;
    NEXT(L) = NULL;
    return OK;
}

void free_node(p_L)
list *p_L;
{
    free(*p_L);
    *p_L = NULL;
}
```

A small example of **allocate_node()** is instructive:

```
Initially
```

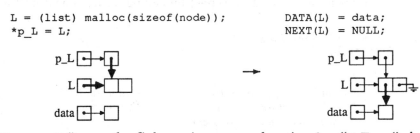

Free_node() uses the C dynamic memory function **free()**. **Free()** destroys the node pointed to by the pointer it is passed, making the space available to the computer for other use. Unfortunately, the pointer passed to **free()** is not automatically made null, but is left pointing to a nonexistent node. This is called a "dangling pointer." These are dangerous because they can be mistaken for valid pointers and used to access and modify memory that may have been reassigned for a different purpose. Therefore, **free_node()** makes the calling routine's pointer **NULL** after calling **free()**. Since no error is possible, **free_node()** is of type **void**.

Continuing with the above illustration, **free_node()** performs the following operations:

```
free(*p_L);                                 *p_L = NULL;
```

Note that **free_node()** does not insure that the fields of the node have already been freed.

4.2.4   Primitive Operations on Linked Lists

In Section 4.1, function prototypes were given for four primitive list operations: initialization, insertion, deletion, and testing for emptiness. The implementation of these functions are described for linked lists.

Initializing a List

The application programmer creates a list using the declaration:

```
list varname;
```

This creates a variable **varname** that must be initialized. The first thing that must be done is to assign a value to that variable. This is done (following the techniques for abstract data types) by calling an initialization function.

```
status init_list(p_L)
list *p_L;
{
    /*
     *   Initialize *p_L by setting the list pointer to NULL.
     *   Always return OK (a different implementation
     *   may allow errors to occur).
     */
    *p_L = NULL;
    return OK;
}
```

Init_list() takes a pointer to the list to be initialized. The list is initialized to be empty by assigning the pointer a value of **NULL**. This function will always return **OK**, since no error can occur with this implementation of init_list().

Status of a List

Emptiness can be determined by checking if a list variable is **NULL**.

```
bool empty_list(L)
list L;
{
    /*
     *   Return TRUE if L is an empty list, FALSE otherwise.
     */
    return (L == NULL) ? TRUE : FALSE;
}
```

Inserting an Item

The **insert()** function inserts an item at the front of a list. The item that was previously at the front of the list is placed after the the new item.

```
status insert(p_L, data)
list *p_L;
generic_ptr data;
{
    /*
     *   Insert a new node containing data as the first item in *p_L.
     */
```

```
        list L;

        if (allocate_node(&L, data) == ERROR)
            return ERROR;
        NEXT(L) = *p_L;
        *p_L = L;
        return OK;
    }
```

Insert() has two arguments, a pointer to a list and the data item to be inserted (a **generic_ptr**). **Allocate_node()** is used to create a new node. If this function fails, **insert()** returns **ERROR**. Otherwise, the **NEXT** field is set to point to the old list (i.e., the first node in the list). This creates a new list. The new list is returned to the calling routines by changing the pointer to the list that was supplied as an argument. Upon successful termination, **insert()** returns **OK**.[2]

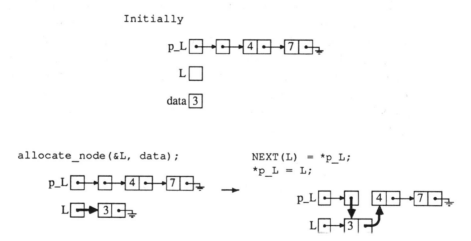

Append

The **append()** function adds a node to the end of a list. The item that was previously last in the list is set to point to the new item.

```
    status append(p_L, data)
    list *p_L;
    generic_ptr data;
    {
```

---

[2]To simplify the pictures, the actual data (as opposed to a pointer) will be shown as part of the node.

```
/*
 *   Append a new node containing data as the last item in *p_L.
 */
list L, tmplist;

if (allocate_node(&L, data) == ERROR)
    return ERROR;

if (empty_list(*p_L) == TRUE)
    *p_L = L;
else {
    for (tmplist = *p_L; NEXT(tmplist)!=NULL; tmplist=NEXT(tmplist)) ;
    NEXT(tmplist) = L;
}
return OK;
}
```

Like **insert()**, **append()** has two arguments, a pointer to a list and a generic pointer. **Allocate_node()** is used to try to create a new node. If this function fails, then **append()** returns **ERROR**. Otherwise, the node is appended to the list. There are two cases that must be considered. If the list is empty, ***p_L** is modified to contain only the new node. If the list already contains at least one item, then it is traversed until the last node is found. The last node's **NEXT** field is then set to point to the new node. Upon successful termination, **append()** returns **OK**.

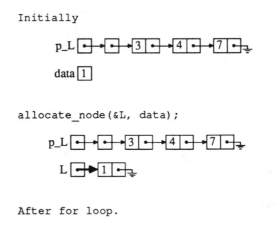

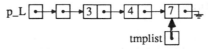

```
NEXT(tmplist) = L;
```

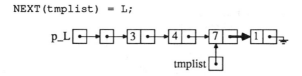

Deleting an Item

The **delete()** function deletes the node at the front of a list and passes back the data that was at the front of the list via a pointer argument. The item that was second in the list becomes first. Deleting the first node in the list is simply a special case of deleting any arbitrary node in the list. Therefore, the function **delete()** can be implemented based on another primitive operation, **delete_node()**.

```
status delete(p_L, p_data)
list *p_L;
generic_ptr *p_data;
{
    /*
     *   Delete the first node in *p_L and return the DATA in p_data.
     */
    if (empty_list(*p_L))
        return ERROR;

    *p_data = DATA(*p_L);
    return delete_node(p_L, *p_L);
}
```

Delete() has two arguments, a pointer to a list and a pointer to a place in which to put the data that was stored in the deleted node. Since it is an error to try to delete from an empty list, **ERROR** is returned if the list is empty. Otherwise, **delete()** copies the data stored in the first node in the list to the argument **p_data** and deletes the first node via a call to **delete_node()**.

```
status delete_node(p_L, node)
list *p_L;
list node;
{
    /*
     *   Delete node from *p_L.
     */
    if (empty_list(*p_L) == TRUE)
        return ERROR;
```

```
    if (*p_L == node)
        *p_L = NEXT(*p_L);
    else {
        list L;
        for (L = *p_L; L != NULL && NEXT(L) != node; L = NEXT(L)) ;

        if (L == NULL)
            return ERROR;
        else
            NEXT(L) = NEXT(node);
    }
    free_node(&node);
    return OK;
}
```

Delete_node() has two arguments: a pointer to the list to modify, and the node to delete. If the node to be deleted is the first one in the list, the list pointer, **p_L** is advanced. Otherwise, the list is traversed to find the node that points to the one to be deleted. If it is found, its **NEXT** field is set to point to the node after the one to be deleted, and the node itself is deleted with a call to **free_node()**. If the node cannot be found in the list, then **ERROR** is returned.

To understand **delete_node()**, it is helpful to trace the operation in two cases: when the first node is deleted, and when a middle node is deleted. Deleting the first node is done as follows:

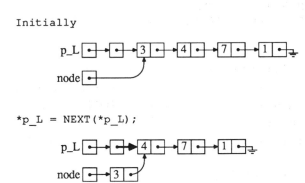

Deleting any other node is done as follows:

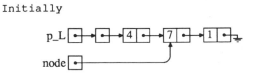

After for loop

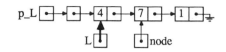

NEXT(L) = NEXT(node);

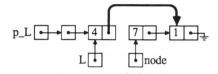

Although they are very short, **append()**, **insert()**, and **delete_node()** are quite sophisticated. Understanding these algorithms provides the groundwork for understanding any function that operates on linked lists.

4.3 Application: Adding Polynomials

The first application to be developed is representative of an entire class of problems ideally suited for linked lists: polynomial arithmetic. In this section, a program is developed to handle just one operation on polynomials, addition.

A polynomial is of the form

$$\sum_{i=0}^{n} c_i x^i$$

where c_i is the coefficient of the ith term, and n is the degree of the polynomial. Some examples are

$$5x^2 + 3x + 1$$
$$12x^3 - 4x$$
$$50x^{20} + 10x^{10} - 5x^3 - 4x^2 + 2x + 1$$

It is not necessary to write terms of the polynomials in descending order of degree. In other words, the two polynomials $x + 1$ and $1 + x$ are equivalent.

To add two polynomials, terms with the same degree are grouped together and the coefficients are added:

$5x^2$	+	$3x$	+	1
		$2x$	−	8
$5x^2$	+	$5x$	−	7

$10x^3$	+	x^2			+	10
				$8x$	−	4
$10x^3$	+	x^2	+	$8x$	+	6

4.3.1   Polynomial Addition Program Design

The program for adding polynomials decomposes into three parts:

1. Read the two polynomials.
2. Add them.
3. Print the sum.

Polynomials should be viewed as an abstract data type. As such, it should be possible to develop an implementation in which there is a fixed set of functions on which an internal representation of polynomials (to those functions) can be manipulated. Since polynomials can be developed in an abstract manner, no function other than the polynomial primitive operation functions has to know the implementation details. Of course, the software implementation of the abstract data type polynomial should be considered carefully. In particular, how should the polynomials be represented? Should any constraints be placed on input or output?

These sort of questions relate to the degree of "perfection" of the software model of the polynomial abstract data type. Initially, it will be assumed that in a single polynomial, no term may be entered with the same degree as a previously entered term. That is, $5x^3 + 10x + 4x^2 + 2x$ is not valid input because there are two terms of degree 1. The user will not be constrained to enter the polynomials in order of degree. However, the output will not be in any particular order either. Furthermore, the addition of polynomials will be a destructive operation. That is, setting $S = A + B$ (where S, A, and B are polynomials) will leave A and B in an indeterminate state. A better software model is developed in the Exercises.

A set of function prototypes for polynomials can be developed.

```
status read_poly(polynomial *p_poly);
void write_poly(polynomial poly);
status add_poly(polynomial *p_poly1, polynomial *p_poly2);
void destroy_poly(polynomial *p_poly);
```

Although, in general, abstract data types should not have side effects, this implementation develops functions that are used because of their side effects. **Read_poly()** reads standard input for the terms of a polynomial and **write_poly()** writes the polynomial to standard output. To make the point that **add_poly()** is not a true representation of the addition function, it is defined to perform the operations

```
p_poly1 = p_poly1 + p_poly2;
p_poly2 = 0;
```

Destroy_poly() is used to delete an entire polynomial. Whenever functions exist to create objects, functions should also exist to delete them.

4.3.2   Polynomial Driver

With the interface to polynomials fully defined, the main routine for this program is very small:

```
main()
{
    /*
     *  Read two polynomials, add them, and print the result.
     */
    polynomial poly1, poly2;

    printf("Enter the first polynomial:\n");
    if (read_poly(&poly1) == ERROR) {
        printf("error in reading polynomial\n");
        exit(1);
    }
    printf("Enter the second polynomial:\n");
    if (read_poly(&poly2) == ERROR) {
        printf("error in reading polynomial\n");
        exit(1);
    }
    printf("    ");
    write_poly(poly1);
    printf("\n+ ");
    write_poly(poly2);
    if (add_poly(&poly1, &poly2) -- ERROR) {
        printf("error adding polynomials\n");
        exit(1);
    }
    printf("\n= ");
    write_poly(poly1);
    printf("\n");
    destroy_poly(&poly1);
    destroy_poly(&poly2);
}
```

The driver uses the polynomial routines to perform all the low-level operations. The bulk of the code in this routine is used for formatting the output and performing error checking.

4.3.3   Polynomial Data Type Implementation

There are several methods one could use for maintaining information about the polynomial terms. The obvious choice is a linked list, where each node in the list holds information about a single term. There are two items associated with each term: the coefficient of the term, and the degree.

```
typedef list polynomial;

typedef struct term {
    int coefficient;
    int degree;
} term;
```

Reading Polynomials

Read_poly() reads the terms of a polynomials and creates the internal data structure. Thought must be given as to how the user can indicate that there are no more terms to be entered. There are at least two alternatives. The program could, after each term is entered, ask if there are more terms to be entered. This method would be very annoying. It is better for the user to indicate completion without the computer constantly asking the same question. One way to do this is to have the user enter out-of-range data as a flag to indicate the end of input. It is not always possible to "find" out-of-range data, but in this case, input can be terminated when a term of $0x^0$ is entered (that is, with a coefficient of 0 and a degree of 0).

```
status read_poly(p_poly)
polynomial *p_poly;
{
    /*
     *   Read standard input for coefficients and degrees and create
     *   a list of terms (a polynomial).   Input is terminated when
     *   0,0 is entered.
     */
    int coef;
    int degree;

    if (init_list(p_poly) == ERROR)
        return ERROR;

    do {
        printf("\tEnter coefficient, degree (0,0 when done): ");
        scanf(" %d,%d", &coef, &degree);
```

```
        if (coef != 0)
            if (term_insert(p_poly, coef, degree) == ERROR)
                return ERROR;
    } while (coef != 0 || degree != 0) ;
    return OK;
}
```

This function uses a list interface routine **term_insert()** that allocates the **term** structure and inserts the item into the list of terms.

Writing Polynomials

Writing polynomials is simply a matter of traversing the list and writing out the individual terms. This could use the (newly defined) list primitive operation **traverse()**. This function would have two parameters, a list and a function to call with each item in the list:

```
status traverse(list L, status (*p_func_f)());
```

With that function defined, both **write_poly()** and the associated function **write_term()** are quite short:

```
void write_poly(poly)
polynomial poly;
{
    /*
     *  Output a polynomial.
     */
    traverse(poly, write_term);
}

status write_term(p_term)
term *p_term;
{
    /*
     *  Output a term of a polynomial.
     */
    printf(" + %dx^%d", p_term->coefficient, p_term->degree);
    return OK;
}
```

Of course, **write_term()** outputs the same thing every time it is called:

$$+ \text{coef } x^{degree}$$

This causes output such as

$$+5x^3 + -2x^2 + 1x^0$$

Ideally, the leading plus sign should be eliminated and instead of adding a negative number, as in "$+ - 2x^2$," a positive number should be subtracted ($-2x^2$). Techniques for doing this are discussed in the Exercises.

Adding Polynomials

The algorithm for adding polynomials implemented here takes two lists, **L1** and **L2**, and sets **L1** to **L1 + L2**.

```
for each node, term, in list L1
    find the node, match_term, with the same degree in L2
        and delete it
    update the coefficient of term
        COEF(term) = COEF(term) + COEF(match_term)
Put the remaining items in L2 in L1
```

This algorithm requires a primitive function that will find a node in a list with a particular key. Once this node has been found, then the primitive operation **delete_node()** can be used to delete it. This primitive operation will be called **find_key()**:

```
status find_key(list L, generic_ptr key, int (*p_cmp_f)(), list *p_keynode);
```

The parameters to this function are the list to search, the search key, a comparison function, and a pointer to the location in which the node should be placed.

Another primitive operation required is one to traverse the list. **Traverse()** could be used, but more than one parameter would be required (both the data node and the second list have to be passed). Therefore, a more flexible method of iterating over the entire list is needed. This function, **list_iterator**, would return the "next" node each time it is called. Coupled with a method in which the **DATA** field could be accessed in an implementation-independent fashion, each term could be visited.

Two techniques could be used to allow a function to have access to data returned in a previous invocation. One would be to use **static** local data. This would be appropriate if it were guaranteed that calls to the function would never be interspersed (i.e., no attempt were made to traverse two lists node by node). Another technique is to require the last return value as a parameter.

This latter technique is used here. The first time the function is called, NULL should be passed as the "last return value."

```
list list_iterator(list L, list lastreturn);
```

With the observation that the **DATA** macro allows one to access the **data** field of a node in an implementation-independent fashion, **add_poly()** can be coded:

```
status add_poly(p_poly1, p_poly2)
polynomial *p_poly1, *p_poly2;
{
    /*
     *   Polynomial p_poly1 += p_poly2;
     *   p_poly2 = 0;
     */
    list lastreturn = NULL;
    list match_node;
    term *p_term;
    term *p_match_term;
    int coef, degree;

    while ( (lastreturn = list_iterator(*p_poly1, lastreturn)) != NULL) {
        p_term = (term *) DATA(lastreturn);
        if (find_key(*p_poly2,(generic_ptr)p_term,cmp_degree,&match_node)
          == OK) {
            p_match_term = (term *) DATA(match_node);
            p_term->coefficient += p_match_term->coefficient;
            delete_node(p_poly2, match_node);
            free(p_match_term);
        }
    }
    while (empty_list(*p_poly2) == FALSE) {
        if (term_delete(p_poly2, &coef, &degree) == ERROR)
            return ERROR;
        else if (term_insert(p_poly1, coef, degree) == ERROR)
            return ERROR;
    }
    return OK;
}

int cmp_degree(p_term1, p_term2)
term *p_term1, *p_term2;
{
    return p_term1->degree - p_term2->degree;
}
```

This function uses a list interface routine **term_delete()** that deletes the first node in a list and returns the coefficient and degree that was in the **term** stored in that node.

Deleting Polynomials

Since a polynomial is a linked list, all that is needed is a function to delete an entire linked list. This could be written as a loop consisting of calls to **delete()**, but instead a new primitive operation, **destroy()**, will be defined. This function will have two arguments, a pointer to the list to be deleted and a function for deleting the data stored in each node:

```
void destroy(list *p_L, void (*p_func_f)());

void destroy_poly(p_poly)
polynomial *p_poly;
{
    destroy(p_poly, free);
}
```

The second argument to **destroy()** is the C library function **free()**.

4.3.4   List Interface Routines for Polynomials

Routines to add (and delete) nodes to (from) a linked list were developed (Section 4.2.4). **Insert()** adds a node into a list with the assumption that the **DATA** field already points to the appropriate application data. In order to use that routine in a program, it will always be necessary to allocate space for the data (either dynamically or statically). Once space has been found, the data can be copied and a pointer to that space can be stored in the **DATA** field. This function is performed for polynomials using **term_insert()**.

```
status term_insert(p_L, coef, deg)
list *p_L;
int coef;
int deg;
{
    /*
     *  Insert a term structure in a p_L using coef and deg as the data.
     */
    term *p_term = (term *) malloc(sizeof(term));

    if (p_term == NULL)
        return ERROR;
```

```
    p_term->coefficient = coef;
    p_term->degree = deg;
    if (insert(p_L, (generic_ptr) p_term) == ERROR) {
        free(p_term);
        return ERROR;
    }
    return OK;
}
```

Term_insert() dynamically allocates a **term** structure and copies the coefficient and degree into the space allocated. It then calls the linked list function **insert()** to perform the actual insertion of the data into the linked list. Note that **term_insert()** is implementation-independent. As long as there exists a function to insert into the list that takes the list and a **generic_ptr** as arguments, whether the list is implemented as an array or as a linked list is irrelevant to this function.

Delete_term() uses the **delete()** primitive operation to delete the first node from a list. **Delete_term()** retrieves the **term** structure from the deleted node and returns the coefficient and degree values via passed parameters:

```
status term_delete(p_L, p_coef, p_deg)
list *p_L;
int *p_coef;
int *p_deg;
{
    /*
     *   Delete a node from p_L. Return the data stored in
     *   the node in p_coef and p_deg.
     */
    term *p_term;

    if (delete(p_L, (generic_ptr *) &p_term) == ERROR)
        return ERROR;
    *p_coef = p_term->coefficient;
    *p_deg = p_term->degree;
    free(p_term);
    return OK;
}
```

4.3.5 Additional List Primitive Operations

Several prototypes for primitive operations were described in the development of the polynomial addition program. The function stubs can now be expanded.

Traverse

Traverse() is a recursive function in which an application-defined function is called with the data stored in each node.

```
status traverse(L, p_func_f)
list L;
status (*p_func_f) ();
{
    /*
     * Call p_func_f() with the DATA field of each node in L.
     * If p_func_f() ever returns ERROR, this function returns ERROR.
     */
    if (empty_list(L))
        return OK;

    if ((*p_func_f)(DATA(L)) == ERROR)
        return ERROR;
    else
        return traverse(NEXT(L), p_func_f);
}
```

If the application-defined function returns **ERROR**, traversal of the list is halted and **traverse()** returns **ERROR**.

Finding Specific Nodes

To find a particular node while maintaining polymorphic data structures requires a comparison function to be passed as an argument. **Find_key()** uses this technique to locate a node based on a key specified by the application.

```
status find_key(L, key, p_cmp_f, p_keynode)
list L;
generic_ptr key;
int (*p_cmp_f)();
list *p_keynode;
{
    /*
     *   Find the node in L that has a data—matching key.
     *   If the node is found, it is passed back in *p_keynode.
     *   OK is returned.  p_cmp_f() is a comparison function
     *   that returns 0 when there is a match.
     */
    list curr = NULL;

    while ( (curr = list_iterator(L, curr)) != NULL) {
```

```
        if ((*p_cmp_f)(key, DATA(curr)) == 0) {
            *p_keynode = curr;
            return OK;
        }
    }
    return ERROR;
}
```

This function uses the **list_iterator()** primitive operation to visit each node in the list. If the comparison function **p_cmp_f()** returns 0, a match has been found. The function returns **OK** and the node is returned via the parameter **p_keynode**.

List Iterator

The list iterator is a function that when called repeatedly returns each node of the list. This implementation requires that the previously returned value be passed as an argument. To begin the iteration, **NULL** is passed as the "last return value."

```
list list_iterator(L, lastreturn)
list L, lastreturn;
{
    /*
     *  Return each item of L in turn. Return NULL
     *  after the last item has been returned.
     *  lastreturn is the value that was returned last.
     *  If lastreturn is NULL, start at the beginning of L.
     */
    return (lastreturn == NULL) ? L : NEXT(lastreturn);
}
```

Destroying an Entire List

When a list is no longer needed, it should be destroyed and all its nodes freed. The naive approach to destroying a list:

```
status destroy(p_L)
list *p_L;
{
    if (empty_list(p_L) == FALSE) {
        destroy(&NEXT(*p_L));
        free_node(p_L);
    }
```

```
        return OK;
    }
```

does not work correctly. Although all the nodes will be deleted, the space used by the data (which may have been dynamically allocated) is never freed.[3]

The correct version of **destroy()** has two parameters, the list to be destroyed and a pointer to a function. The function that is passed (if not **NULL**) will be called with the **generic_ptr** data stored in each node before the node is deleted.

```
    void destroy(p_L, p_func_f)
    list *p_L;
    void (*p_func_f)();
    {
        /*
         *  Delete every node in *p_L.
         *  If p_func_f() is nonnull, call it with the data stored
         *  in each node.
         */
        if (empty_list(*p_L) == FALSE) {
            destroy(&NEXT(*p_L), p_func_f);
            if (p_func_f != NULL)
                (*p_func_f)(DATA(*p_L));
            free_node(p_L);
        }
    }
```

Note the order in which the nodes are deleted. By recursively calling **destroy()** before deleting the node, the list is essentially deleted backwards (i.e., that last node is deleted first and the first node is deleted last). This is done because it is not possible to access the **NEXT** field of a deleted node. The iterative counterpart of this function would use a temporary variable to store the **NEXT** field as the list was destroyed (in order).

4.4   Application: Graphical Display List

Another application that can use linked lists is one that is normally handled by graphics packages or by the hardware in graphics workstations. In computer graphics, a display list is a set of graphics commands that are logically combined together to yield a single entity. This entity, a *display list*, can be manipulated and displayed as though it were a single graphical primitive.

---

[3]Storage that can no longer be accessed but that has not been properly freed is called *garbage*.

What constitutes a true graphical primitive depends on the implementation of the graphics system. Examples of typical primitives are lines, circles, and rectangles. To display a primitive, one must give absolute coordinates for the various parameters. For example, to display a rectangle, one must give the coordinates of opposite corners, as in:

rectangle 5, 5, 10, 10

which indicates a rectangle with corners at (5,5), (5,10), (10,10), and (10,5). To display a line, one must give the endpoints of the line:

line 0, 0, 10, 0

which indicates that a line should be drawn from the Cartesian coordinates[4] (0,0) to (10,0).

Suppose one wanted to animate the previously defined rectangle and line. What would be necessary to show them moving off to the right (i.e., X coordinate increasing)? One would have to erase the rectangle and the line and then redraw them with the X coordinate increased by 1. The following sequence of operations would occur:

```
color white
rectangle 5, 5, 10, 10
line 0, 0, 10, 0
color black
rectangle 5, 5, 10, 10
line 0, 0, 10, 0
color white
rectangle 6, 5, 11, 10
line 1, 0, 11, 0
color black rectangle 6, 5, 11, 10
line 1, 0, 11, 0
etc.
```

Certainly, an operation such as this would be placed in a loop. However, suppose that instead of two primitives, there were 80 primitives to be animated! Clearly, it would be desirable to have a method in which one could operate on all 80 primitives with a small set of operations.

A display list provides this feature. By incorporating the graphical primitives that make up a single logical object into a display list, one can call for

---

[4]Two-dimensional Cartesian coordinates are written as (x, y).

the displaying of the list as necessary. This in itself, however, does not allow one to draw the same object in different positions. That requires being able to change the actual coordinates in the primitives at a time between the access of the display list and the drawing of the primitive.

Although many data transformations are possible, only one will be considered here: *translation*. A primitive is translated by adding values to the X and Y coordinates prior to drawing. With this single transformation, it is possible to draw multiple copies of an object. Also, animating an object is straightforward:

```
Let L represent the display list.
translate 0,0
color white
draw L
color black
draw L
translate 1,0
color white
draw L
color black
draw L
etc.
```

The program to be developed in this section simulates the creation and editing of a display list.

4.4.1 Display List Program Design

Display list routines are not accessible by a user. Instead, they are part of a programmer's library. The display list routines that will be developed here perform the following functions: creation of a new list, adding new primitives to the list, editing a list, closing a list, and drawing the primitives in the list. Another function is needed to set the translation values. These routines will operate in a similar manner to existing software packages and graphics hardware.

In this case, it was decided not to use a **typedef** statement to create a "special" type for display lists. Instead, the **list** type is used. As such, the following prototypes can be developed:

```
list *newobject(void);
void endobject(void);
int line(int x1, int y1, int x2, int y2);
```

```
int rectangle(int x1, int y1, int x2, int y2);
int circle(int x, int y, int radius);
int mark(int value);
int editobject(list *object, int mark_value, int replaceflag);
```

In order to create a display list, **newobject()** is called. This function returns some sort of reference to the new display list. Note that the package maintains the notion of a current display list (and hence only one display list can be "open" at a time). Subsequent calls to graphics primitive functions **point()**, **line()**, **circle()**, and **rectangle()** cause those primitives to be added to the display list, but not drawn on the screen. Closing a display list so that no new primitives will be added is done with **endobject()**. Calls to primitive functions when no display list is open causes those primitives to be drawn.

Another feature available in some graphics systems is the ability to edit a display list. In order to do this, marks must be placed in the list indicating the positions at which editing can occur. This is done with **mark()**. Given that the marks exist, it is then possible to reopen a list to insert new primitives immediately after a mark using the function **editobject()**.

These functions all return **int** values. The actual values are unimportant as an error-handling routine can be considered as part of the package.

```
#define E_NOOBJ 1
#define E_NOSPACE 2
#define E_DELETE 3
#define E_BADPARAM 4
#define E_NOMARK 5
#define E_CNT 5

char *display_error(int err_num);
```

This error handler returns an error message (a string) based on the error code passed as a parameter.

4.4.2 Implementation of Display List Routines

There are two obvious choices for the implementation of display lists. Hardware implementations use arrays. Many software implementations also use arrays. The reason for this is speed (array access is faster than linked list access). However, there is a problem with array implementations. The ability to edit a display list is limited. In particular, as new items are added after the marker, the items that were previously there are deleted. Furthermore, only up to as many items as were there previously can be added.

By using a linked list, editing can be more powerful. Instead of simply replacing the primitives that follow a marker, the programmer can optionally specify that the existing primitives should follow the new primitives. Therefore, a linked list implementation can be used, where each node in the list represents a single graphical primitive. The actual representation of the graphical primitives in the linked list is

```
#define LINE 1
#define RECTANGLE 2
#define CIRCLE 3
#define MARK 4

typedef struct display_node {
    int type;
    int value_1, value_2, value_3, value_4;
} display_node;
```

where **type** is the type of primitive (as given by the preprocessor defines), and **value_i** are the parameters required by the primitive. This definition of a node is valid only because the types of primitives that are supported by this system have at most four parameters and the parameters are all of the same type.

Since the graphics primitive functions (**line()**, **rectangle()**, and **circle()**) operate differently, depending on whether a display list is open, a **static** global variable is required by the package to indicate this fact. At first thought, it may seem that all that is necessary is to maintain a **static** global variable which is the list that is currently open. Then, as primitive functions are called, the new nodes could be appended to the list. However, it is not possible to distinguish if a list is open with a single list variable. A second variable could be used for this purpose.

An alternative implementation uses a **static** global variable that is a pointer to a list (**list ***). This implementation has a few advantages. First, an open or closed display list is determined by whether the **static** global variable is **NULL** (indicating closed). Second, note that **newobject()** must return some indication to the programmer of how to access the display list. If **newobject()** returns a **list**, the value maintained by the application program will be incorrect as soon as the first primitive graphical function is called.

Recall that when an item is added to a list, a pointer to a **list** must be passed as a parameter. This is because the **list** variable may change if an item is inserted at the front of the list. Since the application programmer's **list** variable will not be the one used by the display list package, problems will result.

Another thing to consider is the difference between adding items to a new list and editing a list. A full discussion on this topic will be deferred, but by examining the editing aspect of display lists, the following stands out: there are different editing modes. Specifically, there are three ways of modifying a list:

1. Items can be appended to the list. This occurs when adding items to a new list.

2. Items in the list can be replaced with new items. This is equivalent to replacing the contents of existing nodes in the list. This occurs when editing a list.

3. Items can be inserted at arbitrary points in the list and the items after it are unchanged. This is equivalent to adding new nodes to the middle of the list. This occurs when editing a list.

A **static** global variable is required to indicate the current editing mode:

```
#define EDIT_APPEND 0
#define EDIT_REPLACE 1
#define EDIT_INSERT 2
static list *p_current_list;
static int edit_mode;
static int translate_x, translate_y;
```

The last declaration indicates the current translation values.

Initializing the Package

The initialization routine sets up package parameters.

```
void display_init()
{
    /*
     *   Initialize the display list package.
     */
    p_current_list = NULL;
    edit_mode = EDIT_APPEND;
    translate_x = translate_y = 0;
}
```

Display_init() initializes the global variables. No currently open display list is indicated by setting **p_current_list** to **NULL**. The default **edit_mode** is append, and the primitives that are displayed will be translated by 0 units (i.e., not at all).

Creating New Objects

A display list, which represents a new object, is created with a call to **newobject()**. All subsequent primitives will be added to the current display list and not drawn.

```
list *newobject()
{
    /*
     *   Create a new display list by malloc'ing a list.
     *   This routine returns NULL if there is an error.
     */
    edit_mode = EDIT_APPEND;
    p_current_list = (list *) malloc(sizeof(list));
    if (p_current_list)
        init_list(p_current_list);
    return p_current_list;
}
```

Newobject() returns a value that is a pointer to a list (**list ***). Therefore, the primary task of this function is to dynamically allocate a new list. This is done using **malloc()**. If the list is successfully allocated, then it is initialized. A key to understanding this and all subsequent functions is remembering that **p_current_list** is a *pointer* to a *list*. Hence, when the list primitive functions (like **init_list()**) are called, passing **p_current_list** as a parameter does not require taking its address.

This function returns **p_current_list**. Note that if the allocation fails, **p_current_list** will be **NULL**, which is consistent with no display list being open. Assuming the memory allocation is successful, variables are configured as follows:

p_current_list

(type: list *)   (type: list)

Closing a Display List

Although not quite the dual of a **newobject()**, a function is required to indicate that primitives should no longer be added to a display list. This function is **endobject()**.

```
void endobject()
{
    /*
     *   Close a display list.
     */
```

```
        edit_mode = EDIT_APPEND;
        p_current_list = NULL;
}
```

Endobject() indicates that no display list is open by setting **p_current_list**
to **NULL**. Note that it does not free the space that was dynamically allocated.
That space represents the start of the display list, and, although the programmer is no longer adding to the list, it is incorrect to assume that the list is no
longer needed.

Graphical Primitives

There are five graphical primitives: point, line, rectangle, circle, and marker.
With the exception of the last, the implementation of these primitives follows
the same pattern:

```
if no display list is currently open
    draw the primitive
else
    add the primitive to the current display list
```

Since these primitives all do the same thing, it is logical to merge the common
components into one parameterized function.

```
static int _primitive(type, v1, v2, v3, v4)
int type;
int v1, v2, v3, v4;
{
    if (p_current_list == NULL) {
        display_node *p_node = allocate_display_node(type,v1,v2,v3,v4);
        if (p_node == NULL)
            return E_DELETE;
        draw_primitive(p_node);
        free_display_node(p_node);
        return 0;
    }
    switch (edit_mode) {
        case EDIT_REPLACE:
        case EDIT_INSERT:
            break;
        case EDIT_APPEND:
            if (display_append(p_current_list,type,v1,v2,v3,v4)==ERROR)
                return E_NOSPACE;
            p_current_list = &NEXT(*p_current_list);
            break;
```

```
        }
      return 0;
  }


  int line(x1, y1, x2, y2)
  int x1, y1, x2, y2;
  {
      return _primitive(LINE, x1, y1, x2, y2);
  }

  int rectangle(x1, y1, x2, y2)
  int x1, y1, x2, y2;
  {
      return _primitive(RECTANGLE, x1, y1, x2, y2);
  }

  int circle(x, y, radius)
  int x, y, radius;
  {
      return _primitive(CIRCLE, x, y, radius, 0);
  }

  int mark(value)
  int value;
  {
      return _primitive(MARK, value, 0, 0, 0);
  }
```

Although the actual graphical primitive functions could be eliminated in favor of _primitive(), that has not been done. From the application programmer's point of view, it is more logical to have separate functions for each primitive. It makes sense to try to unify much of the code in the package, but doing so should not impact the user of such code.

The first thing _primitive() does is to check if a display list is currently open. If not, it sets up the parameters to function **draw_primitive()**, which draws the primitive. If a display list is open, then the item is inserted. There are three modes of insertion into the current display list. One mode is for inserting items into a new display list. The other two have to do with editing an existing display list. As such, this version of _primitive() only deals with the **EDIT_APPEND** case. In this case, the new primitive is appended to the current display list using **display_append()**. Then **p_current_list** is moved to point to the node just added. Although not seemingly necessary, one reason for the assignment to **p_current_list** is to avoid the need to traverse the entire display list to add an item to the end. **P_current_list** will always point to the last item in the display list (clearly NOT the same thing that was returned to the user). Note that by using the **NEXT** macro, implementation independence is maintained.

The functions accessed by the application programmer are simple. **Line()**, **rectangle()**, **circle()**, and **mark()** all make calls to _primitive(). An example of how a display list is built up in **EDIT_APPEND** by _primitive() is instructive.

```
line(0,0,1,1); ... _primitive(LINE,0,0,1,1);
After display_append().
```

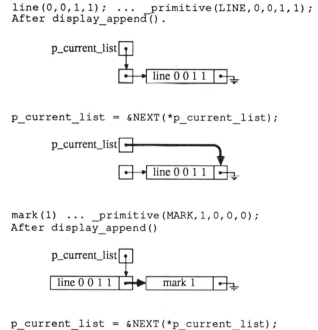

```
mark(1) ... _primitive(MARK,1,0,0,0);
After display_append()
```

Error Handling

The return value of the functions in the display list package is an error code. The error codes are defined in the preprocessor, and the mnemonics for the code give a hint as to exactly what the error is. In order to simplify the user interface for the application programmer, however, the display package also includes a function that returns a formatted string corresponding to the error value passed.

```
#define E_NOOBJ 1
#define E_NOSPACE 2
```

```
#define E_DELETE 3
#define E_BADPARAM 4
#define E_NOMARK 5
#define E_CNT 5

char *display_error(err_num)
int err_num;
{
    static char *errors[E_CNT+1] = {
        "system error",
        "no object current open",
        "out of memory",
        "deletion failed",
        "invalid edit parameter",
        "mark not found"
    };

    if (err_num < 1 || err_num > E_CNT)
        err_num = 0;
    return errors[err_num];
}
```

No assumption is made as to how the application programmer wants to
handle errors. By returning an error number (or 0 if no error occurs), the application programmer is free to follow whatever path of execution is necessary,
whether it be printing a message or aborting the program (or anything else).

Editing Existing Objects

Once a display list has been created and closed (with **newobject()** and **en-
dobject()**), it can only be edited if marks have been set through calls to the
graphical primitive function **mark()**. Those marks represent locations in the
display list at which modifications can be made. To open a display list for
editing requires a call to **editobject()**. Once a list is opened for editing, the
same graphical primitive function calls are used to modify the list.

```
int editobject(object, mark_value, replaceflag)
list *object;
int mark_value;
int replaceflag;
{
    /*
     *  When editing a list, must create dummy list (to work
     *  in the place of the dynamically allocated list when creating
     *  a new list) so that p_current_list can point to it.
     */
```

```
          static list editlist;
          list mark_node;

          if (replaceflag != EDIT_REPLACE && replaceflag != EDIT_INSERT)
              return E_BADPARAM;
          if (find_mark(object, mark_value, &mark_node) == ERROR)
              return E_NOMARK;

          p_current_list = &editlist;
          *p_current_list = mark_node;
          edit_mode = replaceflag;
          return 0;
      }
```

Editobject() has three arguments: the display list to be edited, the value of the mark at which editing begins, and a flag indicated the editing mode. The first step **editobject()** does is verify its parameters. If **replaceflag** is not either **EDIT_REPLACE** (meaning items following the mark should be replaced with the new primitives) or **EDIT_INSERT** (meaning previously existing primitives should follow the new primitives), then an error code is returned. Next, the list node containing the current mark is found with a call to **find_mark()**. This function is an interface routine to the list function, **find_key()**, which performs list searches in a general fashion.

If the mark node is not found, an error is returned. Otherwise, editing should begin with nodes following the node that is returned. This is accomplished by setting **p_current_list** to point to the mark node. First, **p_current_list** is initialized to point to a valid address for a list. Note that in the case of creating a new display list, the list is dynamically allocated. When editing a list, however, no new list is being created. Therefore, **p_current_list** is set to the address of a **static** variable that represents the list to be edited. Then the first node of this list is set to be the mark node.

This sequence of actions is most easily understood by use of diagrams.

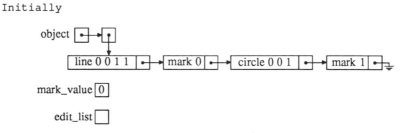

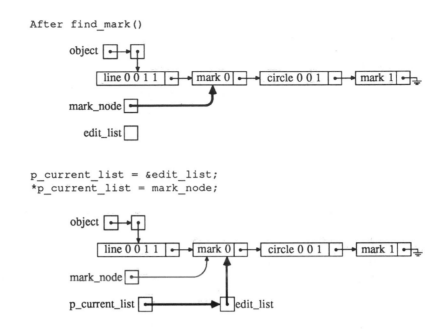

Now _**primitive()** can be implemented for all cases. If the editing mode is **EDIT_INSERT**, then new items will be inserted immediately after the node referenced by **p_current_list** and previously existing nodes will follow that new node. If the editing mode is **EDIT_REPLACE**, then the node immediately following **p_current_list** is deleted, and the new node is inserted.

```
static int _primitive(type, v1, v2, v3, v4)
int type;
int v1, v2, v3, v4;
{
    /*
     *   Add a primitive of type with parameters v1-4 to the display list.
     *   The method of adding depends upon the editmode.
     */
    list nextnode;
    int rtype, r1, r2, r3, r4;

    /*
     *   If no list, just draw the primitive.
     */
    if (p_current_list == NULL) {
        display_node *p_node = allocate_display_node(type,v1,v2,v3,v4);
        if (p_node == NULL)
            return E_DELETE;
        draw_primitive(p_node);
```

```
            free_display_node(p_node);
            return 0;
    }


    /*
     *   p_current_list always points to the address of the NEXT
     *   field of the node in the list immediately before the
     *   intended location for update.
     */
    switch (edit_mode) {
        case EDIT_INSERT:
        case EDIT_REPLACE:
            /*
             *   nextnode (NEXT(*p_current_list)) represents the first node
             *   of a list to be updated.  If mode is insert, then the new
             *   node goes before nextnode.  If it is replace, nextnode is
             *   deleted, then the new node is inserted.  Note that if there
             *   is no next node, then we fall through to the append case.
             */
            if (NEXT(*p_current_list) != NULL) {
                nextnode = NEXT(*p_current_list);

                if (edit_mode == EDIT_REPLACE &&
                    display_delete(&nextnode,&rtype,&r1,&r2,&r3,&r4)==ERROR)
                      return E_DELETE;

                if (display_insert(&nextnode,type,v1,v2,v3,v4)==ERROR)
                      return E_NOSPACE;

                NEXT(*p_current_list) = nextnode;
                p_current_list = &NEXT(*p_current_list);
                break;
            }
            /*
             *   will fall through when replacing existing primitives and
             *   the end of the list is reached.
             */
        case EDIT_APPEND:
            /*
             *   append the node to the end of *p_current_list. Whenever we
             *   are in this mode, p_current_list will always be pointing to
             *   the last node.
             */
            if (display_append(p_current_list,type,v1,v2,v3,v4)==ERROR)
                  return E_NOSPACE;
            p_current_list = &NEXT(*p_current_list);
            break;
    }
```

```
        return 0;
    }
```

Focusing attention on the **EDIT_INSERT** and **EDIT_REPLACE** cases, note that the editing mode only matters if there are nodes following the current node. If there are not, then control falls through to the **EDIT_APPEND** case. Assuming there are nodes following the current node, then **nextnode** is set to point to the list beginning with the first node after ***p_current_list** (remember, **p_current_list** is a pointer to a list). If the **edit_mode** is **EDIT_REPLACE**, then **nextnode** is deleted using an interface routine to the list primitve operation **delete()**. When this happens, **nextnode** will now point to the start of the modified list.

Regardless of the edit mode, at this point, the new primitive can be inserted at the head of the list beginning with **nextnode**. Since **nextnode** should be the node pointed to by **NEXT(*p_current_list)**, the two nodes are joined, creating a single list that contains the new primitive. ***P_current_list** is then modified to point to the node just added. This assignment is necessary so that subsequent nodes are added to the list being edited in the correct location.

An example helps clarify the flow of control.

```
Initially: _primitive(RECTANGLE, 2, 2, 3, 3);
```

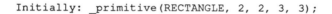

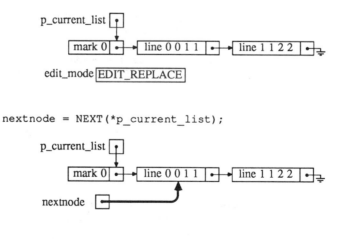

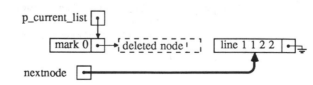

After display_insert()

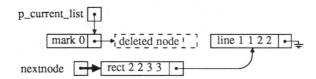

```
NEXT(*p_current_list) = nextnode;
p_current_list = &NEXT(*p_current_list);
```

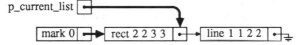

Drawing a Display List

By using **traverse()**, drawing a display list is quite simple. For the present purposes, a display list will be "drawn" by printing the contents to standard output.

```
void drawobj(p_L)
list *p_L;
{
    /*
     *   "Draw" the contents of a display list.
     */
    traverse(*p_L, draw_primitive);
}

status draw_primitive(p_node)
display_node *p_node;
{
    /*
     *   "Draw" the graphic primitive.
     */
    int newvalue_1 = p_node->value_1;
    int newvalue_2 = p_node->value_2;
    int newvalue_3 = p_node->value_3;
    int newvalue_4 = p_node->value_4;

    switch (p_node->type) {
        case LINE:
        case RECTANGLE:
            newvalue_1 += translate_x;
            newvalue_2 += translate_y;
```

```
                newvalue_3 += translate_x;
                newvalue_4 += translate_y;
                printf("%s %d %d %d %d\n",
                    (p_node->type == LINE) ? "line" : "rectangle",
                    newvalue_1, newvalue_2, newvalue_3, newvalue_4);
                break;
            case CIRCLE:
                newvalue_1 += translate_x;
                newvalue_2 += translate_y;
                printf("circle %d %d %d\n", newvalue_1, newvalue_2, newvalue_3);
                break;
            case MARK:
                printf("mark %d\n", newvalue_1);
                break;
            default:
                printf("unknown primitive type %d\n", p_node->type);
        }
        return OK;
    }

    void translate(x, y)
    int x, y;
    {
        translate_x = x;
        translate_y = y;
    }
```

The last function in this set, **translate**(), is the routine that the application programmer can use to set the transformations to be applied to the primitives of a display list prior to their being output.

4.4.3   List Interface Routines for Display Lists

In the code for _**primitive**(), it was assumed that routines for inserting, appending, and deleting nodes from a list already existed. Also, **editobject**() assumed the existence of a routine that returned the list node containing a particular key. Those routines do exist, except that they operate on data that is of type **generic_ptr**. Therefore, a set of routines have to be developed that provide an interface between the list primitive operations and the display list package. These routines should operate in the same way as the corresponding list primitive operations, except that their parameters are tailored for this specific application.

The routines for adding and deleting **display_nodes** from a list follow.

```
status display_append(p_L, type, v1, v2, v3, v4)
```

```
list *p_L;
int type;
int v1, v2, v3, v4;
{
    /*
     *   Append a display node to p_L populated with type and v1-4.
     */
    status ret_code;
    display_node *p_key = allocate_display_node(type, v1, v2, v3, v4);

    if (p_key == NULL)
        return ERROR;
    ret_code = append(p_L, (generic_ptr) p_key);
    if (ret_code == ERROR)
        free_display_node(p_key);

    return ret_code;
}

status display_insert(p_L, type, v1, v2, v3, v4)
list *p_L;
int type;
int v1, v2, v3, v4;
{
    /*
     *   Insert a display node in p_L populated with type and v1-4.
     */
    status ret_code;
    display_node *p_key = allocate_display_node(type, v1, v2, v3, v4);

    if (p_key == NULL)
        return ERROR;
    ret_code = insert(p_L, (generic_ptr) p_key);
    if (ret_code == ERROR)
        free_display_node(p_key);

    return ret_code;
}

status display_delete(p_L, p_type, p_v1, p_v2, p_v3, p_v4)
list *p_L;
int *p_type;
int *p_v1, *p_v2, *p_v3, *p_v4;
{
    /*
     *   Delete a node from p_L. Return the data stored in
     *   the node in p_type and p_v1-4.
     */
```

```
        display_node *p_node;

        if (delete(p_L, (generic_ptr *) &p_node) == ERROR)
            return ERROR;

        *p_type = p_node->type;
        *p_v1 = p_node->value_1;
        *p_v2 = p_node->value_2;
        *p_v3 = p_node->value_3;
        *p_v4 = p_node->value_4;
        free_display_node(p_node);

        return OK;
}

display_node *allocate_display_node(type, v1, v2, v3, v4)
int type;
int v1, v2, v3, v4;
{
        /*
         *   Allocate and initialize a display node.   Return the new node.
         */
        display_node *p_node = (display_node *) malloc(sizeof(display_node));

        if (p_node == NULL)
            return NULL;
        p_node->type = type;
        p_node->value_1 = v1;
        p_node->value_2 = v2;
        p_node->value_3 = v3;
        p_node->value_4 = v4;

        return p_node;
}

void free_display_node(p_node)
display_node *p_node;
{
        free(p_node);
}
```

The routines for adding to the list, **display_insert()** and **display_append()**, have six parameters: a pointer to the list to be modified, and the type and applicable data values to be added. These routines allocate a new display node and then call the corresponding list primitive function to perform the actual modification to the list. If an error occurs in the list primitive function, the space allocated for the **display_node** is freed.

Display_delete() operates in a similar fashion. It calls the list primitive operation, **delete()**, and if successful, copies the data out of the **display_node** into its parameters and deletes the **display_node**. If **delete()** fails, **display_delete()** returns **ERROR.**

The fourth interface routine **find_mark()** searches a linked list and returns the node whose mark value matches the value supplied as an argument. This is done by setting up the parameters to the list primitive operation **find_key()**.

```
status find_mark(p_L, mark_value, p_mark_list)
list *p_L;
int mark_value;
list *p_mark_list;
{
    /*
     *  Find the "mark" node in p_L with mark_value.  Return the node
     *  in p_mark_list.
     */
    status ret_code;
    display_node *p_key = allocate_display_node(MARK, mark_value, 0, 0, 0);

    if (p_key == NULL)
        return ERROR;

    ret_code = find_key(*p_L, (generic_ptr) p_key, mark_cmp, p_mark_list);
    free(p_key);
    return ret_code;
}

int mark_cmp(p_node1, p_node2)
display_node *p_node1, *p_node2;
{
    int match = (p_node1->type == MARK && p_node2->type == MARK
                    && p_node1->value_1 == p_node2->value_1);
    return match == 0;
}
```

Given the mark value, **find_mark()** temporarily allocates a **display_node** to use as the search key. It then calls **find_key()**, passing the key and a comparison function. **Find_mark()** returns the value of **find_key()** after it frees the space used by the search key.

4.4.4 A User Interface

The best user interface to this application is graphical. Since graphics devices may not be accessible to the average reader (and teaching graphics is not the intent of this book), a simple text-based interface will be developed instead. This interface presents the user with a menu that has items corresponding to each of the display list functions described.

Since the display list routines require that the parameters be supplied in the call to the routine, routines must be developed that solicit this information from the user. These routines will then call routines in the display list library.

```
#define MAXOBJECTS   20

main()
{
    static struct menuoptions {
        char *string;
        void (*f)();
    } menu[] = {
        { "Create a new display list", new_display },
        { "Edit a display list", edit_display },
        { "Close current list", close_display },
        { "Add a line", add_line },
        { "Add a circle", add_circle },
        { "Add a rectangle", add_rectangle },
        { "Add a marker", add_mark },
        { "Set translation", set_translate },
        { "Print display list", print_display },
        { "Exit the program", quit }
    };
    int menusize = sizeof(menu) / sizeof(struct menuoptions);
    list *display_lists[MAXOBJECTS];
    int listcnt = 0;
    int i, choice;

    display_init();

    while (TRUE) {
        for (i = 0; i < menusize; i++) {
            fprintf(stderr, "\t%d -- %s\n", i+1, menu[i].string);
        }
        fprintf(stderr, "Enter your choice: ");
        scanf("%d", &choice);
        if (choice > 0 && choice <= menusize) {
            (*menu[choice-1].f)(display_lists, &listcnt);
        }
    }
}

void new_display(l, p_cnt)
list *l[];
```

```c
int *p_cnt;
{
    if (*p_cnt == MAXOBJECTS) {
        fprintf(stderr, "Can't create any more display lists\n");
        return;
    }
    l[*p_cnt] = newobject();
    if (l[*p_cnt] == NULL) {
        fprintf(stderr, "Creation of new display list failed!\n");
        return;
    }
    (*p_cnt)++;
    fprintf(stderr, "New display list is %d\n", *p_cnt);
}


void edit_display(l, p_cnt)
list *l[];
int *p_cnt;
{
    int listno, markno, ins_rep;
    int rc;

    if (*p_cnt == 0) {
        fprintf(stderr, "No lists to edit\n");
        return;
    }
    do {
        fprintf(stderr, "Which list to edit (1-%d)? ", *p_cnt);
        scanf("%d", &listno);
    } while (listno < 1 || listno > *p_cnt);
    fprintf(stderr, "Edit beginning at what marker number? ");
    scanf("%d", &markno);
    do {
        fprintf(stderr, "0 -- replace existing primitives with new\n");
        fprintf(stderr, "1 -- insert new before existing primitives\n");
        fprintf(stderr, "Enter your choice: ");
        scanf("%d", &ins_rep);
    } while (ins_rep != 0 && ins_rep != 1) ;

    rc = editobject(l[listno-1], markno,
            (ins_rep == 0) ? EDIT_REPLACE : EDIT_INSERT);
    if (rc) {
        fprintf(stderr, "display error: %s\n", display_error(rc));
    }
}

void close_display()
```

```
{
    endobject();
}

void add_line()
{
    int x1, y1, x2, y2;
    int rc;

    fprintf(stderr, "Enter the endpoints of the line in the form x1, y1, x2, y2\n");
    fprintf(stderr, "    (example: 0, 0, 10, 0): ");
    scanf("%d,%d,%d,%d", &x1, &y1, &x2, &y2);
    rc = line(x1, y1, x2, y2);
    if (rc != 0) {
        fprintf(stderr, "display error: %s\n", display_error(rc));
    }
}


void add_rectangle()
{
    int x1, y1, x2, y2;
    int rc;

    fprintf(stderr, "Enter the coordinates of opposite corners of the rectangle\n");
    fprintf(stderr, "in the form x1, y1, x2, y2 (example: 0, 0, 10, 0): ");
    scanf("%d,%d,%d,%d", &x1, &y1, &x2, &y2);
    rc = rectangle(x1, y1, x2, y2);
    if (rc != 0) {
        fprintf(stderr, "display error: %s\n", display_error(rc));
    }
}

void add_circle()
{
    int x1, y1, x2, y2;
    int rc;

    fprintf(stderr, "Enter coordinates of center and radius in the form x, y, r\n");
    fprintf(stderr, "    (example: 0, 0, 10): ");
    scanf("%d,%d,%d", &x1, &y1, &x2);
    rc = circle(x1, y1, x2);
    if (rc != 0) {
        fprintf(stderr, "display error: %s\n", display_error(rc));
    }
}

void add_mark()
{
```

```
        int x1;
        int rc;

        fprintf(stderr, "Enter marker number: ");
        scanf("%d", &x1);
        rc = mark(x1);
        if (rc != 0) {
            fprintf(stderr, "display error: %s\n", display_error(rc));
        }
}

void set_translate()
{
        int x, y;

        fprintf(stderr, "Enter the translation values (example: 10, 5): ");
        scanf("%d,%d", &x, &y);
        translate(x, y);
}

void print_display(l, p_cnt)
list *l[];
int *p_cnt;
{
        int listno;

        if (*p_cnt == 0) {
            fprintf(stderr, "No lists to display\n");
            return;
        }
        do {
            fprintf(stderr, "Which list to display (1-%d)? ", *p_cnt);
            scanf("%d", &listno);
        } while (listno < 1 || listno > *p_cnt) ;
        drawobj(l[listno-1]);
}

void quit()
{
        exit(0);
}
```

The main program has an array of menu items. The array contains a menu string and a pointer to the function that performs the corresponding task. An infinite loop is entered in which the menu is printed, user input is obtained, and the corresponding function is executed. The program is terminated when the user chooses to "quit" the program. Function **quit**() invokes the C library function **exit()**. Note that an array of 20 (**MAXOBJECTS**) display lists is declared in this routine and passed to each of the menu functions. Although it may seem unreasonable for the application program to limit the user to a small number of lists, it is far better for the limiting factor to be the application routines, not the library routines. Also note that the array is passed to each of the menu functions, even though not all functions are set up to receive the parameters. This is necessary because some of the functions require this information. Only those that need the variables have the arguments declared.

4.5   Exercises

1. Write the following list primitive operations:

   (a)   `bool equal(list L1, list L2, int (*p_cmp_f)());`

   Equal() returns **TRUE** if the **DATA** field of each node in list **L1** points to data equal to that of the node in the same position in **L2**.

   (b)   `bool set_equal(list L1, list L2, int (*p_cmp_f)());`

   Set_equal() returns **TRUE** if the set of values of the nodes in **L1** is the same as the set of values of the nodes in **L2**. Order does not matter with this function.

   (c)   `status copylist(list L1, list *p_L2);`

   Copylist() makes a copy of **L1** and sets **p_L2** to point to the new list. This function returns **ERROR** if any of the insertions into the new list fail. Can there potentially be memory allocation problems if this function is used? *Hint:* What happens when the data in list **L1** is deleted?

   (d) Develop a **copylist()** function that also copies the data stored in the node. *Hint:* By using the C **sizeof** operator, the application-defined data can be duplicated in an application-independent manner.

   (e)   `status appendlist(list *p_L1, list *p_L2);`

   Appendlist() takes the nodes in **p_L1** and moves them to the end of **p_L2**. Should **p_L1** be modified? If so, in what way? If not, why not?

2. What are the conditions when an array implementation of a list may be preferable to a linked list implementation?

3. The polynomial printing function **write_poly()** could generate nicer output by eliminating the leading plus sign, using subtraction instead of adding negative numbers and when raising X to the 0th power, not writing the X at all. For example, instead of writing:

$$+1x^4 + 5x^3 + -2x^2 + 1x^0$$

the output

$$x^4 + 5x^3 - 2x^2 + 1$$

would look much nicer.

Rewrite this function using the following techniques:

(a) Continue using the **traverse()** primitive operation, but pass an extra argument indicating whether **write_term()** is writing the first term. To do this, learn how C handles functions with variable numbers of arguments and modify **traverse()** to use those constructs.

(b) Use the **list_iterator()** primitive operation.

(c) Which do you prefer? Why? Are there specific times when one technique should be used over the other?

4. Modify the semantics of **add_poly()** so that it does not modify its parameters. The function prototype should be

```
status add_poly(polynomial *p_sum, polynomial p1, polynomial p2);
```

5. Develop a **subtract_poly()** function:

```
status subtract_poly(polynomial *p_diff, polynomial p1,
                     polynomial p2);
```

where p_diff $= p1 - p2$.

6. Develop a **multiply_poly()** function:

```
status multiply_poly(polynomial *p_product, polynomial p1,
                     polynomial p2);
```

where p_product $= p1 \times p2$.

7. Modify the polynomial program so that polynomials are printed in descending order by degree. Furthermore, when a coefficient becomes 0 (through addition, multiplication, or subtraction), delete it from the list. *Hint:* Create the list primitive operation **insert_order()** to insert the terms in the correct order.

8. Write a program to add, subtract, multiply, and divide integers of arbitrary length.

9. Write a program to add, subtract, multiply, and divide floating-point numbers of arbitrary length.

10. Write a function to delete all duplicate values from a list. For example, (1 2 2 3 3 2 3 3 5) becomes (1 2 3 5). Note that the list is not necessarily sorted and the first occurrence of each value should be the one that is retained. This should be done in an application-independent fashion.

CHAPTER
FIVE

STACKS AND
QUEUES

In this chapter, the most basic data structures are presented: stacks and queues. These data structures are considered basic because, unlike linked lists, there is a fixed set of primitive operations that are associated with them.

5.1   The Stack

The stack is one of the most commonly used data structures. Consider a stack of trays in a cafeteria. Clean trays are added to the stack by being placed at the top. As trays are needed, they are removed from the top. Thus, the tray at the bottom was the first one added and will be the last one removed; the tray at the top was the last one added and will be the first one removed.

The stack data structure is characterized as "last in, first out," or *LIFO*. Graphically, a stack can be viewed as a vertical structure with the top of the stack at the top of the picture.

Viewed horizontally, the stack grows to the left with an artificial bottom-of-stack marker, Λ, indicating the bottom of the stack.

Λ
a Λ
a b Λ
a c Λ

There are only five primitive operations associated with a stack: *init_stack*, *empty_stack*, *push*, *pop*, and *top*. *Init_stack* is analogous to the operation *init_list*, as it is executed once to initialize the stack data structure. The boolean operator *empty_stack* is analogous to the *empty_list* as it indicates the state of the stack (i.e., empty or not empty).[1] *Push* adds a new item to the top of the stack, whereas *pop* deletes the item on the top and returns the item removed. *Top* returns the item at the top of the stack without removing it from the stack. *Top* does not actually access the stack, but is instead a composite of *pop* and *push*. It is an error to *pop* (or *top*) an empty stack.

These definitions describe the types of parameters that one has to pass to C functions that implement the stack data type. To maintain true data abstraction, all data placed on the stack must be cast to a **generic_ptr**. Furthermore, the assumption is made that anything that adds to a data structure can generate some sort of error, depending on the implementation (e.g., a full stack or memory allocation failure). This yields the following function prototypes:

```
status init_stack(stack *p_S);
bool empty_stack(stack *p_S);
status push(stack *p_S, generic_ptr data);
status pop(stack *p_S, generic_ptr *p_data);
status top(stack *p_S, generic_ptr *p_data);
```

5.2   Application: Parenthesis Checker

The first application to be developed is a parenthesis checker. The parenthesis checker considers three sets of grouping symbols: the standard parentheses "()," braces "{}," and brackets "[]." For each line of input, it verifies that for each left parenthesis, brace, or bracket, there is a corresponding closing symbol and that the symbols are appropriately nested. Some examples of valid input lines are

---

[1]Some texts also consider another boolean operator, *full_stack*, which indicates whether the stack is full.

Valid Input
( )
{ } [ ]
({ [ ] [ ] })
[{ { { } ( ) } [ ] } [ ] { }]

Some examples of invalid input lines are

Invalid Input	
Input	Error
)	No matching open symbol
[	Missing closing symbol
{]	Incorrect nesting of symbols

5.2.1   The Parenthesis-Checker Algorithm

The algorithm used to solve this problem uses a stack to maintain a record of
the left parentheses (brackets, braces) as they occur. Since the corresponding
right symbol must match the last left-hand symbol seen, the LIFO property
of the stack is ideally suited to this problem.

```
For each character, c, in the input line:
    if c is a left symbol, push it on the stack
    if c is a right symbol then
        if the stack is empty then
            error:  "No matching open symbol"
        otherwise
            pop a symbol, s, off the stack.
            if s doesn't correspond to c
                error:  "Incorrect nesting of symbols"
If the stack is not empty then
    error:  "Missing closing symbol(s)"
    clear the stack
```

This algorithm can be refined to C code one line at a time. The first line
indicates a loop based on the input line. The input will be stored in a line
buffer (character array) called **buffer** and a pointer variable **ptr** will be used
to access the individual characters. The end of the buffer will be indicated by
the null character (the standard string termination character).

To push or pop a character, the primitive operations previously described
can be used, but not directly. As with lists, the stack functions expect data to

be of type **generic_ptr**. Therefore, new memory locations must be allocated for each character pushed onto the stack (and that memory must be freed when the item is popped).

Since characters will be pushed onto the stack, **push_char()** and **pop_char()** will perform memory management and interface with the stack primitive operations. Prototypes for these functions are

```
status push_char(stack *p_S, char p);
status pop_char(stack *p_S, char *p_c);
status top_char(stack *p_S, char *p_c);
```

The translation of the remaining steps in the algorithm is straightforward.

```
#define ERR_PUSH   "Error in pushing symbol (character #%d).\n"
#define ERR_POP    "Error in popping symbol to match character #%d.\n"
#define ERR_MATCH \
    "Incorrect closing symbol '%c' (character #%d).  Expecting '%c'.\n"
#define ERR_EOL    "Unexpected end of input line.  Expecting:\n\t"

main()
{
    /*
     *  A parenthesis matcher.  Ensures that (){}[] are properly nested.
     */
    char c, *ptr, buffer[BUFSIZ];
    bool error;
    stack S;

    init_stack(&S);
    /*
     *  Prompt and read a line of data.  The loop is entered as
     *  long as end of file has not been reached and the line
     *  read is not empty.
     */
    printf("? ");
    while (gets(buffer) != NULL && buffer[0] != '\0') {
        error = FALSE;
        /*
         *  Process each character on the line.
         */
        for (ptr = buffer; *ptr != '\0' && error == FALSE; ptr++) {
            switch (*ptr) {
                case '(':
                case '-':
                case '[':
                    if (push_char(&S, *ptr) == ERROR) {
                        error = TRUE;
```

```
                            printf(ERR_PUSH, ptr - buffer + 1);
                    }
                  break;
               case ')':
               case '"':
               case ']':
                  if (pop_char(&S, &c) == ERROR) {
                      error = TRUE;
                      printf(ERR_POP, ptr - buffer + 1);
                      break;
                  }
                  /*
                   *  The symbol popped must match the input symbol.
                   */
                  if (*ptr != matching_symbol(c)) {
                      error = TRUE;
                      printf(ERR_MATCH, *ptr, ptr - buffer + 1,
                          matching_symbol(c));
                  }
                  break;
            }
        }
        if (error == TRUE)
            /*
             *  If an error occurs, clear the stack for the next line
             *  of input.
             */
            while (empty_stack(&S) == FALSE)
                pop_char(&S, &c);
        else if (empty_stack(&S) == TRUE)
            printf("Valid input.\n");
        else {
            /*
             *  If there is something on the stack, there were not
             *  enough closing parentheses (braces, brackets).
             */
            printf(ERR_EOL);
            while (empty_stack(&S) == FALSE) {
                pop_char(&S, &c);
                printf("%c ", matching_symbol(c));
            }
            printf("\n");
        }
    printf("? ");
    }
}

char matching_symbol(c)
```

```
char c;
{
    /*
     *   Return  the  opposite  symbol  of  c.
     */
    switch (c) {
      case '(':   return ')';
      case ')':   return '(';
      case '-':   return '"';
      case '"':   return '-';
      case '[':   return ']';
      case ']':   return '[';
    }
    /*  can't get here  */
    return 0;
}
```

The **while** loop in **main()** will be entered as long as **gets()** (which reads a line of input from standard input and stores it in its parameter) does not return **NULL** and the user did not enter an empty line. Once inside the loop, the above algorithm is applied with the addition of informative error messages. The character number in error is determined through the use of pointer arithmetic. The expected input is determined through **matching_symbol()**, which returns the symbol opposite the one that is passed as a parameter. Furthermore, whenever an error does occur, **error** is set and the line is immediately discarded.

5.2.2   Stack Interface Routines for Characters

Push_char() and **pop_char()** are not primitive operations. Their form is not dependent on the actual implementation of the stack data structure. These functions are merely an interface to the true stack primitive operations.

```
status push_char(p_S, c)
stack *p_S;
char c;
{
    /*
     *   Push  the  character  c  onto  the  stack.
     */
    char *p_c = (char *) malloc(sizeof(char));

    if (p_c == NULL)
        return ERROR;
    *p_c = c;
```

```
        if (push(p_S, p_c) == ERROR) {
            free(p_c);
            return ERROR;
        }
        return OK;
}

status pop_char(p_S, p_c)
stack *p_S;
char *p_c;
{
    /*
     *  Pop the stack.   Return the character in p_c.
     */
    char *p_data;

    if (pop(p_S, &p_data) == ERROR)
        return ERROR;

    *p_c = *p_data;
    free(p_data);
    return OK;
}

status top_char(p_S, p_c)
stack *p_S;
char *p_c;
{
    /*
     *  Return the top character from the stack in p_c.
     */
    char *p_data;

    if (top(p_S, &p_data) == ERROR)
        return ERROR;

    *p_c = *p_data;
    return OK;
}
```

Push_char() allocates space for the character with a call to **malloc()**. If no space is available, the character is not pushed onto the stack and the **push_char()** returns **ERROR**. Otherwise, **push_char()** returns the same value as **push()**.

Pop_char() pops an item off the stack via a call to **pop()**. If that function returns **ERROR**, **pop_char()** returns **ERROR**. Otherwise, the item popped is copied to **pop_char()**'s parameter, the memory space is freed, and **OK** is returned.

An execution trace of the program showing the contents of the stack after each iteration of the **for** loop shows how the program works. Given the input [ ] ({ })

*ptr	S
'['	'[' Λ
']'	Λ
'('	'(' Λ
'{'	'{' '(' Λ
'}'	'(' Λ
')'	Λ

The next example gives a stack trace when invalid input is given. The input line (( ]) has a right bracket where a right parenthesis is expected:

*ptr	S
'('	'(' Λ
'('	'(' '(' Λ
']'	Λ

When the right bracket character is processed, the character at the top of the stack is not the matching symbol, so **error** is set to TRUE, an error message is displayed, and the stack is cleared.

5.3   Stack Implementation: Static Arrays

There are at least three techniques for modeling stacks in a programming language. A commonly used method is to use static arrays. Since access to the stack is limited to one end of the array, no holes can appear in the middle of the array. However, there is a problem when the amount of data to be stored in the stack is not known in advance or cannot be accurately predicted. If a small array is declared, the program may run out of space; if a large array is declared, the program may be wasting space much of the time.

Nevertheless, given the parenthesis checker, it is easy to predict the maximum size of the stack. Since the stack is emptied after each line of input, it only has to be large enough to hold a single line of input (about 80 characters). Therefore, the **MAXSTACKSIZE** will be chosen to be 100, slightly more than the amount predicted.

The next thing to consider is how to access an array of **generic_ptr**'s. One method would simply have an **int** index into the array, so that the top of the stack may be accessed as

$$array[top] = \ldots$$

A more efficient method is to use a pointer into the array to directly access the top of the stack. This leads to the following definitions for the stack:

```
#define MAXSTACKSIZE 100

typedef struct {
    generic_ptr base[MAXSTACKSIZE];
    generic_ptr *top;
} stack;
```

The member **top** will always point to the space one position *after* the current top of the stack. This means that **top** points to the position for the next item to be pushed onto the stack. When the stack is empty, **top** will point to the zeroth position in the array.

```
#define current_stacksize(p_S) ((p_S)->top - (p_S)->base)

status init_stack(p_S)
stack *p_S;
{
    /*
     *   Initialize the stack to empty.
     */
    p_S->top = p_S->base;
    return OK;
}

bool empty_stack(p_S)
stack *p_S;
{
    /*
```

```
   *    Return TRUE if stack is empty, FALSE otherwise.
   */
  return (p_S->top == p_S->base) ? TRUE : FALSE;
}

status push(p_S, data)
stack *p_S;
generic_ptr data;
{
  /*
   *    Push data on p_S.  If there is no room, return ERROR.
   */
  if (current_stacksize(p_S) == MAXSTACKSIZE)
      return ERROR;

  *p_S->top = data;
  p_S->top++;
  return OK;
}

status pop(p_S, p_data)
stack *p_S;
generic_ptr *p_data;
{
  /*
   *    Pop the top value of of p_S and put in p_data.
   */
  if (empty_stack(p_S) == TRUE)
      return ERROR;

  p_S->top--;
  *p_data = *p_S->top;
  return OK;
}

status top(p_S, p_data)
stack *p_S;
generic_ptr *p_data;
{
  /*
   *    Return the value at the top of the stack without
   *    removing it.
   */
  if (pop(p_S, p_data) == ERROR)
      return ERROR;

  return push(p_S, *p_data);
}
```

As was predicted earlier, it is possible for **push()** to return an error because the implementation of the abstract data type is not perfect. The concept of "stack" does not recognize the notion of a limited stack, but rather deals with infinite store. In this implementation, there is a case in which **push()** will fail — when the difference between **top** and **base**, the base of the stack array, is equal to **MAXSTACKSIZE** (i.e., the stack is full).

5.4   Application: Graphical Region Filling

A more practical application for a stack is graphical region filling.[2] In computer graphics, there are several types of regions. The type of region that will be considered here is called an interior-defined four-connected region. A region is "filled" by changing its color to a new color.

An interior-defined region is characterized by all the elements (actually called *pixels* for "picture elements") of the region having the same color. "Four-connected" means that the pixels of the region must be "touching" each other at one of four positions (north, south, east, west). An example of the valid connections in a four-connected region is shown by the filled circles in the diagram:

In the remaining examples in this section, the color of a pixel in an image is given by an integer between 0 and 9 (inclusive). Instead of showing filled circles, the images will be given as text, where the color $(0-9)$ will be listed.

Using the text format, the above four-connected region could be represented as

$$1 \ 0 \ 1$$
$$0 \ 0 \ 0$$
$$1 \ 0 \ 1$$

Note that the pixels outside of the region need not (and probably would not) have the same color:

$$2 \ 0 \ 4 \ 6 \ 0$$
$$0 \ 0 \ 1 \ 4 \ 0$$
$$5 \ 0 \ 0 \ 8 \ 0$$
$$1 \ 0 \ 0 \ 8 \ 0$$
$$0 \ 1 \ 0 \ 0 \ 0$$

---

[2]A more complete discussion of region filling can be found in J. Foley and A. Van Dam, *Fundamentals of Interactive Computer Graphics* (Reading, MA: Addison Wesley, 1982).

The largest region in this example consists of 14 pixels with color 0.

To fill a an interior-defined region, it is necessary to give a starting position for the fill algorithm, the current color, and the new color desired. For example, assume the pixels are numbered with the top left corner being (0,0) and the bottom right corner being (4,4) where the first number in the pair represents the row number and the second represents the column. The goal is to fill the region starting at (1,1), initial color 0, with the color 7. With an initial image as before, the algorithm should yield

```
2 7 4 6 7
7 7 1 4 7
5 7 7 8 7
1 7 7 8 7
0 1 7 7 7
```

Note that the pixel in the lower left corner (4,0) remains at 0 since there is no chain starting at (1,1) consisting of four-connected pixels of the same color to that point.

5.4.1   The Fill Algorithm

The algorithm that will be used to solve this problem uses a stack to maintain a record of the pixels to be examined. That is, given a particular pixel that is known to be in the region, the pixels that are four-connected must be examined to determine if they are in the region.

```
Push the starting point on the stack
While the stack is not empty:
    pop a point, p, off the stack
    if the color of p == old color
        push the 4-connected points on the stack
        set the color of p to the new color
```

In order to develop a complete program to implement this algorithm on an alphanumeric display, three items are needed. In particular, unlike the parenthesis checker, this application is not inherently interactive. Therefore, a driver will allow the user to input the data that is needed by the fill algorithm. This driver is discussed after the algorithm implementation.

Second, an interface to the image is needed. This image interface must allow the program to read the current color of a pixel, change the color of a pixel, and "display" the image on the screen. Furthermore, the image has to be created. This will be done by assuming that there exists a file containing the pixel colors that can be input into the program. This leads to the following function prototypes:

```
int init_image(char *filename);
int read_pixel(int x, int y);
int write_pixel(int x, int y, int color);
void display_image(void);
```

The last thing that is needed is an implementation of the stack abstract data type. The implementation given in the previous section could be used, but it will be shown in the next section that there may be a better way. Note that regardless of the method of implementation, the stack primitive operations do not change. What does change, however, is the type of the data to be pushed onto the stack. As always, the stack actually maintains a pointer to the data. Therefore, interface routines are needed between the application and the stack primitive operations to allow for the pushing and popping of (X, Y) coordinate pairs onto the stack. **Push_xy()** and **pop_xy()** will perform this function:

```
status push_xy(stack *p_S, int x, int y);
status pop_xy(stack *p_S, int *p_x, int *p_y);

#define INIT_ERR "Error initializing stack.  Region not filled.\n"
#define PUSH_ERR \
    "Error adding to stack.  Region may not be totally filled.\n"

#define PUSH_XY(p_S, x, y) \
        if (push_xy(p_S, x, y) == ERROR) { \
            printf(PUSH_ERR); \
            continue; \
        }

void fill(x, y, old_color, new_color)
int x, y, old_color, new_color;
{
    /*
     *    Perform a interior-defined 4-connected fill
     */
    stack S;

    if (init_stack(&S) == ERROR) {
        printf(INIT_ERR);
        return;
    }
    push_xy(&S, x, y);
    while (! empty_stack(&S)) {
```

```
        pop_xy(&S, &x, &y);
        if (read_pixel(x, y) == old_color) {
            write_pixel(x, y, new_color);
            PUSH_XY(&S, x, y - 1);
            PUSH_XY(&S, x, y + 1);
            PUSH_XY(&S, x - 1, y);
            PUSH_XY(&S, x + 1, y);
        }
    }
}
```

There are two particular items of interest in this implementation of the fill algorithm. The first is a stylistic point: the use of a preprocessor macro to perform error checking during the push operation. Since there are four items pushed onto the stack sequentially with four nearly identical statements all requiring the same type of error checking, a preprocessor macro is ideal. To add the check for an error condition in each of those statements poses no particular hardship on the programmer, but it can obscure the meaning of the code. By using the macro, the program performs the error checking as efficiently as if the programmer had included the error checking in line, but without unnecessarily cluttering the code.

The other item of interest has to do with exactly what is pushed onto the stack. Suppose the fill algorithm is to start at pixel (0,0). The first thing the program does is push that onto the stack. The **while** loop is entered, (0,0) is popped off the stack, and the four adjacent pixels are pushed on the stack.

1, 0
-1, 0
0, 1
0, -1

Eventually, $(-1, 0)$ will be popped off the stack and a comparison will be made between the current color of that pixel and the old color of the region. Note, however, that that pixel does not exist. There can be no color associated with it. This problem is handled by requiring that both **read_pixel()** and **write_pixel()** return -1 if an attempt is made to access an invalid pixel. Since -1 is an invalid color, no new color will match it and no further attempt will be made to access the pixel.

5.4.2 The Program Driver

Since the fill algorithm is not interactive, a driver has to be developed that will gather the appropriate information from the user and invoke the fill routine.

The driver developed here is straightforward:

1.   Get the name of the file containing the image
2.   Initialize the image package
3.   If there is an error
          exit the program
4.   Display the image and get a valid starting point
          If (-1,-1) is entered
                  exit the program (normal termination)
5.   Display the color of the starting pixel and
          get a valid new color
6.   Perform the fill operation
7.   Go to step 4

```
main()
{
    /*
     *  Provides a user interface for the fill algorithm.
     */
    char filename[BUFSIZ];
    int x, y, old_color, new_color;

    printf("Enter image file name: ");
    scanf("%s", filename);
    if (init_image(filename) == -1) {
        printf("Error initializing the image.\n");
        exit(1);
    }
    while (TRUE) {
        display_image();
        printf("Enter the point at which the fill should start (x, y): ");
        scanf("%d, %d", &x, &y);
        if (x == -1 && y == -1)
            break;
        old_color = read_pixel(x, y);
        do {
            printf("Pixel color is %d.  Enter the new color: ", old_color);
            scanf("%d", &new_color);
        } while (old_color == new_color || new_color<0 || new_color>9) ;
        fill(x, y, old_color, new_color);
    }
    printf("All done.\n");
}
```

5.4.3   The Image Functions

Since a graphics display is a two-dimensional screen (as is the CRT), the image
will be modeled as a two-dimensional array of integers (that represent colors).
The maximum size of the screen will arbitrarily be chosen to be 100.

```
#define SCREENMAX 100

static int screen[SCREENMAX][SCREENMAX];
static int xmax, ymax;
```

The variables **xmax** and **ymax** are used to hold the actual dimensions of
the image after it is initialized. Note that these variables are declared **static**.
In this implementation, the image functions will be placed in a single file and
the variables needed are global to all the functions in the file. To prevent other
functions from accessing these variables, however, they are declared as **static**,
which limits their scope to the functions in the file in which they are declared.

Read_pixel() returns the value stored in the array that represents the
screen. **Write_pixel**() stores a value in the array. **Display_image**() writes the
array to standard output. The only slightly complicated function is the one
that initializes the image, **init_image**(). The code for all these functions is
presented first, then **init_image**() is discussed in detail.

```
int init_image(filename)
char *filename;
{
    /*
     *   Read the image file called filename.  The first line of the
     *   image should contain the number of rows and columns of the
     *   image.  An "image" is just a set of digits representing
     *   colors at each pixel.
     */
    FILE *fd = fopen(filename, "r");
    char linebuffer[BUFSIZ];
    int row, col;

    if (fd == NULL)
        return −1;

    /* first read image size */
    fgets(linebuffer, BUFSIZ, fd);
    sscanf(linebuffer, "%d %d", &xmax, &ymax);
    if (xmax < 0 || ymax < 0) {
        fprintf(stderr, "Invalid image dimensions (%d,%d).\n", xmax, ymax);
        fclose(fd);
```

```
                return -1;
        }
        for (row = 0; row < xmax; row++) {
            if (fgets(linebuffer, BUFSIZ, fd) == NULL) {
                fprintf(stderr, "Missing %d rows in data file\n",
                    xmax - row);
                break;
            }
            col = 0;
            while (col < ymax) {
                if (linebuffer[col] == '\n') {
                    fprintf(stderr, "Missing %d columns on line %d.\n",
                        ymax - col, row);
                    for ( ; col < ymax; screen[row][col++] = 0) ;
                } else {
                    screen[row][col] = linebuffer[col] - '0';
                    col++;
                }
            }
        }
        xmax = row;
        fclose(fd);
        return 0;
}

int read_pixel(x, y)
int x, y;
{
        /*
         *  Return the color at pixel x,y
         */
        if (x < 0 || x >= xmax || y < 0 || y >= ymax)
            return -1;

        return screen[x][y];
}

int write_pixel(x, y, color)
int x, y, color;
{
        /*
         *  Set the color at pixel x,y to color
         */
        if (x < 0 || x >= xmax || y < 0 || y >= ymax)
            return -1;

        return screen[x][y] = color;
}
```

```
void display_image()
{
    /*
     *  "Display" an image by writing the dimensions and then
     *  printing the "color" at each pixel.
     */
    int row, col;

    printf("Dimensions: %d x %d\n", xmax, ymax);
    for (row = 0; row < xmax; row++) {
        printf("%3d ", row);
        for (col = 0; col < ymax; col++)
            printf("%1d", screen[row][col]);
        putchar('\n');
    }
    putchar('\n');
}
```

Init_image() initializes the screen by reading pixel values from a file, where the first line of the file gives the proposed image size and the subsequent lines represent rows of pixel values. Were error checking to be eliminated from **init_image()**, the function would be very short.

There is no need for the first line of the data file to contain the image size, since it can be determined by reading the file. However, it is included for verification. Should subsequent lines of the data file contain too few columns or if the file should end without enough rows of data, an error can be reported. Note that the errors are written to standard output. Although this means that the image subsystem has side effects, which is an undesirable feature, this method is used for simplicity.

5.4.4   Stack Interface Routines for X-Y Coordinates

The interface routines for coordinates are very similar to that for characters, except that a structure representing the X-Y coordinate pair must be allocated.

```
typedef struct {
    int x, y;
} point;

status push_xy(p_S, x, y)
stack *p_S;
int x, y;
{
    /*
     *  Push the point (x,y) on the stack by allocating a point
```

```
      *   structure and using the stack primitive operation push().
      */
     point *pt = (point *) malloc(sizeof(point));

     if (pt == NULL)
         return ERROR;

     pt->x = x;
     pt->y = y;
     if (push(p_S, (char *) pt) == ERROR) {
         free(pt);
         return ERROR;
     }
     return OK;
}
status pop_xy(p_S, p_x, p_y)
stack *p_S;
int *p_x, *p_y;
{
     /*
      *   Pop a point off the stack and return the data in p_x and p_y.
      */
     point *pt;

     if (pop(p_S, (generic_ptr *) &pt) == ERROR)
         return ERROR;

     *p_x = pt->x;
     *p_y = pt->y;
     free(pt);
     return OK;
}
```

5.5 Stack Implementation: Dynamic Arrays

The fill algorithm is quite straightforward in its use of the stack. For each
point popped off the stack, either zero or four points are pushed onto the
stack. Exactly how big can the stack grow (see the Exercises)? It is easy
to picture a region of 1000 points, so clearly a stack size of 100 would be
inadequate. Alternatively, it is possible that no region will be larger than 50
points.

The stack should allow for as many points as possible without allocating
huge amounts of storage that may not be used. An alternate implementation
is required.[3] Instead of using a static array to represent the stack, it would be

---

[3]Or a different fill algorithm might suffice.

ideal if a dynamic array could be used. That is, the stack should start small
and be able to grow as needed.

Not all computer languages support this concept, but it is implemented
nicely in C using pointers and the dynamic memory functions **malloc()** and
realloc(). To use those functions, it is necessary to represent the base of the
stack as a pointer:

```
#define STACKINCREMENT 100

typedef struct {
    generic_ptr *base;
    generic_ptr *top;
    int stacksize;
} stack;
```

Since a pointer does not actually reserve any space for the stack, the stack
initialization routine must be changed to allocate space. Furthermore, whenever an item is pushed, it must be determined whether the stack is full. If
it is, a larger piece of memory must be allocated and the existing stack data
copied into that space before the new item can be added.

```
status init_stack(p_S)
stack *p_S;
{
    /*
     *    Allocating space for the stack and initialize it to empty.
     */
    p_S->base = (generic_ptr *)malloc(STACKINCREMENT*sizeof(generic_ptr));
    if (p_S->base == NULL)
        return ERROR;

    p_S->top = p_S->base;
    p_S->stacksize = STACKINCREMENT;
    return OK;
}

status push(p_S, data)
stack *p_S;
generic_ptr data;
{
    /*
     *    Push data onto p_S.  If there is no more room in the
     *    stack, allocate a larger chunk of memory.
     */
    if (current_stacksize(p_S) == p_S->stacksize) {
        generic_ptr *newstack = (generic_ptr *) realloc(p_S->base,
```

```
                         (p_S->stacksize+STACKINCREMENT)*sizeof(generic_ptr *));
        if (newstack == NULL)
            return ERROR;
        p_S->base = newstack;
        p_S->top = p_S->base + p_S->stacksize;
        p_S->stacksize += STACKINCREMENT;
    }
    *p_S->top = data;
    p_S->top++;
    return OK;
}
```

Init_stack() allocates space for **STACKINCREMENT generic_ptr**'s and sets the stack base to point to the space allocated. Furthermore, it indicates the amount of space allocated (**stacksize**), and sets **top** to point to **base**, indicating an empty stack.

Push() first checks to see if all of the allocated space has been used up. If it has not, then it adds the item to the stack. If all the allocated space has been used, then the stack must grow. This is done by using the C library function **realloc()**. **Realloc()** takes two arguments: a pointer to the space that is too small, and the amount of space that is desired (*not* the amount of space to add). **Realloc()** will allocate new contiguous space (the amount requested), copy the data from the old space into the newly allocated space, and return a pointer to that new space. Furthermore, it will free up the old space. This means that if **realloc()** is successful, the pointer that is passed as a parameter to that function may no longer point to valid space.[4] Therefore, **base** is set to the address returned and **top** is adjusted to point to the offset within the new space that represents the top of the stack. If **realloc()** returns **NULL**, there was not enough contiguous space available, so push() returns **ERROR**. In this case, the stack remains unchanged.

The remaining functions **pop()** and **top()** are unchanged from the **static** array implementation.

5.6 Application: Mathematical Notation Translation

Programs that perform language translation often use stacks. One example of such a program is one that translates from one *infix* notation to *postfix*

---

[4]It is possible that **realloc()** will find enough contiguous space starting immediately after the "old" space. In this case, all it need do is mark that additional space as no longer available for allocation and return the original pointer.

notation. Although human beings are quite used to seeing mathematical expressions in infix notation, as in $a + b \times c$, the notation is actually rather complex. Using this notation, a nontrivial set of rules must be be applied to the expression in order to determine the final value. These rules, which are taken for granted, involve concepts such as operator precedence and associativity.

Using infix notation (where operators are placed between the operands), one cannot tell the order in which the operators should be applied by looking at the expression. Therefore, whenever an expression contains more than one operator, precedence rules are applied to decide which operator and operands are evaluated first. The standard rules for precedence dictate that parentheses are evaluated first, followed by unary minus, multiplication and division, and, lastly, addition and subtraction. All these operators are left associative, which means that if there is more than one operator of the same precedence, the leftmost operator is applied first.

There is an alternate notation called postfix notation, where the operator is written immediately following its operands, as in $ab+$. To evaluate the expression, it is scanned left to right. As operands are encountered, they are placed on a stack. When an operator is encountered, it takes the top one or two operands (depending upon the operator) off the stack, applies the operator and places the result back on the stack. At the end of the expression, the stack should contain only one value, the result of evaluating the entire expression. Note that since the operands appear immediately before the operator, there is no need for operator precedence *or* for parentheses to group operations.

The following are some examples of equivalent expressions in the two notations.

Postfix	Infix
$abc \times +$	$a + b \times c$
$abc + \times$	$a \times (b + c)$
$abc - \times d/$	$a \times (b - c)/d$
$ab \times cd \times +$	$a \times b + c \times d$

The problem addressed in this section is to develop a program that, given a valid infix expression, determines the corresponding expression in postfix notation.

5.6.1   The Infix-to-Postfix Algorithm

The algorithm used to solve this problem uses a stack to maintain the set of operators for which the operands have not yet appeared. Although variables appear in a postfix expression in the same order as in the corresponding infix expression (and hence can be output as soon as they are encountered), the order in which the operators are output depends upon precedence. That is, precedence must be considered between the input operator and the operator on the top of the stack when determining the appropriate action to take.

The first thing to note is, if the stack is empty, any operator that is encountered in the input will be pushed onto the stack. Next, consider the input $a + b \times c$. In this case, $+$ will be on the top of the stack when $\times$ is encountered. Since $\times$ has precedence over $+$, it must be evaluated before $+$. However, $\times$ can not be output because only one of its operands has already been output. Therefore, the operator will be pushed onto the stack. Alternatively, consider the input $a \times b + c$. For this input, $\times$ will be on the stack when $+$ is encountered in the input. Since the operator on the stack has precedence over the input operator and both of its operands have been output, it will be popped and printed. This leads to two rules for conversion of infix expressions to postfix notation:

> If the precedence of the input operator is greater than the precedence of the stack operator, push the input operator on the stack.

> If the precedence of the stack operator is greater than (or equal to) the precedence of the input operator, pop and print the stack operator.

Parentheses are the next "operators" to be considered. Since a left parenthesis starts a grouping in which all operators must be applied before (or when) the right parenthesis is encountered, it should be pushed onto the stack. This seems to fit nicely with the pattern encountered with the other operators, since parentheses have the highest precedence. An exception occurs when there are two left parenthesis in a row in the input. In this case, the top of the stack is a left parenthesis and the input is also a left parenthesis. The previous rule indicates that the stack should be popped, but the appropriate action is always to push left parentheses onto the stack.

To handle this problem, consider two types of precedence: stack precedence and input precedence. Input precedence is as expected: parenthesis, multiplication and division, and addition and subtraction. Stack precedence, however, is slightly modified. When an operator is on the stack, it has the same precedence as the input precedence except for the left parenthesis. The stack precedence of the left parenthesis should be lower than $+$ and $-$. This forces any operator encountered immediately after the left parenthesis to be pushed onto the stack.

When a right parenthesis appears in the input, it indicates the end of a group, so all operators that appear in the group should be printed (if that hasn't already occurred). This is done by popping and printing until a left parenthesis appears on the top of the stack. The left parenthesis is then popped off the stack and discarded (as is the right parenthesis).

At the end of input, all operators on the stack should be popped and printed. Note that if a left parenthesis remains on the stack, there was an error in the expression (no corresponding right parenthesis).

These observations lead to the following algorithm:

```
for each character, c, in the input line:
    if c is a variable, output c
    if c is an operator then
        /* let t be on the top of the stack */
        while the stack is not empty and
        stack priority(t) >= input priority(c)
            pop the stack and output t
        push c onto the stack
    if c is a right parenthesis
        while the stack is not empty and
        the stack top is not "("
            pop the stack and output t
        pop the "(" off the stack
while the stack is not empty
    pop the stack and output the operator
```

5.6.2   Infix-to-Postfix Implementation

There are several aspects of this algorithm that must be considered before any code can be written. The first thing to consider is how to parse the input. There are two pieces of information associated with each character: the type (e.g., operator, variable, or right parenthesis) and the value. A function will read and parse each line of input. Each time the function is called, it will return a pointer to a **static** buffer containing two fields, the type and value of the next input character. Another type of input character will signify the end of line. This leads to the following structure definition and function prototype:

```
#define BOTTOMMARKER '$'

typedef enum { EOF_T, EOL_T, OPERATOR_T, VARIABLE_T, RIGHTPAREN_T } inputtype;
```

```
typedef struct {
    inputtype tokentype;
    char tokenvalue;
} tokendata;

tokendata *gettoken();
```

The next consideration is how to handle the input and stack precedence. This is quite easy using two functions, one that takes a character as an argument and returns the input precedence and the other that returns the stack precedence of the item on the top of the stack.

```
int stackprec(stack *p_S);
int inputprec(char c);
```

Each of these functions simply does a table lookup and returns the appropriate precedence. Precedence values can be arbitrary as long as the relationships described in the previous section are maintained:

Operator	Precedence	
	Input	Stack
(	3	0
×/	2	2
+−	1	1
$		-1

The last line of the table represents a special "bottom-of-stack" indicator. Using a *sentinel* value such as this is a way to eliminate multiple conditions in a loop. In particular, note the stack priority of the sentinel is the lowest of all the operators. The loop that pops the stack while the stack priority is higher than the input priority will always terminate when the sentinel symbol is reached. This eliminates the need for checking for an empty stack.

As with the parenthesis checker program, characters will be pushed onto the stack. Functions **push_char()** and **pop_char()** as described previously can be used as the interface to the stack primitive operations.

```
#define PUSH(s, c) \
    if (push_char(s, c) == ERROR) { \
        printf("Fatal error in pushing symbol on stack.\n"); \
        exit(1); \
    }
#define POP(s, c) \
    if (pop_char(s, c) == ERROR) { \
```

```
            printf("Fatal error in popping symbol off stack.\n"); \
            exit(1); \
        }
#define TOP(s, c) \
        if (top_char(s, c) == ERROR) { \
            printf("Fatal error in top operation.\n"); \
            exit(1); \
        }

main()
{
    /*
     *  Perform an infix–to–postfix language translation.
     *  Algorithm:
     *      If precedence(input) > precedence(stack), push(input)
     *      otherwise while (prec(stack) >= prec(input)) pop and print.
     *  Infix expressions must be complete on 1 line.
     */
    stack S;
    tokendata *p_token;
    char stacksymbol;
    bool eofreached = FALSE;

    init_stack(&S);
    PUSH(&S, BOTTOMMARKER);
    do {
    p_token = gettoken();
        switch (p_token->tokentype) {
      case EOF_T:
            eofreached = TRUE;
            break;
            case VARIABLE_T:
                printf("%c ", p_token->tokenvalue);
                break;
            case OPERATOR_T:
                while (stackprec(&S)>=inputprec(p_token->tokenvalue)) {
                    POP(&S, &stacksymbol);
                    printf("%c ", stacksymbol);
                }
                PUSH(&S, p_token->tokenvalue);
                break;
            case RIGHTPAREN_T:
                do {
                    POP(&S, &stacksymbol);
                    if (stacksymbol == BOTTOMMARKER) {
                        printf("Error in expression.\n");
                        skiptoeol();
                        clearstack(&S);
```

```
                        break;
                    }
                    if (stacksymbol != '(')
                        printf("%c ", stacksymbol);
                } while (stacksymbol != '(') ;
                break;
        case EOL_T:
            TOP(&S, &stacksymbol);
            while (stacksymbol != BOTTOMMARKER) {
                POP(&S, &stacksymbol);
                if (stacksymbol == '(') {
                    printf("Error in expression.\n");
                    clearstack(&S);
                } else
                    printf("%c ", stacksymbol);
                TOP(&S, &stacksymbol);
            }
            putchar('\n');
            break;
        }
    } while (eofreached == FALSE) ;
}

int stackprec(p_S)
stack *p_S;
{
    /*
     *  Return the precedence of the character at the top of the stack.
     *  The precedence values here are related to those in inputprec()
     *  and must be maintained for the algorithm to work correctly.
     */
    char topsymbol;

    TOP(p_S, &topsymbol);
    switch (topsymbol) {
      case '(':
          return 0;
      case '*':
      case '/':
          return 2;
      case '+':
      case '-':
          return 1;
      case '$':
          return -1;
      default:
          printf("Unknown symbol on stack: %c\n", topsymbol);
          return -1;
```

```
    }
    printf("Reached an unreachable section of code!\n");
    return -1;
}

inputprec(c)
char c;
{
    /*
     *  Return the input precedence of c.  The precedence values here
     *  are related to those in stackprec() and must be maintained for
     *  the algorithm to work correctly.
     */
    switch (c) {
      case '(':
          return 3;
      case '*':
      case '/':
          return 2;
      case '+':
      case '-':
          return 1;
      default:
          printf("Unknown operator in input: %c\n", c);
          return -1;
    }
    printf("Reached an unreachable section of code!\n");
    return -1;
}


void skiptoeol()
{
    /*
     *  Read tokens (and discard) tokens until the end of the line has
     *  been reached.
     */
    tokendata *p_token;

    do {
    p_token = gettoken();
    } while (p_token->tokentype!=EOL_T && p_token->tokentype!=EOF_T) ;
    putchar('\n');
}

void clearstack(p_S)
stack *p_S;
{
```

```
/*
 *    Empty the contents of the stack and push the BOTTOMMARKER
 *    back on.
 */
char c;

while (empty_stack(p_S) == FALSE)
    POP(p_S, &c);
PUSH(p_S, BOTTOMMARKER);
}
```

An execution trace of the program showing the contents of the stack just before testing the condition of the **do** loop shows how the program works. Given the input (a + b) * c + d

*ptoken	S	program output
OPERATOR_T, '('	'(' '$' Λ	
VARIABLE_T, 'a'	'(' '$' Λ	a
OPERATOR_T, '+'	'+' '(' '$' Λ	a
VARIABLE_T, 'b'	'(' '$' Λ	a b
RIGHTPAREN_T, ')'	'$' Λ	a b +
OPERATOR_T, '*'	'*' '$' Λ	a b +
VARIABLE_T, 'c'	'*' '$' Λ	a b + c
OPERATOR_T, '+'	'+' '$' Λ	a b + c *
VARIABLE_T, 'd'	'+' '$' Λ	a b + c * d
EOF_T	'$' Λ	a b + c * d +

The only deviation from the algorithm described is the error checking. As in a previous application, preprocessor macros are used to handle errors that occur within the stack primitive operations, although, in this case, the program is terminated when an error occurs. Furthermore, a minimal amount of input error checking is performed. Although the problem description claims that the input will be a *valid* infix expression, what should the program do if an invalid expression is input?

There are three conditions that can occur when an invalid infix expression is input: (1) the program could crash, (2) the program could discard the bad input line and continue (or exit), or (3) the program could give incorrect results. Under most circumstances, it is unacceptable for a program to terminate abnormally. It is also undesirable for a program to propagate bad input by assuming that it is valid and giving equally bad output.[5] The ideal situation is for the program to recognize invalid input and not to process it at all.

---

[5]This leads to the well-known adage, "Garbage in, garbage out."

The previous program will not terminate abnormally due to bad input. Although it can recognize problems with nesting of parentheses (and will output an error message), no claim is made that it will catch all possible errors in input.

5.6.3 The Lexical Analyzer

The last piece of code needed to make a complete program is the lexical analyzer, which takes a stream of input characters and turns it into tokens. In this program, the single function **gettoken()** does the lexical analysis:

```
tokendata *gettoken()
{
    /*
     *   Return a token (a pointer to a static location). Buffer
     *   contains an entire input line and bufptr points to the
     *   next character to be scanned.
     */
    static bool eof = FALSE;
    static char buffer[BUFSIZ], *bufptr = NULL;
    static tokendata token;
    char *operators = "+-*/(";

    if (eof == TRUE) {
    token.tokentype = EOF_T;
        return &token;
    }

    if (bufptr == NULL) {
    /*
     *   No data currently in buffer, so read an entire line
     */
        printf("? ");
        if ((bufptr = gets(buffer)) == NULL || *bufptr == '\0') {
            eof = TRUE;
        token.tokentype = EOF_T;
        return &token;
        }
    }

    while (isspace(*bufptr))
        bufptr++;

    if (*bufptr == '\0')
        token.tokentype = EOL_T;
    else if (*bufptr == ')')
```

```
        token.tokentype = RIGHTPAREN_T;
    else if (strchr(operators, *bufptr) != NULL)
    /*
     *  character is in the list of operators
     */
        token.tokentype = OPERATOR_T;
    else
        token.tokentype = VARIABLE_T;

    token.tokenvalue = *bufptr;

    if (token.tokentype == EOL_T)
        bufptr = NULL;
    else
        bufptr++;

    return &token;
}
```

Gettoken() uses several **static** local variables: **eof** indicates whether the end of the file has been reached, **buffer** contains the current input line, **bufptr** is a pointer to the next character to be analyzed, and **token** will contain the information that is examined by the calling routine.

The first thing that is checked is if the end of the file has been reached. If so, the token type **EOF_T** is returned. Next, if **bufptr** is equal to 0, this means that a new line of input must be read. If the end of the file is reached or the user enters a blank line, **eof** is set to 1 and the token type **EOF_T** is returned.[6]

The routine skips any white space in the input. The next set of statements determines the type of token to be returned. If the line is blank, then the end-of-line token type will be returned. If the character being examined is a right parenthesis, then that token type will be returned. If the character being examined is in the list of operators, then the operator token type will be returned. This is determined by using the standard library function **strchr()**, which has two arguments: a string and a character. It returns either a pointer into the string, which is the first occurrence of that character, or **NULL**, which means the character does not occur in the string. If the input token is none of the above, then it must be a variable.

The last thing **gettoken()** does is set up **bufptr** for the next call of the function by moving it to the next character position.

---

[6]The only reason why a flag must be used to remind the program that the end of the file has been reached is because some implementations of C reset the end-of-file flag on the standard input stream.

5.7   Stack Implementation: List Functions

In examining the linked list functions **insert()** and **delete()**, one can see that **insert()** adds a node to the beginning of a list, whereas **delete()** deletes the first node in the list. Therefore, if only these two functions are used to add and remove items from the list (and no other list manipulation functions are used), then the list has the "last-in, first-out" property that characterizes stacks. This makes it very simple to implement a stack in terms of a list:

```
typedef list stack;

status init_stack(p_S)
stack *p_S;
{
    return init_list(p_S);
}

bool empty_stack(p_S)
stack *p_S;
{
    return empty_list(*p_S);
}

status push(p_S, data)
stack *p_S;
generic_ptr data;
{
    return insert(p_S, data);
}

status pop(p_S, p_data)
stack *p_S;
generic_ptr *p_data;
{
    return delete(p_S, p_data);
}
```

Now the advantage of having functions that do not print error messages can be seen. Suppose that the list function **insert()** printed the message "list insertion error" and terminated the program, rather than communicating errors via a return value. In a stack implementation, an error message about lists is quite confusing. From the point of view of the user, the program contains no lists, only stacks. The confusion could easily be compounded given additional layers of abstraction. It is better to have error conditions passed along via return values, so that the highest-level function can take appropriate action. For example, **push()** is passing along an error status generated by **malloc()**, and conveyed through **allocate_node()** and **insert()**.

Even though this implementation of the stack is totally different from the previous implementations, the stack primitive operation **top()** does not change, because **top()** does not access the stack directly. Instead, it uses **pop()** and **push()** to perform its function.

5.8   The Queue

The queue is the dual of the stack. Operations on a queue are similar to a line at a movie theater box office: people enter the line at the back and exit at the front (first come, first served). With a queue, data items are placed at the rear and removed from the front. This means that items are removed from a queue in the same order in which they were added (in contrast to a stack in which items are removed in the opposite order). Thus, queues are said to be "first in, first out," or FIFO, data structures.

Graphically, a queue can be viewed as a horizontal structure with the "front" of the queue at the left end of the picture. As items are added to the queue, they will be shown at the right end:

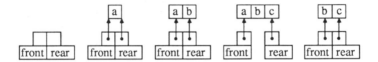

There is only a small set of primitive operations associated with this data structure: *init_queue*, *empty_queue*, *qadd*, and *qremove*. *Init_queue* is performed once to initialize the queue. It essentially puts the queue in an empty state. *Empty_queue* is a boolean operator indicating the state of the queue (i.e., empty or not empty). *Qadd* adds an item to the back of the queue, and *qremove* deletes the item at the front the queue. It is an error to attempt to remove an item from an empty queue.

These functions describe the types of parameters that have to be passed to C functions that implement the queue data type. As with the previous data structures, all data to be placed onto the queue must be cast to **generic_ptr**. Furthermore, the assumption that any operation that adds to a data structure may fail (in practice) is also applied to queues. This yields the following function prototypes:

```
status init_queue(queue *p_Q);
bool empty_queue(queue *p_Q);
```

```
status qadd(queue *p_Q, generic_ptr data);
status qremove(queue *p_Q, generic_ptr *p_data);
```

5.9   Application: Operating System Simulation

The application to be developed that uses a queue is an operating system simulation. Although an operating system performs many tasks and has many facilities whose use must be scheduled (e.g., CPU, I/O devices), the program developed here will only consider a single CPU with no special I/O handling and all tasks having the same priority. In particular, jobs will enter the system at a random interval, with each job requiring a random amount of time to complete. Since only one job can be executed at a time, the scheduling algorithm will allow jobs to run in the order in which they entered the system. Each job will be allowed a maximum of 15 time units in which to complete before it is preempted. That is, a job will be given 15 time units to complete; if it hasn't completed within that time, it will be placed back into the queue and the next job will be executed. When the preempted job is started again, it will continue from the point at which it was preempted. The goal of this simulation is to determine the average amount of time a job will wait in the queue (this is an indicator of the quality of the scheduling algorithm).

There are basically three events that can occur in this simulation: jobs can enter the system from one of two terminals, a job can run to completion, or a job may use its allotted CPU time and be preempted. It has already been stated that the CPU time limit is always 15 time units. The other two events, however, cannot be static. The simulation would not provide any interesting results if the job submittal and run times were constant values. Instead, random numbers for these times will be used. However, it is desirable that the random numbers be in some reasonable range, or at least have an average at (or around) a predictable value. This can be done be using an exponential distribution about some mean value, which is given by the formula:

$$value = T \times \ln(\text{random number})$$

By using this formula, approximately two-thirds of the values returned will be less than or equal to T. Time between job submittals will be $T = 8$ and the average run time will be $T = 15$.

5.9.1   The Simulation Algorithm

There are only three types of events to be handled by the simulation algorithm:

```
get next event
if next event is "job submittal"
    add the job to the queue
    if the CPU isn't busy
        start up the first job in the queue
else if next event is "job completed"
    do end of job statistics
    start up the first job in the queue
else if next event is "cpu timeout"
    place the job in the CPU back in the queue
    start up the first job in the queue
```

There are two approaches as to how long the simulation should run. One approach is to execute the simulation for a certain amount of time (where time is measured by the simulation clock) The other approach is to continue the simulation until a certain number of jobs have completed execution. Since, in general, a large number of jobs must be completed for the statistical data gathered to have any meaning, this implementation will be limited by the latter measure.

```
#define SUBMITONE 0
#define SUBMITTWO 1
#define JOBCOMPLETE 2
#define CPUTIMEOUT 3

#define MAXEVENTS 4

main()
{
    /*
     *  Perform a operating system simulation until 100 jobs have
     *  completed.  Use a "first come, first served" scheduling strategy.
     */
    queue cpuq;
    int entry;

    init_events();
    init_stats();
    init_queue(&cpuq);

    while (jobscompleted() < 100) {
        switch (entry = next_entry()) {
          case SUBMITONE:
          case SUBMITTWO:
            submitjob(&cpuq, entry);
```

```
          break;
        case JOBCOMPLETE:
          finishjob(&cpuq);
          break;
        case CPUTIMEOUT:
          requeuejob(&cpuq);
          break;
      }
    }
    print_stats();
}
```

An integer is returned by **next_entry()**, which signifies the next event to occur. The handling and the determining of events is coordinated in the event subsystem.

5.9.2   The Event Subsystem

The event subsystem is governed by a system clock and a table listing the amount of time remaining until each possible event can occur. The system clock starts at 0 and the job submittal events are initialized according to the exponential distribution. As opposed to looping as though the system clock were "ticking," the clock is advanced to the time at which the next event will occur. This can be done safely, as only the events listed in the table can cause a change of state in the simulation:

```
#define MEANSUBMIT 8
#define MEANRUN 15
#define CPULIMIT 20

static int systemclock;
static int EventTable[MAXEVENTS];
#define UNUSED 1000

typedef struct {
    int basetime;
    int elapsedtime;
    int runtime;
} job;

static job currentjob;

void init_events()
{
    /*
```

```
        *   An event table stores the time when the next event of a particular
        *   type should occur.   There are four events -- two job submittal
        *   events, a job completion event, and a cpu time-out event.  Jobs
        *   are submitted based on an exponential distribution.   Initially,
        *   no jobs are running, so time-out and completion times are not used.
        */
    long now;

    srand(time(&now));

    EventTable[SUBMITONE] = expdistr(MEANSUBMIT);
    EventTable[SUBMITTWO] = expdistr(MEANSUBMIT);
    EventTable[JOBCOMPLETE] = UNUSED;
    EventTable[CPUTIMEOUT] = UNUSED;
    systemclock = 0;
    currentjob.runtime = 0;
}


int next_entry()
{
    /*
     *   Determine what is the next event to occur.   Advance the system
     *   clock to that time and return the event for processing.
     */
    int event = 0;
    int i;

    for (i = 1; i < MAXEVENTS; i++)
        if (EventTable[i] < EventTable[event])
            event = i;

    advance_clock(EventTable[event]);
    return event;
}

int advance_clock(incr)
int incr;
{
    /*
     *   Advance the clock by decrementing the times for events to
     *   occur and incrementing the global system clock.
     */
    int i;

    for (i = 0; i < MAXEVENTS; EventTable[i++] -= incr) ;
    return systemclock += incr;
}
```

```
status submitjob(p_Q, event)
queue *p_Q;
int event;
{
    /*
     *   Submit a job for running by adding it to the queue.  Call
     *   startjob() to start the job.
     */
    if (qadd_job(p_Q, systemclock, 0, expdistr(MEANRUN)) == ERROR)
        return ERROR;

    printf("%5d Submitting job\n", systemclock);
    EventTable[event] = expdistr(MEANSUBMIT);
    return startjob(p_Q);
}

status startjob(p_Q)
queue *p_Q;
{
    /*
     *   Start a job.  If there is already a job running, do nothing.
     *   Otherwise, take the first job out of the queue and start it
     *   by setting the time-out and job-completion events.
     */
    int base, elapse, runtime;

    if (currentjob.runtime != 0)
        return OK;

    if (empty_queue(p_Q) == TRUE)
        return OK;

    if (qremove_job(p_Q, &base, &elapse, &runtime) == ERROR)
        return ERROR;

    /*
     *   The current job remaining run time is pulled out of the
     *   information stored with the job in the queue.  The elapsed
     *   time the job has already been waiting in the queue (used
     *   for statistics) is updated.
     */
    currentjob.runtime = runtime;
    currentjob.elapsedtime = elapse + systemclock - base;
    EventTable[CPUTIMEOUT] = CPULIMIT;
    EventTable[JOBCOMPLETE] = runtime;
    printf("%5d Starting job\n", systemclock);
    return OK;
}
```

```
status finishjob(p_Q)
queue *p_Q;
{
    /*
     *  A job is finished.   Update the statistics and start another job.
     */
    EventTable[CPUTIMEOUT] = UNUSED;
    EventTable[JOBCOMPLETE] = UNUSED;
    accumulate_stats(currentjob.elapsedtime);
    currentjob.runtime = 0;
    printf("%5d Finishing job\n", systemclock);
    return startjob(p_Q);
}

status requeuejob(p_Q)
queue *p_Q;
{
    /*
     *  A cpu time out has occurred.   Put the current job back on
     *  the queue (decrement the remaining run time by the amount
     *  of time just spent in the CPU).   Start another job.
     */
    EventTable[CPUTIMEOUT] = UNUSED;
    EventTable[JOBCOMPLETE] = UNUSED;
    if (qadd_job(p_Q, systemclock, currentjob.elapsedtime,
            currentjob.runtime - CPULIMIT) == ERROR)
        return ERROR;

    currentjob.runtime = 0;
    printf("%5d Requeueing job\n", systemclock);
    return startjob(p_Q);
}

int expdistr(meantime)
int meantime;
{
    /*
     *  Return a random number in an exponential distribution about
     *  meantime.   This routine assumes that rand() returns an
     *  int between 0 and 32767.
     */
    return (int) (-meantime * log( rand() / 32767.0 )) ;
}
```

Init_events() initializes the event table and provides a seed for the random-number generator. It also indicates that no job is currently running by setting the amount of run time needed for the current job to complete to be 0.

Next_entry() determines which event is to occur next by finding the smallest time in the event table. The system clock is then advanced to the time found. When the system clock is advanced, the event table is modified to reflect the amount of time that was skipped (in function **advance_clock()**). One subtle, but very important, point is that the "job completed" event must be checked before the "CPU time-out" event. Since it is possible for both events to occur at the same time, it is necessary to ensure that a job with 0 time units left to run is not requeued, but, instead, marked as completed.

The remaining functions perform the actual events. **Submitjob()** adds a job to the CPU queue via a call to the queue interface routine **qadd_job()**. Since a queued job consists of the time at which it was queued, the amount of time it has spent thus far in the queue, and the amount of run time needed to complete, this information is passed as parameters to **qadd_job()**. **Submitjob()** sets the event table entry to a random value representing the amount of time that must elapse before the submit event should occur. The last operation this function performs is invoke **startjob()**, which will start a CPU job if no job is currently running and if there is a job waiting in the CPU queue. A job is started by removing it from the queue and setting the "job complete" and "CPU time-out" events to the appropriate values.

Finishjob() marks the job that is in the CPU as finished. This is done by resetting the "job complete" and "CPU time-out" events to an **UNUSED** value and setting the current job run time to 0. Furthermore, statistical information is maintained through **accumulate_stats()**. Lastly, **startjob()** is invoked to start a job in the now-idle CPU.

Requeuejob() is invoked when the CPU time limit has been reached. This function adds the job currently in the cpu to the queue and moves the first job in the queue into the CPU. Note that when a job is requeued, the elapsed time spent in the queue may be nonzero, as the job has already been on the queue. Furthermore, the amount of time left until the job completes will be less than the original run time, since the job was just executing for **CPULIMIT** time units.

5.9.3   The Statistical Subsystem

Many statistics can be maintained for operating system simulations. The information of interest for this simulation is very basic: the average time a job spends in the CPU queue. To calculate this value, the total amount of time in the queue and the number of jobs are needed.

```
static long total_qtime;
static int jobcount;
```

```
void init_stats()
{
    /*
     *    Initialize statistics subsystem.  Only interested in the
     *    total number of jobs and the amount of time spent in the
     *    queue.
     */
    total_qtime = 0;
    jobcount = 0;
}

void accumulate_stats(qtime)
int qtime;
{
    /*
     *    Update statistics.
     */
    jobcount++;
    total_qtime += qtime;
}

void print_stats()
{
    /*
     *    Compute and print total and average time a job was queued.
     */
    printf("%-10s%-10s%s\n", " ", "Total", "Average");
    printf("%-10s%-10ld%.2f\n", "CPU Q:", total_qtime,
            total_qtime / (float) jobcount);
}

int jobscompleted()
{
    /*
     *    Return the number of jobs completed.
     */
    return jobcount;
}
```

5.9.4   Queue Interface Routines for Job Data

The queue interface routines are similar to the stack counterparts. They allow
for application-dependent access to the polymorphic queue primitive operations. For the simulation, three items of information are retained for each job
in the queue: the amount of run time needed to complete, the amount of time
already spent in the queue, and the time at which the job is entered into the

queue. The latter two items are used together in order that the statistical data
can be gathered.

```
typedef struct {
    int basetime;
    int elapsedtime;
    int runtime;
} job;

status qadd_job(p_Q, base, elapse, run)
queue *p_Q;
int base, elapse, run;
{
    /*
     *   Allocate a job structure, initialize it, and add it to the queue.
     */
    job *p_j = (job *) malloc(sizeof(job));

    if (p_j == NULL)
        return ERROR;

    p_j->basetime = base;
    p_j->elapsedtime = elapse;
    p_j->runtime = run;

    if (qadd(p_Q, (generic_ptr) p_j) == ERROR) {
        free(p_j);
        return ERROR;
    }
    return OK;
}

status qremove_job(p_Q, p_base, p_elapse, p_run)
queue *p_Q;
int *p_base, *p_elapse, *p_run;
{
    /*
     *   Remove a node from the queue and return the job data in
     *   p_base, p_elapse, and p_run.
     */
    job *p_j;

    if (qremove(p_Q, (generic_ptr *) &p_j) == ERROR)
        return ERROR;

    *p_base = p_j->basetime;
    *p_elapse = p_j->elapsedtime;
    *p_run = p_j->runtime;
```

```
        free(p_j);
        return OK;
}
```

Qadd_job() allocates space for the job data structure and copies the information into the allocated space. If no space is available, **ERROR** is returned. Otherwise, **qadd_job()** returns the same value as **qadd()**.

Qremove_job() removes an item from the queue via a call to **qremove()**. If that function returns **ERROR**, **qremove_job()** returns **ERROR**. Otherwise, the information that was removed from the queue is copied into the functions parameters, the memory space is freed, and **OK** is returned.

5.9.5   Simulation Results

The messages indicating the state of the system tell the user that the program is actually doing something. The information that is really needed from a simulation program is the statistics printed at program termination. If the statistics are to be reliable, they require a large set of data, hence the program termination condition.

One run of this simulation program showed an average time in the queue of 509.09 time units. Is this good or bad? In Chapter 7 another scheduling policy is discussed. By comparing the average time in the queue of this policy with the other, the relative merits of each can be assessed.

5.10   Queue Implementation: List Functions

A linked list provides a general method of storing data that allows for access of any of the members of the list in any order. As such, it can be used as a building block for the queue data structure.

In examining the linked list functions **append()** and **delete()**, one can see that **append()** adds a node to the end of a list, whereas **delete()** deletes the first node in the list. Therefore, if only these two functions are used to add and remove items from the list (and no list manipulation functions are used), then the list has the "first-in, first-out" property that characterizes queues. This makes it very simple to implement a queue in terms of a list:

```
typedef list queue;
status init_queue(p_Q)
queue *p_Q;
{
    return init_list(p_Q);
```

```
}

bool empty_queue(p_Q)
queue *p_Q;
{
    return empty_list(*p_Q);
}

status qadd(p_Q, data)
queue *p_Q;
generic_ptr data;
{
    return append(p_Q, data);
}

status qremove(p_Q, p_data)
queue *p_Q;
generic_ptr *p_data;
{
    return delete(p_Q, p_data);
}
```

A series of additions and deletions from the queue show how the list is manipulated:

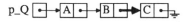

5.11   Queue Implementation: Header Node

In general, the implementation of a queue through the use of a list is a fairly
efficient technique. Of course, this statement can only be made if the list is
efficiently implemented. Looking back to the implementation of list operations
insert() and **append()**, it can be seen that although **insert()** is a very efficient
operation, **append()** is not. **Append()** traverses the entire list in order to find
the end. This makes that function's efficiency dependent on the size of the
list.

One technique of avoiding the traversal of the entire queue (list) each time
an item is added is to keep track of both ends of the queue[7] by defining a
queue to be a list with a special node at the beginning to keep track of this
additional information:

```
typedef struct {
    node *front;
    node *rear;
} queue;

#define FRONT(Q)  ((Q)->front)
#define REAR(Q)   ((Q)->rear)
```

By using this technique, it is necessary to rewrite *only* **qadd()**. However,
by rewriting just that one function, it may not be entirely clear how the queue
primitive operations work together.

```
status init_queue(p_Q)
queue *p_Q;
{
    /*
     *   Initialize  the  queue  to  empty.
     */
    FRONT(p_Q) = NULL;
    REAR(p_Q) = NULL;
    return OK;
}

bool empty_queue(p_Q)
queue *p_Q;
{
    /*
     *   Return  TRUE  if  the  queue  is  empty,  FALSE  otherwise.
     */
```

---

[7]Another technique is described in Chapter 6.

```
        return (FRONT(p_Q) == NULL) ? TRUE : FALSE;
}

status qadd(p_Q, data)
queue *p_Q;
generic_ptr data;
{
    /*
     *  Add data to p_Q.
     */
    list newnode;

    if (allocate_node(&newnode, data) == ERROR)
        return ERROR;

    if (empty_queue(p_Q) == FALSE) {
        NEXT(REAR(p_Q)) = newnode;
        REAR(p_Q) = newnode;
    } else
        FRONT(p_Q) = REAR(p_Q) = newnode;
    return OK;
}

status qremove(p_Q, p_data)
queue *p_Q;
generic_ptr *p_data;
{
    /*
     *  Remove a value from p_Q and put in p_data.
     */
    list nodeinfront;

    if (empty_queue(p_Q) == TRUE)
        return ERROR;

    nodeinfront = FRONT(p_Q);
    *p_data = DATA(nodeinfront);
    if (REAR(p_Q) == FRONT(p_Q))
        REAR(p_Q) = FRONT(p_Q) = NULL;
    else
        FRONT(p_Q) = NEXT(nodeinfront);

    free_node(&nodeinfront);
    return OK;
}
```

Init_queue() sets both the front and rear of the queue to **NULL**. This indicates the empty queue state. **Empty_queue()** checks only the front pointer to see if the queue is empty. Also, it is not necessary to check the rear pointer, because if there is nothing at the front of the queue, there can be nothing at the rear of the queue.

Qadd() first allocates a new node. If the queue is not empty (which is determined by looking at the rear pointer), then the new node is added after the last node in the queue and the rear pointer is changed to point to the node just added. If the queue is empty, then both the front and rear pointers are set to point to the new node.

Qremove() considers three cases. The first case is that there are not any nodes in the queue. This is an error. The second case is that there is exactly one node in the queue. Since both the front and rear pointers will point to that node, both the front and rear pointers will be reset to **NULL**, indicating an empty queue. The last case occurs when there is more than one node in the queue. This case is handled by setting the front pointer to the next item in the queue.

To contrast this with the list implementation, the same sequence of additions and deletions is illustrated.

Initially

qadd(p_Q, A);

qadd(p_Q, B);
NEXT(REAR(p_Q)) = newnode;

REAR(p_Q) = newnode;

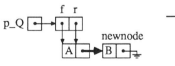

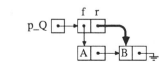

```
qadd(p_Q, C);                                    REAR(p_Q) = newnode;
NEXT(REAR(p_Q)) = newnode;
```

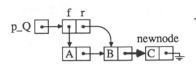
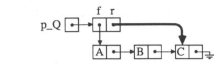

```
qremove(p_Q, p_data);                            FRONT(p_Q) = NEXT(nodeinfront);
```

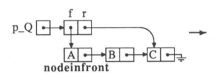
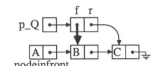

5.12   Exercises

1. Can you think of any other implementations for the stack data type? List
   the merits and deficiencies of the implementations given in this chapter
   and of any other implementations you can think of.

2. Empirically determine how large the stack can grow when filling a 100 ×
   100 region.

3. Write a test program to determine how large the stack can grow during
   execution of the fill algorithm. You may want to modify the stack primitive operations to include some sort of stack size information that can
   be made available to other routines. What should the dimensions of the
   test image be? What should the image look like? Can you exhaust the
   memory of your computer?

4. Since the fill algorithm requires such a large stack, develop and implement a different algorithm that uses a smaller stack. *Hint:* Look for runs
   of pixels and only push the ends onto the stack.

5. Implement unary minus in the infix-to-postfix notation translation program. *Hint:* In infix notation, the minus sign can be either a unary
   or binary operator, recognizable by the context in which the operator
   occurs. This is not the case in postfix notation.

6. Perform complete input error checking in the infix-to-postfix notation translation program. Modify the program so that no output occurs if there is an error in the input.

7. Write a program that translates an infix expression into prefix notation (in prefix notation, the operator precedes its operands).

8. Write a program that remove superfluous parentheses from infix expressions.

9. Develop an implementation for the queue that uses two stacks.

10. Develop an implementation for the queue that uses an array. Note that the front of the queue cannot always be at Array[0] unless the data in the queue is shifted down whenever an item is removed. Since it is extremely inefficient to constantly shift the data, the front pointer should move as necessary. Also, the back pointer should wrap around to the beginning of the array as necessary. Modulo arithmetic can be used for the wraparound. *Hint:* Think carefully about what constitutes an empty queue versus a full queue.

11. Rewrite the queue implementation of Section 5.11 to make use of as many list primitive operations as possible (i.e., minimize the amount of linked list manipulation that is done in the queue functions). It might help to think of the queue header node as

```
typedef struct {
    list front;
    list rear;
} queue;
```

CHAPTER
SIX

ADVANCED LIST STRUCTURES

The basic linked list, described in Chapter 4, can be used without modification in many programs. However, some applications require enhancements to the linked list design. These enhancements fall into three broad categories and yield variations on linked lists that can be used in any combination: circular lists, doubly-linked lists, and lists with header nodes.

6.1   Circular Lists

In a circular linked list, the last node points to the first. Although circular chains may not seem to have "first" or "last" nodes, external pointers provide a frame of reference. For example, the "list" variable used to access the data structure points to the *last* node, so both the first and last can be accessed quickly. For example, a list containing **A**, **B**, and **C** (in that order) is represented as

A new node definition is not needed for circular lists, because the structure of the nodes is the same as that of noncircular lists. However, the primitive operations must take into account the circular nature. In particular, functions that require moving along the entire list can no longer test for the end of the list by comparing the pointer to **NULL**. With a circular list, it is necessary to maintain a pointer to the end of the list and compare the auxiliary pointer used to traverse the list to that value.

Circular lists have the advantage of allowing fast appends. Like noncircular lists, they have a simple, uniform structure (all nodes have the same type) that can be recursively defined. The drawback is the slight increase in the complexity of the primitive operations.

6.1.1   Primitive Operations on Circular Lists

As with linear linked lists, many functions can be developed that operate on the list in a general fashion. Minimally, functions are needed for initialization, insertion, deletion, and testing for emptiness. The implementation of these functions, as well as the append function, is described for circular linked lists. Ideally, if linear linked lists and circular linked lists were implemented in an abstract manner, the two types of lists could be used interchangeably in any program. This is a strong argument for using the same function names in the two implementations. However, different function names will be used here so confusion among the packages is minimized.

Initializing a Circular List

Initialization of a circular linked list is the same as with a linear linked list.

```
status init_circ_list(p_L)
list *p_L;
{
    /*
     *   Initialize *p_L by setting the list pointer to NULL.
     *   Always return OK (a different implementation
     *   may allow errors to occur).
     */
    *p_L = NULL;
    return OK;
}
```

The purpose of the list initialization routine is to set the list to empty. This is done by setting the **list** variable to **NULL**. Since this operation is the same for both linear linked lists and circular linked lists, the same function could have been used.

Status of a Circular List

Circular linked lists are empty when the list variable has a value of **NULL**.

```
bool empty_circ_list(L)
list L;
{
    /*
     *  Return TRUE if L is an empty list, FALSE otherwise.
     */
    return (L == NULL) ? TRUE : FALSE;
}
```

As indicated, an empty list is determined in the same fashion for both linear linked lists and circular linked lists.

Inserting an Item

Inserting an item at the front of a circular linked list requires a different algorithm than with a linear linked list. The **circ_insert()** function performs the insertion and maintains the lists circular properties.

```
status circ_insert(p_L, data)
list *p_L;
generic_ptr data;
{
    /*
     *  Insert a new node containing data as the first item in *p_L.
     */
    list L;

    if (allocate_node(&L, data) == ERROR)
        return ERROR;

    if (empty_circ_list(*p_L) == TRUE) {
        NEXT(L) = L;
        *p_L = L;
    } else {
        NEXT(L) = NEXT(*p_L);
        NEXT(*p_L) = L;
    }
    return OK;
}
```

Like the linear linked list insert routine, **circ_insert()** has two arguments: a pointer to the list and the data item to be inserted. **Allocate_node()** is used to create a new node. If this function fails, then **circ_insert()** returns **ERROR**. Otherwise, the data will be successfully added.

To insert the data into the circular list, there are two cases that must be considered. When the list is empty, the new list will contain exactly one node and the node must be set so that its **NEXT** field points to itself (to make the list circular). The list variable should then be set to point to this node. When the list already contains some data, the list variable, ***p_L**, points to the last node, and that node's **NEXT** field points to the first node in the list. The new node should be inserted between these two. This is done by setting the new node's **NEXT** field to point to the first node in the list (as given by ***p_L**'s **NEXT** field) and making the last node point to the new node. Since the last node of the list has not changed, it is not necessary to modify the list variable.

The algorithm used for these two cases is easily understood using diagrams. The first case is insertion into an empty list:

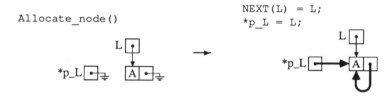

The second case assumes the list already has two nodes containing **A** and **B** (in that order):

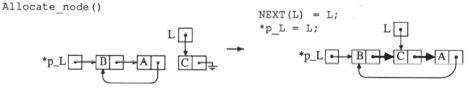

It is important to see that the algorithm is valid even if the list contains only one node.

Appending an Item to a Circular List

The **circ_append()** function adds a node to the end of a circular linked list. Due to the list's structure, it is not necessary to traverse the entire list to perform this operation:

```
status circ_append(p_L, data)
```

```
list *p_L;
generic_ptr data;
{
    /*
     *   Append a new node containing data as the last item in *p_L.
     *   Update *p_L to point to the new last node.
     */
    list L;

    if (allocate_node(&L, data) == ERROR)
        return ERROR;

    if (empty_circ_list(*p_L) == TRUE)
        NEXT(L) = L;
    else {
        NEXT(L) = NEXT(*p_L);
        NEXT(*p_L) = L;
    }
    *p_L = L;
    return OK;
}
```

Since (***p_L**) points to the last node in the list, appending a node entails adding a node after ***p_L** and setting ***p_L** to point to it. As with **circ_insert**(), there are two cases.

If the list is initially empty, then the new node's **NEXT** field should be set to point to the new node. This creates a new circular list. If the list is not empty, then the new node must be inserted after the last node. This is done using the same procedure as with **circ_insert**(). In either case, the list variable must then be modified to point to the new last node. The following diagram illustrates appending **C** to a list containing **A** and **B** (in that order):

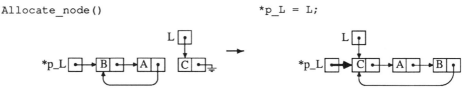

By examining this algorithm closely, it can be seen that the only difference between this function and **circ_insert**() is that in this function, the list variable is modified. This observation leads to the following simplified function:

```
status circ_append(p_L, data)
list *p_L;
generic_ptr data;
```

```
{
    /*
     *  Append a new node containing data as the last item in *p_L.
     *  Update *p_L to point to the new last node.
     */
    if (circ_insert(p_L, data) == ERROR)
        return ERROR;
    *p_L = NEXT(*p_L);
    return OK;
}
```

Deleting an Item

The **circ_delete()** function deletes the first node in a circular linked list and passes back the data that was at the front of the list via a pointer argument. Deleting the first node in the list is a special case of deleting any arbitrary node. Therefore, **circ_delete()** can be implemented based on the primitive operation **circ_delete_node()**.

```
status circ_delete(p_L, p_data)
list *p_L;
generic_ptr *p_data;
{
    /*
     *  Delete the first node in *p_L and return the DATA in p_data
     */
    if (empty_circ_list(*p_L))
        return ERROR;

    *p_data = DATA(NEXT(*p_L));
    return circ_delete_node(p_L, *p_L);
}
```

Circ_delete() has two arguments: a pointer to a list, and a pointer to a place in which to put the data that was stored in the deleted node. Since it is an error to try to delete from an empty list, **ERROR** is returned if the list is empty. Otherwise, **circ_delete()** copies the data stored in the first node in the list, which is given by **NEXT(*p_L)**, to the argument **p_data** and deletes the first node via a call to **circ_delete_node()**.

```
status circ_delete_node(p_L, node)
list *p_L;
list node;
{
    /*
```

```
 *   Delete node from *p_L.
 */
list L;

if (empty_circ_list(*p_L) == TRUE)
    return ERROR;

if (node == NEXT(node))
    /*
     *   Delete the only node in the list.
     */
    *p_L = NULL;
else {
    for (L = NEXT(*p_L); L != *p_L && NEXT(L) != node; L = NEXT(L))  ;
    if (NEXT(L) != node)
        return ERROR;
    NEXT(L) = NEXT(node);
    if (node == *p_L)
        /*
         *   Deleting the last node in the list, so update *p_L
         */
        *p_L = L;
}
free_node(&node);
return OK;
}
```

The general scheme for deleting an arbitrary node is to traverse the list until the node before the one to be deleted is found. That node's **NEXT** field is set to point to the node after the one to be deleted.

Initially

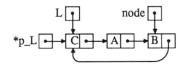

After for loop

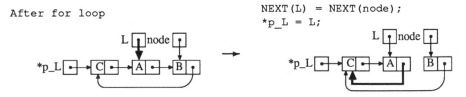

NEXT(L) = NEXT(node);
*p_L = L;

Circ_delete_node() must consider two special cases when deleting an arbitrary node. These cases involve resetting the list pointer. They occur when the only node in the list is deleted and when the last node in the list is deleted (recall the the list pointer points to the last node). In the first case, the list pointer must be set to **NULL**. In the second case, the list pointer must be set to point to the node that is before the last node.

Initially

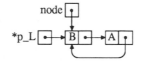

After for loop

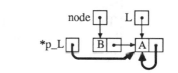

6.2   Application: LISP Subset Interpreter

One application that could benefit from circular linked lists is a LISP interpreter. LISP (**LIS**t **P**rocessing Language) is a computer language in which the linear linked list is the primary structure. Although it may appear most logical to implement a language interpreter using the same structure, a circular linked list will be used in the interpreter to allow for fast appends.

LISP is actually a very simple language. There are two basic data types in LISP: the "atom" and the "list." An atom is a symbolic name (similar to a variable), and a list is a linear linked list containing atoms and/or other lists. Objects in a list are enclosed in parentheses. Some examples of lists are

(a b c)	a list containing three atoms, *a*, *b*, and *c*
(a (b c))	a list containing two objects: the atom *a* and the list *(b c)*
()	an empty list

An expression in LISP is called a *symbolic-expression*, or *s-expression*, and is either an atom or a list. When evaluating s-expressions in a true implementation of LISP, atoms are treated as variables and their values are fetched. In the implementation that will be developed in this section, it will be assumed that the value of an atom is the name of the atom. For example:[1]

---

[1]Computer prompts and responses will be shown in boldface. User input will be in the

> **lisp:** a
> **A**
> **lisp:** z
> **Z**
> **lisp:** name
> **NAME**

Lists are evaluated by treating the first element as a function name and calling the function with the remaining members of the list as arguments after they have been evaluated. Very often, operations have to be performed on expressions without evaluating the expression. The special LISP function **quote** has one argument in which it suppresses further evaluation:

> **lisp:** (quote (this is a list))
> **(THIS IS A LIST)**
> **lisp:** (quote (quote (another list)))
> **(QUOTE (ANOTHER LIST))**

Since **quote** is frequently used, LISP defines a shorthand notation for this function. The apostrophe (') can be used to quote an expression:

> **lisp:** '(this is a list)
> **(THIS IS A LIST)**
> **lisp:** (quote '(another list))
> **(QUOTE (ANOTHER LIST))**

The function **car** has one argument, a list. **Car** returns the first element of the list. If the argument is not a list, an error message is printed:

> **lisp:** (car '(A B C))
> **A**
> **lisp:** (car (car '((sublist 1) arg2 arg3)))
> **SUBLIST**
> **lisp:** (car 'atom)
> **Error evaluating expression**

It is instructive to follow the steps that would be taken by the interpreter to evaluate these examples. The first example **(car '(A B C))** is expanded to **(car (quote (A B C)))**. The function to apply is **car** and its argument is **(quote (A B C))**. The argument is evaluated, which yields the list **(A B C)**. **Car** is then applied to that list, which results in **A**.

---

standard typeface.

The second example further indicates the recursive nature of LISP. (**car (car '((sublist 1) arg2 arg3)))** expands to (**car (car (quote ((sublist 1) arg2 arg3)))).** The **quote** function is evaluated first, yielding **((sublist 1) arg2 arg3).** Then **car** is applied to that value, yielding **(sublist 1).** The outermost **car** is then applied, yielding **SUBLIST.**

The function **cdr**[2] also has one list argument. This function, which is similar to the list basic operation **delete()**, returns a list consisting of its argument without the first element:

> **lisp:** (cdr '(A B C))
> **(B C)**
> **lisp:** (cdr '((SUB 1) (SUB 2)))
> **((SUB 2))**
> **lisp:** (cdr 'atom)
> **Error evaluating expression**

The first example shows a list with three elements, A, B, and C. By taking the **cdr** of this list, the first element is removed and a list containing only the second and third is returned. In the second example, the **cdr** is being taken of a list with two elements, each of which is a list. One might think that since the second element is already a list, it will be returned by **cdr** without modification. However, **cdr** always makes a list of the remaining items. Therefore, a list containing one item (a list) is returned.

The function **cons** is the LISP equivalent of **insert()**. It has two arguments and it creates a new list by inserting the first argument at the front of the second argument. This means that the second argument must be a list:

> **lisp:** (cons 'a '(b c))
> **(A B C)**
> **lisp:** (cons '(a) '(b))
> **((A) B)**
> **lisp:** (cons 'a 'b)
> **Error evaluating expression**

The first example inserts the atom **a** into the list containing **b**, and the second example inserts one list into another. **Cons** does not distinguish between the type of value to be inserted; atoms and lists are inserted in the same fashion (although the results are quite different).

Note that **cdr** and **car** undo a **cons**. Given a list, **cons**'ing the **car** and the **cdr** of that list yields the original list:

---

[2]Pronounced *could'er*.

lisp: (cons (car '(A B C)) (cdr '(A B C)))
(A B C)

There are two arguments to **cons**. Evaluating the first argument, **(car '(A B C))**, yields **A**. Evaluating the second argument, **(cdr '(A B C))**, yields **(B C)**. The result of evaluating the entire expression, **(cons 'A '(B C))**, is **(A B C)**.

One last function that will be in the subset of LISP is **eval**. This function is the inverse of **quote**. Whereas **quote** suppresses evaluation of its arguments, **eval** causes its arguments to be evaluated. Since LISP code has the same structure as LISP data, functions can be modified and executed (using **eval**) at run time. This is one of the greatest strengths of LISP.

lisp: (eval (quote (car '(A B C))))
A

In this example, the data is **(quote (car '(A B C)))**. Although this data is "hard coded" into the example, it is not difficult to imagine circumstances in which it may not be known in advance exactly what code is to be evaluated.

6.2.1   LISP Interpreter Design

The main loop of any LISP interpreter is the "read-eval-print" loop. The read routine scans a LISP s-expression and converts it to an internal format. The eval routine takes the internal representation and creates a new s-expression that represents the value of the s-expression that was input. The print routine will convert the internal representation to something that can be output. Function prototypes can be defined for these functions without deciding upon the internal representation:

```
int read_expression(lisp_expression *p_expression);
int eval_expression(lisp_expression expression, lisp_expression *p_value);
status print_expression(lisp_expression expression);
```

These prototypes assume that regardless of the actual form of the internal representation, the s-expressions will be accessible via the type **lisp_expression**. The first two functions will return an integer error number if an error occurs, and the third function will return an error flag.

6.2.2   LISP Interpreter Program Driver

The program driver for a LISP interpreter is quite short. It implements the "read-eval-print" loop found in all LISP interpreters. It operates by using functions that read an s-expression, evaluate an s-expression, and print an s-expression. This particular implementation also uses a function that prints error messages corresponding to error codes returned by the other functions.

```
#define E_EXIT   -1
#define E_EOF     1
#define E_SPACE   2
#define E_SYNTAX  3
#define E_EVAL    4
#define MAXERROR  5


main()
{
    /*
     *   The read-eval-print loop for a "subset of lisp" interpreter.
     */
    lisp_expression expression, value;
    int rc;

    do {
        printf("lisp: ");
        rc = read_expression(&expression);
        if (rc) {
            printerror(rc);
            continue;
        }
        rc = eval_expression(expression, &value);
        if (rc != E_EXIT) {
            if (rc) {
                printerror(rc);
                continue;
            }
            print_expression(value);
            printf("\n");
        }
    } while (rc != E_EXIT) ;
    printf("Normal termination.\n");
}

printerror(errnum)
int errnum;
{
    /*
     *   Print a "lisp" error message.  The order of the strings in
     *   errmsg is dependent upon the error value "#defines".
     */
    static char *errmsg[] = {
```

```
            "unexpected  end  of  file",
            "out  of  memory  space",
            "syntax  error",
            "error  evaluating  expression"
            };

    if (errnum < 0 || errnum >= MAXERROR) {
        printf("System Error.  Invalid error number: %d\n", errnum);
        return;
    }
    printf("%s\n", errmsg[errnum-1]);
}
```

This driver has three local variables: **expression** is the s-expression that is input by the user, **value** is the s-expression obtained as a result of evaluating **expression**, and **rc** is an integer code returned by the read and evaluate functions.

The loop terminates when the code returned by **eval_expression()** is equal to **E_EXIT**, which means the user entered a LISP expression containing the function **(EXIT)**. The LISP function **exit** causes immediate termination of the program — no further arguments are evaluated. Note, however, that **exit** causes termination when it is evaluated, not when it is input. The ramification of this is that if **(exit)** is an argument to another function, the other function will not be evaluated. This makes both of the following examples valid ways in which to exit the interpreter without errors:

lisp: (exit)
Normal termination.

lisp: (car (exit))
Normal termination.

6.2.3   Internal Representation

Given that circular linked lists will be used as the internal representation of s-expressions, a node in the linked list must be able to contain either a LISP list or a LISP atom. A **union** gives this capability:

```
typedef enum {LIST, ATOM} lisp_type;
typedef list lisp_list;
typedef char *lisp_atom;

typedef struct lisp_node {
    lisp_type type;
```

```
    union {
        lisp_list lisplist;
        lisp_atom atom;
    } value;
} lisp_node, *lisp_expression;
```

Since a **lisp_node** can contain either a list or an atom (but not both at the same time), a flag is stored in the node indicating which type of value is currently stored. The flag variable **type** is a **lisp_type** variable. **List_type** is another name for the enumerated type consisting of **LIST** and **ATOM**. Whenever a value is stored in the **value** field, the **type** will also be specified. The enumerated type value **LIST** corresponds to the **lisp_list** type (which is just another name for a **list**) being stored in the node. The enumerated type value **ATOM** corresponds to the **lisp_atom** type (which is just another name for a **char ***) being stored in the node.

Some preprocessor macros help clarify how the members of the node relate and make the code easier to follow.

```
#define LISP_TYPE(x) (((lisp_expression) x)->type)
#define ATOM_VALUE(x) (((lisp_expression) x)->value.atom)
#define LIST_VALUE(x) (((lisp_expression) x)->value.lisplist)

#define T_VALUE "T"
#define NIL_VALUE "NIL"
#define QUOTE_VALUE "QUOTE"
```

The first macro, **LISP_TYPE**, indicates the type of data stored in the node. The subsequent macros assume that the data is of a particular type and result in access to the corresponding **union** member. Note that these macros do not enforce that the data pulled out of the node is of the same type that was put in. Code for ensuring this should appear prior to each access.

There are two additional issues that must be addressed. In the list routines developed in this chapter and in Chapter 4, a null (or empty) list was represented by a null pointer. In LISP, however, a null list is represented by a special atom. This atom, NIL, is both an atom and the null list. It is represented in input by either the string "nil" or the empty list given by "()." A single internal representation should be used. If the user enters "nil," then no special processing is required because it will be treated as any other atom. If the user enters the empty parentheses, then it must be converted into the NIL atom.

A similar issue is that of the internal representation of an apostrophe. Since the apostrophe is a shorthand notation for **QUOTE**, the obvious solution is to treat it internally as if the user had entered (**QUOTE** ...). By doing this, the internal representation remains consistent, even though the user may view things slightly differently.

6.2.4   Reading S-Expressions

The input routine will organize the user input into a circular linked list, where each node represents either an atom or a subexpression. The algorithm proceeds as follows:

```
if the token is a left parenthesis
    if the next token is a right parenthesis
        create a null list
    otherwise
        until the next token is a right parenthesis do
            recursively read the inner expression
            append the inner expression as a node on
                the current expression list
otherwise if the token is an apostrophe
    expand the apostrophe into (QUOTE ...)  by creating a
    list with the first argument "QUOTE" and appending
    the next expression to that list.
otherwise if the token is a string
    the expression is an atom
```

Before coding can begin, the calling semantics of **read_expression()** should be formalized. In particular, this function will return 0 if the input is successfully read and a nonzero return code (as described before) if an error occurs. The expression that is read will be returned via an argument to the function. The argument will be a pointer to a **lisp_expression** and space will be allocated for the expression and atoms as necessary.

Reading an s-expression involves the same sort of low-level lexical analysis routines as the infix-to-postfix expression translator in Section 5.6, only in this case, the valid tokens are a left parenthesis, a right parenthesis, an apostrophe ('), and a string. Instead of having only a single routine to return the current token, another routine is required that allows one to look ahead at the next token without actually processing it. These two functions will return the data by setting pointers into **static** buffers that contain a field indicating token type and token value.

This yields the following definitions and function prototypes:

```
int read_expression(lisp_expression *p_expression);
lisp_expression new_expression(void);
lisp_atom new_atom(char *string);

#define MAXTOKENLENGTH 32

typedef enum {QUOTE_T,RIGHTPAREN_T,LEFTPAREN_T,STRING_T,EOF_T} inputtype;

typedef struct tokendata {
    inputtype tokentype;
    char tokenvalue[MAXTOKENLENGTH];
} tokendata;

tokendata *gettoken();
tokendata *lookahead();
```

With these building blocks, the recursive function **read_expression()** can be coded:

```
int read_expression(p_expression)
lisp_expression *p_expression;
{
    /*
     *  Read a lisp expression and store it in p_expression.  If no
     *  errors, return 0. Otherwise return the appropriate error flag.
     */
    list expr_list;
    lisp_expression expression, inner_expression;
    tokendata *p_token, *p_next_token;
    lisp_atom value;
    status rc;
    int readerror;

    p_token = gettoken();
    if (p_token >tokentype == EOF_T)
        return E_EOF;

    if ((expression = new_expression()) == NULL)
        return E_SPACE;

    switch (p_token->tokentype) {
        case RIGHTPAREN_T:
            /*
             *  Can't have a lone ')'.
             */
            return E_SYNTAX;
        case STRING_T:
            /*
```

```
     *    Create an atom.
     */
    if ((value = new_atom(p_token->tokenvalue)) == NULL)
        return E_SPACE;
    LISP_TYPE(expression) = ATOM;
    ATOM_VALUE(expression) = value;
    break;
case LEFTPAREN_T:
    /*
     *    The start of a list.
     */
    p_next_token = lookahead();
    if (p_next_token->tokentype == EOF_T)
        return E_EOF;
    if (p_next_token->tokentype == RIGHTPAREN_T) {
        /*
         *    The lookahead token is a ).  This is a null list.
         */
        if ((value = new_atom(NIL_VALUE)) == NULL)
            return E_SPACE;
        LISP_TYPE(expression) = ATOM;
        ATOM_VALUE(expression) = value;
    } else {
        /*
         *    Read the inner expressions.
         */
        init_circ_list(&expr_list);
        do {
            readerror = read_expression(&inner_expression);
            if (readerror != 0)
                return readerror;
            rc = circ_append(&expr_list,
                    (generic_ptr) inner_expression);
            if (rc == ERROR)
                return E_SPACE;
            p_next_token = lookahead();
            if (p_next_token->tokentype == EOF_T)
                return E_EOF;
        } while (p_next_token->tokentype != RIGHTPAREN_T);
        LISP_TYPE(expression) = LIST;
        LIST_VALUE(expression) = expr_list;
    }
    p_token = gettoken();
    break;
case QUOTE_T:
    /*
     *    Got an apostrophe. Create the QUOTE token and make the
     *    next expression the second element in the list.
```

```
                        */
            p_next_token =lookahead();
            if (p_next_token->tokentype == EOF_T)
                return E_EOF;
            if (p_next_token->tokentype == RIGHTPAREN_T) {
                return E_SYNTAX;
            } else {
                init_circ_list(&expr_list);
                if ((inner_expression = new_expression()) == NULL)
                    return E_SPACE;
                if ((value = new_atom(QUOTE_VALUE)) == NULL)
                    return E_SPACE;
                LISP_TYPE(inner_expression) = ATOM;
                ATOM_VALUE(inner_expression) = value;
                rc=circ_append(&expr_list,(generic_ptr)inner_expression);
                if (rc == ERROR)
                    return E_SPACE;
                readerror = read_expression(&inner_expression);
                if (readerror != 0)
                    return readerror;
                rc=circ_append(&expr_list,(generic_ptr)inner_expression);
                if (rc == ERROR)
                    return E_SPACE;

                LISP_TYPE(expression) = LIST;
                LIST_VALUE(expression) = expr_list;
            }
            break;
        }

    *p_expression = expression;
    return 0;
}
```

When **read_expression()** is called, it reads the next token and also allocates
space for the expression to be returned. If either of these operations fails,
the appropriate error code is returned. The next operation performed by this
function depends on the input token.

If the input token is a right parenthesis, a syntax error has occurred and
the corresponding error code is returned. If a string is input, a new atom node
is allocated and the type of the current expression is set to **ATOM**.

For example, the input **A** will yield the following structure:

Note that a **lisp_node** always points to the atom value; atom values should never occur without a corresponding **lisp_node**. This fact becomes important as the other cases are considered.

If the token is a left parenthesis, then the lookahead token is checked. If it is a right parenthesis, then a new atom node with value of **NIL** is allocated. The type of the current expression is set to **ATOM** and the value of the expression is the atom node just allocated. This corresponds to the following structure:

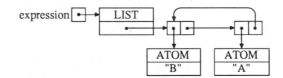

If the lookahead token is not a right parenthesis, then a list of subexpressions is created by recursively invoking **read_expression()** and appending the results to **expr_list**. When the lookahead token becomes a right parenthesis, the end of the sublist is indicated. The value of the current expression becomes the **expr_list** and the type of the expression is a **LIST**. For example, the input (**A B**) corresponds to the following structure:

Note that at this point, the trailing right parenthesis has been found only by **lookahead()**. This means that it is waiting in the input queue. Since the right parenthesis is no longer needed, a call to **gettoken()** will remove it.

If the current token is an apostrophe (**QUOTE_T**), then (provided the lookahead token is not a right parenthesis), the expression returned will be a list whose first element is the atom "QUOTE." This atom is created using **new_expression()** to allocate a new lisp expression node and then calling **new_atom()** to allocate the atom node that is the value of the new expression. The quote atom must be attached to the list via an expression node to remain consistent with how other atoms are created. After this quote expression is added to the **expr_list**, the remaining argument to quote is read with a recursive call and its expression is appended to **expr_list**. The value of the entire expression is the **expr_list** just created and the type is **LIST**. For example, the input '(**A B**) corresponds to the following structure:

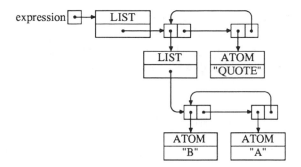

A useful exercise for the reader is to draw a picture of the internal structure that corresponds to the input **(car (cdr '(A B)))**.

6.2.5   Printing S-Expressions

Printing an s-expression is easy since a **lisp_expression** is simply a list. By using the basic circular linked list function, **circ_traverse()**, **print_expression()** is indirectly recursive:

```
status print_expression(expression)
lisp_expression expression;
{
    /*
     *  Format and print an expression to standard output.
     */
    if (LISP_TYPE(expression) == ATOM)
        printf("%s ", ATOM_VALUE(expression));
    else {
        printf("(");
        circ_traverse(LIST_VALUE(expression), print_expression);
        printf(") ");
    }
    return OK;
}
```

Print_expression() is called with a single parameter, the expression to be printed. If the type of the expression is an atom, then the value is printed. If the type of the expression is a list, then an open brace is printed, the list traversal function is called to print the sublist, and then the closing parenthesis is printed.

When **circ_traverse()** is called, it will apply **print_expression()** to each of the nodes in the list. This creates a potential sequence of **print_expression()** calling **circ_traverse()**, which in turn calls **print_expression()**, etc. This indirect recursion will always terminate because of the atoms contained in each list.

6.2.6   Evaluating S-Expressions

The algorithm for evaluating expressions in this language subset is the same as in a complete LISP interpreter with the exception of how atoms are treated. In the subset, the value an atom is the atom name. The value of a list is obtained by assuming the first element of the list is a function name. That first element must be an atom. If it is a list, then an error is indicated. Otherwise, that function is applied to the rest of the arguments in the list after the arguments are evaluated. In both this subset and in standard LISP, the only exception to this rule is if the function is "QUOTE." This function returns its arguments unevaluated. These three cases are explicitly considered in the implementation of **eval_expression()**.

```
int eval_expression(expression, p_value)
lisp_expression expression, *p_value;
{
    /*
     *  Evaluate expression and return the value in p_value.
     */
    list L, arg;
    lisp_atom function_name;
    list sublist;
    lisp_expression subexpr;
    lisp_expression return_value;
    int rc;

    if (LISP_TYPE(expression) == ATOM) {
        *p_value = expression;
        return 0;
    }

    L = LIST_VALUE(expression);

    /*
     *  Get the first list member.  It should be the function name (an atom).
     */
    arg = circ_list_iterator(L, NULL);

    if (LISP_TYPE(DATA(arg)) != ATOM)
```

```
            return E_EVAL;
        function_name = ATOM_VALUE(DATA(arg));

        if (equal_atom(function_name, QUOTE_VALUE)) {
            /*
             *  The function is QUOTE.  There better be one other node
             *  in the list.  Return the other node unevaluated.
             */
            if (circ_length(L) != 2)
                return E_EVAL;
            *p_value = (lisp_expression) DATA(circ_list_iterator(L, arg));
            return 0;
        }
        /*
         *  Evaluate the inner expressions (if there are any).
         */
        init_circ_list(&sublist);
        if (circ_length(L) > 1) {
            /*
             *  Iterate over the inner expressions placing their values in
             *  sublist.  The iterator was initialized in a previous call.
             */
            while ( (arg = circ_list_iterator(L, arg)) != NULL) {
                rc = eval_expression((lisp_expression) DATA(arg), &subexpr);
                if (rc)
                    return rc;
                if (circ_append(&sublist, (generic_ptr) subexpr) == ERROR)
                    return E_EVAL;
            }
        }
        rc = evaluate_function(function_name, sublist, &return_value);
        if (rc)
            return rc;
        *p_value = return_value;
        return 0;
}

evaluate_function(name, args, p_value)
char *name;
list args;
lisp_expression *p_value;
{
    /*
     *  Evaluate the built-in function, name.  Use args as the arguments.
     *  Return the evaluated expression in p_value.  If the function is not
     *  in the built-in list, return an error flag.
     */
    int c_car(), c_cdr(), c_cons(), c_eval(), c_exit();
```

```
#     define MAXBUILTIN 5
      static struct {
          char *func_name;
          int (*f)();
      } builtin[MAXBUILTIN] = {
          { "CAR", c_car },
          { "CDR", c_cdr },
          { "CONS", c_cons },
          { "EVAL", c_eval },
          { "EXIT", c_exit }
      };
      int i;

      for (i = 0; i < MAXBUILTIN; i++) {
          if (strcmp(name, builtin[i].func_name) == 0)
              return builtin[i].f(args, p_value);
      }
      return E_EVAL;
}
```

Eval_expression() checks to see if the expression consists of an atom. If so, then the result is the same as the expression (in this version of the interpreter, the value of an atom is its name). Otherwise, the expression is a list and must be evaluated using the rules for evaluating lists. First, a check is made to ensure that the first node in the list is an atom (representing the function to be applied). Note the use of the **circ_list_iterator()** primitive operation. This function (like its linear linked list counterpart) returns each node of a list in turn. The first time it is called, it will return the first node in the list. When there are no more items left in the list, it will return **NULL**. Note that, on this call, it is not necessary to check to ensure that the value returned by **circ_list_iterator()** is nonnull, since null lists are replaced by **NIL** atoms in **read_expression()**.

If the function name corresponds to the function name for the quote function (i.e., "quote"), then the result is the second item in the list (unevaluated). Before this value can be returned, however, the length of the list is verified to be exactly 2. This can be done with the **circ_length()** primitive operation.

If the function to be applied is not the **quote** function, then the arguments must be evaluated. First, a check is made to see if there are any arguments to evaluate. If there are, **eval_expression()** is called recursively to perform the evaluation, with the result being placed in the variable **subexpr**. This value is then appended to **sublist**. After all the arguments (if there are any) have been evaluated, **evaluate_function()** is called. This C function applies the LISP function to the list of arguments and places the result in **return_value**.

Note that return codes are constantly checked within **eval_expression()** and if at any point an error is indicated, the function returns.

Evaluate_function() is quite simple. The C function maintains an array containing the valid (built-in) function names and the corresponding C routine that performs the operation. The C routine is called with the argument list and a pointer variable for storing the result.

```c
int c_exit(arglist, p_return)
list arglist;
lisp_expression *p_return;
{
    /*
     *  Exit the lisp interpreter by setting the exit flag.
     */
    return E_EXIT;
}

int c_car(arglist, p_return)
list arglist;
lisp_expression *p_return;
{
    /*
     *  (car arglist) in p_return. arglist must
     *  contain a single node that is a list.  The first node in
     *  that list is returned.
     */
    lisp_expression car_list;

    if (circ_length(arglist) != 1)
        return E_EVAL;
    car_list = (lisp_expression) DATA(nth_node(arglist, 1));
    if (LISP_TYPE(car_list) != LIST)
        return E_EVAL;
    *p_return = (lisp_expression)DATA(nth_node(LIST_VALUE(car_list),1));
    return 0;
}

int c_cdr(arglist, p_return)
list arglist;
lisp_expression *p_return;
{
    /*
     *  (cdr arglist) in p_return.  Arglist must contain a single node
     *  that must be a list. Create a new expression that contains
     *  all but the first element of that list.  This function
     *  modifies its argument.
     */
```

```
        lisp_expression expression;
        lisp_expression cdr_list;
        list car_node;

        if (circ_length(arglist) != 1)
            return E_EVAL;
        cdr_list = (lisp_expression) DATA(nth_node(arglist, 1));
        if (LISP_TYPE(cdr_list) != LIST)
            return E_EVAL;
        if ((expression = new_expression()) == NULL)
            return E_EVAL;
        /*
         *  Get rid of the first argument.  Note that the space for the
         *  expression is not freed.
         */
        car_node = nth_node(LIST_VALUE(cdr_list), 1);
        free(DATA(car_node));
        if (circ_delete_node(&LIST_VALUE(cdr_list), car_node) == ERROR) {
            return E_EVAL;
        }
        if (empty_circ_list(LIST_VALUE(cdr_list)) == TRUE) {
            /*
             *  Expression should be the NIL atom.
             */
            LISP_TYPE(expression) = ATOM;
            ATOM_VALUE(expression) = new_atom(NIL_VALUE);
            if (ATOM_VALUE(expression) == NULL)
                return E_SPACE;
        } else {
            LISP_TYPE(expression) = LIST;
            LIST_VALUE(expression) = LIST_VALUE(cdr_list);
        }
        *p_return = expression;
        return 0;
}

int c_cons(arglist, p_return)
list arglist;
lisp_expression *p_return;
{
        /*
         *  (cons arglist) in p_return.  Arglist must contain two items,
         *  the second of which must be a list.  The first item is inserted
         *  at the front of the other list. This function modifies its
         *  argument.
         */
        lisp_expression arg1, arg2;
```

```
        if (circ_length(arglist) != 2)
            return E_EVAL;

        arg1 = (lisp_expression) DATA(nth_node(arglist, 1));
        arg2 = (lisp_expression) DATA(nth_node(arglist, 2));
        if (LISP_TYPE(arg2) != LIST)
            return E_EVAL;
        if (circ_insert(&LIST_VALUE(arg2), (generic_ptr) arg1) == ERROR)
            return E_EVAL;
        *p_return = arg2;
        return 0;
}

c_eval(arglist, p_return)
list arglist;
lisp_expression *p_return;
{
    /*
     *   (eval arglist) in p_return.
     */
    if (circ_length(arglist) != 1)
        return E_EVAL;
    return eval_expression((lisp_expression) DATA(arglist), p_return);
}
```

The built-in functions operate as expected. **C_exit()** does not modify its parameters at all. By returning **E_EXIT**, it sets an error flag that will propogate all the way to **main()**

C_car() performs the LISP **car** operation. Since **car** should have only one argument, the C routine verifies that this is the case. It then ensures that the one argument is a **LIST**. If it is, then the return value is the value of the first item in that list. If any of these checks fail, the appropriate error value is returned.

To get the first item in the list, the primitive operation **nth_node()** is used. This function has two arguments: the list and the number of the node desired, with 1 being the first node. To get the last node, −1 should be passed as the node number. If the desired node doesn't exist, this function will return **NULL**.

C_cdr() performs the LISP **cdr** operation. Like **car**, **cdr** requires its single argument to be a list. Creating the resultant expression, however, is slightly more complicated. Since **cdr** requires the result to be a list, a new expression node must be allocated and set to type **LIST**. The value stored in this new node is the same as the argument to **cdr** except that the first item must be removed from the list. The node is deleted using list primitive operations.

If the remaining list is empty, the value of **cdr** should be the **NIL** atom. Otherwise, the resulting list is returned. As an example of how this function works, assume it is called with **arglist** corresponding to (**A B C**):

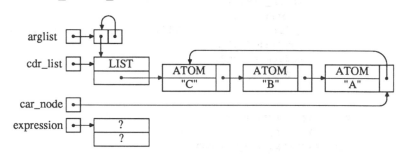

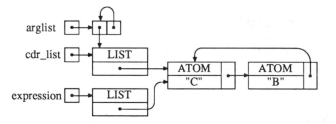

C_cons() requires two arguments, with the second argument being a list. It then inserts the first argument at the front of its second argument. That modified list is returned.

C_eval() is included to show how easy it is to use data as a program. This function requires one argument and calls **eval_expression()** to evaluate that argument. Since **eval_expression()** calls **c_eval()**, which in turn calls **eval_expression()**, this function is indirectly recursive.

There is a problem with several of these functions as they are written. They have undesirable side effects. **C_cdr()** and **c_cons()** both modify the first argument to the function even though the result is returned via the second argument. A solution to this problem is proposed in the exercises.

6.2.7   The Lexical Analyzer

The lexical analyzer required in this section is slightly more advanced than the one developed in Section 5.6. This lexical analyzer allows one to "look ahead" at the next token while still leaving it in the input queue. This is limited in that only a single token lookahead is permitted, but it is sufficient for its current use.

```
static tokendata *p_lookahead = NULL;

tokendata *gettoken()
{
    /*
     *   Return a token.  If p_lookahead is not NULL, return (and clear)
     *   that lookahead token. Otherwise, "toggle" tokenindex and
     *   store the returned token in token[tokenindex].
     */
    static tokendata token[2];
    static int tokenindex = 0;
    tokendata *p_token;
    char *p_value;
    int c;

    if (p_lookahead != NULL) {
        p_token = p_lookahead;
        p_lookahead = NULL;
        return p_token;
    }

    tokenindex = (tokenindex + 1) % 2;
    p_token = &token[tokenindex];
    p_value = p_token->tokenvalue;
    /*
     *   Skip white space.
     */
    do {
        if ((*p_value = getchar()) == EOF) {
            p_token->tokentype = EOF_T;
            return p_token;
        }
    } while (isspace(*p_value));

    p_value[1] = 0;
    switch (*p_value) {
        case '\'':
            p_token->tokentype = QUOTE_T;
            break;
        case '(':
            p_token->tokentype = LEFTPAREN_T;
            break;
        case ')':
            p_token->tokentype = RIGHTPAREN_T;
```

```
                break;
          default:
                *p_value = toupper(*p_value);
                p_value++;
                while ((c = getchar()) != EOF && isalpha(c))
                    *p_value++ = toupper(c);
                *p_value = '\0';
                if (c != EOF)
                    ungetc(c, stdin);
                p_token->tokentype = STRING_T;
        }
      return p_token;
}


tokendata *lookahead()
{
    /*
     *   Return the lookahead token.  If p_lookahead is non-NULL use it,
     *   otherwise, set p_lookahead with a call to gettoken().
     */
    if (p_lookahead == NULL)
        p_lookahead = gettoken();
    return p_lookahead;
}
```

Lookahead is implemented by using two **static** buffers and a lookahead variable. If **p_lookahead** is non-**NULL**, then a lookahead token has been scanned. In that case, **gettoken()** will return that value and clear **p_lookahead**. Otherwise, the next token to be read will be stored in one of the two **static** buffers (always alternating between the two). Two buffers are used to allow concurrent storage of the current token and the lookahead token.

6.2.8   Low-Level LISP Routines

There are two routines that are used to allocate the LISP expression data structures and another routine that is used to examine atoms. These routines are used in place of explicit list interface routines.

```
lisp_expression new_expression()
{
    return (lisp_expression) malloc(sizeof(lisp_node));
}


lisp_atom new_atom(s)
char *s;
{
```

```
        char *dest = malloc(sizeof(char)*(strlen(s)+1));

        if (dest)
            strcpy(dest, s);
        return dest;
}

int equal_atom(atom1, atom2)
lisp_atom atom1, atom2;
{
        return strcmp(atom1, atom2) == 0;
}
```

New_expression() uses **malloc()** to allocate a new **lisp_node**. **New_atom()** uses **malloc()** to allocate space for enough characters to store the string that is passed as an argument. If **malloc()** is successful, then the string value is copied into the new space. The last function, **equal_atom()** returns a nonzero value if the two atoms passed are the same. If they are not the same, then zero is returned.

6.2.9   Additional Circular List Primitive Operations

In the development of the LISP interpreter, several prototypes for circular list primitive operations were described.

Circular List Iterator

The circular list iterator is a function that when called repeatedly returns each node of the list. This implementation requires that the previously returned value be passed as an argument. To begin the iteration, **NULL** is passed as the "last return value." Note that special care must be taken to identify the end of the list.

```
  list circ_list_iterator(L, lastreturn)
  list L;
  list lastreturn;
  {
      /*
       *   Return each item of L in turn. Return NULL
       *   after the last item has been returned.
       *   lastreturn is the value that was returned last.
       *   If lastreturn is NULL, start at the beginning of L.
       */
      if (lastreturn == NULL)
```

```
            return (L) ? NEXT(L) : NULL;
        else
            return (lastreturn == L) ? NULL : NEXT(lastreturn);
}
```

Circular List Length

Circ_length() returns the number of nodes in a circular linked list.

```
int circ_length(L)
list L;
{
    /*
     *  Return the number of nodes in L.
     */
    list lastreturn;
    int length;

    length = 0;
    lastreturn = NULL;
    while ( (lastreturn = circ_list_iterator(L, lastreturn)) != NULL)
        length++;
    return length;
}
```

Finding Nodes Based On Position

Finding a node based on its position in the list requires specifying a base position. The obvious base position for a list is the first node. However, should that be node 1 or node 0? It was arbitrarily chosen to make node 1 the first node. The last node can be accessed by specifying −1.

```
list nth_node(L, number)
list L;
int number;
{
    /*
     *  Return the number'th node of L.   The first node is 1.
     *  To get the last node, number should be −1.  If there aren't
     *  enough nodes in the list, return NULL.
     */
    list tmp;

    if (empty_circ_list(L) == TRUE)
        return NULL;
```

```
        if (number == -1)
            return L;

    tmp = L;
    do {
            tmp = NEXT(tmp);
            number--;
    } while (number > 0 && tmp != L);
    return (number != 0) ? NULL : tmp;
}
```

This function also ensures that the node requested exists. That is, if a request is made for node 8 in a list with only seven elements, **NULL** is returned.

Traversing a List

The function **circ_traverse()** is used to apply an application-defined function to the data stored in each node of the list.

```
status circ_traverse(L, p_func_f)
list L;
status (*p_func_f)();
{
    /*
     * Call p_func_f() with the DATA field of each node in L.
     * If p_func_f() ever returns ERROR, this function returns ERROR.
     */
    list tmp;

    if (empty_circ_list(L) == TRUE)
        return OK;

    tmp = L;
    do {
        tmp = NEXT(tmp);
        if ((*p_func_f)(DATA(tmp)) == ERROR)
            return ERROR;
    } while (tmp != L) ;
    return OK;
}
```

If the list is empty, then **circ_traverse()** returns, indicating success. Otherwise, **tmp** is used to traverse the list. It is initialized to point to the *last* node in the list. The loop is entered and **tmp** is set to point to the next node (which will be the first node the first time through the loop). The passed function is then applied. The condition for exiting the loop is that **tmp** points to the last item in the list (equal to **L**).

The order in which operations are performed in this function is very important. Careful thought must be given to functions that operate on a circular structure so as to ensure that all the nodes are visited in the correct order and that the termination condition is proper. In this routine, **tmp** is modified at the top of the loop, whereas the test for termination is not until the bottom of the loop. Since **tmp** can be set to the last node in the list, the passed function will be applied to it and *then* the loop will be terminated.

Writing this function using **circ_list_iterator()** is left as an exercise.

6.3 Doubly-Linked Lists

A limitation of both linear linked lists and circular linked lists is that the list can be traversed in only one direction. Also, with both these types of lists, deleting an arbitrary node requires traversing the list from the start to locate the node that points to the one to be deleted. Doubly-linked lists make these operations efficient.

Each node in a doubly-linked list contains two pointers: one to the previous node and one to the next node.

A new node definition is required for this type of list. Formally, a doubly-linked list and this new type of node is defined as follows:

- A doubly-linked list is a pointer to a "double-node" or is null.

- A double-node has three fields:

  1. a **datapointer** field, which points to the data element
  2. a **prev** field, which points to the previous node in the list
  3. a **next** field, which points to the next node in the list

The first node in the list has a **NULL prev** field. The last node in the list has a **NULL next** field. With this definition, it is no longer required that the head of the list be used as the sole entry point into the list. Since any node can be found by using the **prev** or **next** pointers, any node can be used to access the list.

6.3.1   C Representation of Double-Nodes

As with the other list structures, the nodes of a doubly-linked list will contain pointers to the data. This enables the C implementation of the list basic operations to be independent of the type of data maintained in the list.

```
typedef struct double_node double_node, *double_list;

struct double_node {
    generic_ptr datapointer;
    double_list next;
    double_list prev;
};

#define DATA(L) ((L)->datapointer)
#define NEXT(L) ((L)->next)
#define PREV(L) ((L)->prev)
```

This definition is very similar to the definition for linear linked lists, including the use of preprocessor macros for accessing the members of the structure. Many of the properties of singly-linked lists also apply to doubly-linked lists. In particular, the use of a **generic_ptr** for the data requires the programmer to develop a layer of routines on top of the doubly-linked list functions to manage storage for the data elements.

The application developer's functions should not be confused with the functions for allocating and freeing nodes, which are internal to the doubly-linked list package. The application programmer must interface with operations on lists. Conversely, the functions within the list package must consider operations on nodes. In Section 4.2.3, an interface was developed for managing memory for nodes in a linear linked list. A similar set of functions must be developed for doubly-linked lists. Since these functions are almost identical to the ones previously described, they are presented without comment.

```
status allocate_double_node(p_L, data)
double_list *p_L;
generic_ptr data;
{
    double_list L = (double_list) malloc(sizeof(double_node));

    if (L == NULL)
        return ERROR;

    *p_L = L;
    DATA(L) = data;
    NEXT(L) = NULL;
```

```
        PREV(L) = NULL;
        return OK;
}

void free_double_node(p_L)
double_list *p_L;
{
        free(*p_L);
        *p_L = NULL;
}
```

6.3.2   Primitive Operations on Doubly-Linked Lists

As a basis of comparison, some of the operations that were developed for linear linked lists and circular linked lists will be developed for doubly-linked lists. However, since doubly-linked lists allow for more general access, the functions should make no assumptions about the list being passed. With linear linked lists and circular lists, it did not matter whether the list being passed was actually the first node of the list or a pointer to a node in the middle of some larger list. In the latter case, it was up to the application programmer to ensure that the "larger" list was maintained correctly. The list operations always assumed that the node was the first in the list.

This is the only assumption possible based on the structure of a linear (or circular) linked list. With a doubly-linked list however, the structure provides more information about a node's position within a list. With this extra information, the doubly-linked list functions can ensure that the "larger" list is maintained correctly.

Initializing a Doubly-Linked List

A doubly-linked list is initialized to be empty.

```
status init_double_list(p_L)
double_list *p_L;
{
        /*
         * Initialize *p_L by setting the list pointer to NULL.
         * Always return OK (a different implementation
         * may allow errors to occur).
         */
        *p_L = NULL;
        return OK;
}
```

This initialization routine is the same as with the other types of lists.

Status of a List

A doubly-linked list is empty when the list variable has a value of **NULL**.

```
bool empty_double_list(L)
double_list L;
{
    /*
     *  Return TRUE if L is an empty list, FALSE otherwise.
     */
    return (L == NULL) ? TRUE : FALSE;
}
```

Since an empty list is the same for all three types of list structures, the function that checks the status of the list is the same.

Inserting an Item

The operation of inserting an item at the front of a doubly-linked list is slightly more complicated than the corresponding operation for linear linked lists. This is because the **PREV** pointer must be maintained.

```
status double_insert(p_L, data)
double_list *p_L;
generic_ptr data;
{
    /*
     *  Insert a new node containing data as the first item in *p_L.
     */
    double_list L;

    if (allocate_double_node(&L, data) == ERROR)
        return ERROR;

    if (empty_double_list(*p_L) == TRUE) {
        PREV(L) = NEXT(L) = NULL;
    } else {
        NEXT(L) = *p_L;
        PREV(L) = PREV(*p_L);
        PREV(*p_L) = L;
        if (PREV(L) != NULL)
            NEXT(PREV(L)) = L;
    }
    *p_L = L;
```

```
    return OK;
}
```

Double_insert() has two arguments: a pointer to the list, and the data item to be inserted. It is not required that the list pointer ***p_L** point to the first item in the list. If successful, this function will modify ***p_L** to point to the list beginning with the node just added.

This function first calls **allocate_double_node**() to allocate a new node **L** for the doubly-linked list. If successful, then two cases must be considered. If the list is initially empty, the **NEXT** and **PREV** fields of the new node are set to **NULL**. This indicates that the new node is both the first and last node of the list. If the list is not empty, the **NEXT** field of the new node is set to point to ***p_L** and the **PREV** field of the new node is set to point to the **PREV** field of ***p_L**. This will allow the new node to be placed between the nodes **PREV(*p_L)** and ***p_L**. Now those nodes must be modified to point to the new node. Since ***p_L** follows the new node, its **PREV** field is set to point to the new node. Similarly, since the node pointed to by **PREV(L)** comes before the new node (**L**), its **NEXT** field is set to point to the new node. Since **PREV(L)** is potentially **NULL**, this condition is checked prior to the assignment. Note that it is this assignment that removes the assumption that ***p_L** is the first node in the list.

Two examples will help clarify the steps taken in this function. In the first example, the head of a list containing three nodes is passed to **double_insert**():

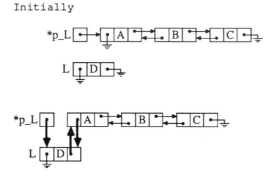

The second example starts with the same list of three nodes, but instead of passing the true head of the list, a pointer to the second node will be passed.

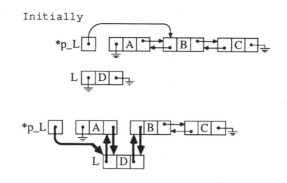

Appending an Item

The append operation for doubly-linked lists, **double_append()**, is very similar to that for linear linked lists. This function, which will be required by the application to be developed, is left as an exercise (see Exercise 7).

Deleting an Item

The **double_delete()** function deletes the first node in a doubly-linked list and passes back the data that was at the front of the list via a pointer argument. As with its circular and linear linked list counterparts, this function represents a special case of deleting an arbitrary node in the list. Therefore, **double_delete()** can be implemented based upon the primitive operation **double_delete_node()**.

```
status double_delete(p_L, p_data)
double_list *p_L;
generic_ptr *p_data;
{
    /*
     *  Delete the first node in *p_L and return the DATA in p_data
     */
    if (empty_double_list(*p_L) == TRUE)
        return ERROR;

    *p_data = DATA(*p_L);
    return double_delete_node(p_L, *p_L);
}
```

Double_delete() has two arguments: a pointer to the list, and a pointer to a location in which to place the data that was in the deleted node. It is not required that the list pointer point to the first item in the list. Since it is an error to try to delete from an empty list, **ERROR** is returned if the list is empty. Otherwise, **double_delete()** copies the data stored in the first node in the list to the argument **p_data** and deletes the first node via a call to **double_delete_node()**.

```
status double_delete_node(p_L, node)
double_list *p_L;
double_list node;
{
    /*
     *   Delete node from *p_L.
     */
    double_list prev, next;

    if (empty_double_list(*p_L) == TRUE)
        return ERROR;

    prev = PREV(node);
    next = NEXT(node);

    if (prev != NULL)
        NEXT(prev) = next;
    if (next != NULL)
        PREV(next) = prev;

    if (node == *p_L) {
        if (next != NULL)
            *p_L = next;
        else
            *p_L = prev;
    }

    free_double_node(p_L);
    return OK;
}
```

Since each node in a doubly-linked list points to the previous and next nodes, there is no need for a list traversal. Instead, all that is required is for the **PREV** and **NEXT** fields of the next and previous nodes, respectively, to be modified. In the implementation, the cases where one or both of the neighboring nodes are null (i.e., the node to be deleted is either the first or the last) must be considered. Furthermore, if the node to be deleted, **node,** is equal to the list pointer passed, **p_L**, then the parameter must be modified. If this is the case, then ***p_L** is set to the next node if there is one. If there is no next node, then ***p_L** is set to the previous node. If ***p_L** is the last node in the list, then this has the effect of setting ***p_L** to **NULL**.

Two of these cases are illustrated. When deleting a middle node from a list, the following sequence is followed:

Initially

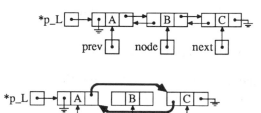

When deleting the first node from a list, the following sequence is followed:

Initially

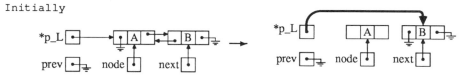

The observant reader will have already noticed that it is not necessary to pass a list pointer to **double_delete_node()**. In previous implementations, the list pointer was used to find the node that pointed to the node to be deleted. With doubly-linked lists it is not used at all (except to be modified when necessary). With this in mind, **double_delete_node()** could be written with a single parameter. However, since doubly-linked lists are being implemented as an abstract data type with a corresponding set of primitive operations, it may not be clear to the application how to maintain a single "list pointer" representing the object that is a doubly-linked list.

6.4 Application: Simple Line Editor

A line editor is a type of text editor. Minimally, a text editor allows one to enter data, edit existing data, and delete existing data. Most modern editors are full-screen editors. With a full-screen editor, the user has control over which section of the file is displayed on the screen, and it is possible to edit any part of a file just by moving the cursor to that position on the screen and typing the new data.

Interfaces to line editors are less sophisticated. The user can display a line and perform operations on that line. In order to view that line in the context of the rest of the file, the user must give a command that will print a section of the file. This does not imply that a screen editor is more powerful than a line editor. A fully functioned line editor can perform the same operations as a fully functioned screen editor. The only difference is the user interface. In this section, a simple text editor is developed.

6.4.1   Line-Editor Design

In designing the line editor, the first thing to consider is what capabilities should be included. Some possible functions are

- Read a file.
- Write any portion of the current data to a file.
- Display any portion of the current data.
- Insert new lines.
- Delete lines.
- Move lines around.
- Make changes to any subset of existing lines.
- Insert the contents of a file within the current data.

User Paradigm

The user's view of the program is the best place to begin the design. It must be decided how the user will view the data (the user *paradigm*). The program then becomes an implementation of that paradigm. First, consider the exact operations that will be implemented (a subset of the previous list):

- Read a file.
- Write a file (using the **w** command).
- Insert a line (using the **i** command).
- Delete a set of lines (using the **d** command).
- Move a set of lines (using the **m** command).
- Quit (exit) the editor (using the **q** command).

Since the editor is a line editor, the user needs some way to reference lines. A natural solution is to give each line a number and allow the user to reference lines by using the line number. The first line number will always be line 1.

Oftentimes, however, the user may want to refer to the last line. Knowing that the first line is always line 1 does not tell the user the last line number. Although the program could continually display the last line number, this is awkward. One alternative is to allow the user to enter a very large number and if that number is greater than the actual number of lines in the file, then the last line is used. This, too, is awkward. A better alternative is to give the last line a label that the user can use to reference it. One choice is a dollar sign (**$**). Therefore, to print (display) the last line, the user could enter

p$

The second-to-last line can be accessed by referencing the one before the last line, as in

p$−1

Given this method of accessing lines in the file, consider how the previous commands would operate. This can be done by imagining an editing session (% is the computer prompt):

```
% edit
Enter the name of the file to edit: somefile.c
4 lines read.
cmd: p1,$
1    main()
2    {
3      printf("Hello, world!\n");
4    }
cmd: i3
      printf("Entering program.\n");
  .
cmd:
```

The insert command will insert lines before the line number given. The end of the text is signified by a period on a line by itself. Suppose the user realizes that there should be some output before "Hello, world!" What line number should be given to the insert command? One approach is to make the user count the number of lines input so that **i4** could be entered.

A better approach is to invent a new line reference: the current line. It will always be the last line referenced and will have the label "**.**" (period). When lines are inserted, the current line will not change. So entering another in the previous example can be done as follows:

```
cmd: i.
    printf("Here is the text: ");
cmd: p1,$
1    main()
2    {
3        printf("Entering program.\n");
4        printf("Here is the text: ");
5        printf("Hello, world!\n");
6    }
cmd:
```

With this new construct, thought must be given as to what the current line becomes with each command. There are several ways in which the current line can be set for each command. Arbitrarily, it was decided that upon reading a file, the current line will be the last line in the file. When lines are printed, the current line will be the last line printed. When lines are inserted, the current line will be the line after the last line inserted. When lines are deleted, the current line will be the line after the last line deleted. If the last line of the file was deleted (meaning there is no line following it), the current line will be the last line of the file.

Thus far, the following commands have been alluded to: print, insert, and delete. The print command takes a range of line numbers, where a range is a single line reference or two line references separated by a comma. Note that a line reference can be relative as in $.+1$ or $\$-1$. If the print command is executed without any line reference, it is as though p. were entered. The insert command uses a single line reference. This indicates the line before which the data is added. The end of the data to be inserted is indicated by a line containing just a period. The delete command takes a range of line numbers and deletes those lines.

The move command takes a range of line numbers and moves those lines to before the current line. It is an error for the current line to be included within the range.

```
cmd: p3
3        printf("Entering program.\n");
cmd: m4,5
cmd: p1,$
```

```
1      main()
2      {
3              printf("Here is the text:  ");
4              printf("Hello, world!\n");
5              printf("Entering program.\n");
6      }
cmd: p
5              printf("Entering program.\n");
cmd: m3,6
invalid line specification.
cmd:
```

The write command without an argument will write the entire set of lines to the file named when the program was invoked. If a file name argument is given, this command will write the data to the file named. The quit command exits the program. If the user has modified any of the data, this command gives a warning that the data should be saved. Continuing with the above example:

```
cmd: q
File modified. Enter W to save, Q to discard.
cmd: w
6 lines written.
cmd: q
%
```

Internal Representation

Since the user views the data file as a collection of lines to be edited, it is logical for the program to take the same view. However, before choosing the obvious internal representation for the data, consider some requirements of the program: each line of text must be accessible individually; it must be possible to determine the line number of each line and since lines can be reordered, added, and deleted, the line number must be able to be modified quickly. The representation must be able to handle an arbitrarily large number of lines and data per line. Furthermore, the operations of adding or deleting lines at any point in the file must be efficient as they will be performed often.

The obvious choice is some sort of list of lines. An array representation of the list would be ideal in that the line numbers could be quickly determined based on the element in the array. However, adding and deleting from the middle of an array is inefficient because a hole must be created (or filled in) by shifting all subsequent elements. Using a singly-linked linear linked list would be more efficient, however problems would appear with relative line numbers.

If a doubly-linked list is used (with each node storing exactly one line), both insertion and deletion can be performed very efficiently. Furthermore, relative line referencing (as in $.-1$) can be implemented by traversing either the **PREV** or **NEXT** pointers as necessary. The only open question concerns the type of information to store in each node of the list. One choice is to store the string data and a line number. This has the advantage of being able to determine the line number very quickly. The disadvantage of this approach is that every time lines are added, deleted, or moved, the entire list will have to be traversed to store the new line numbers. The question reduces to which operation will be performed most often. If it is expected that line numbers will be needed more often than insertions and deletions, then the line numbers should be stored with the data. However, since an editor is being developed, it is safe to assume that editing will done more frequently than displaying of text. It follows that the line numbers should be computed as needed and not stored with the data.

Since only a single data type will be stored in the list, it is not necessary to define a structure for the element data. Of course, interface routines for appending information to a doubly-linked list will still be required to dynamically allocate (and free) the storage for the character strings that are input.

One other design issue is that of determining the program modules. Actually, this too is rather obvious. There will be a single function for each of the editing commands, and the parameters to the functions will be the arguments to the editing command, the current line, and the current data list. Since each of these functions will need to parse the line number specification (which is the argument to most of the editing commands), a subfunction should perform this task. This subfunction will have five arguments. The line specification to be parsed, a pointer to the head of the data list, and a pointer to the current line will be passed in. The function will return a pointer to the starting line and a pointer to the ending line via the remaining two parameters.

```
int printlines(char *linespec,double_list *p_head,double_list *p_current);
int deletelines(char *linespec,double_list *p_head,double_list *p_current);
int insertlines(char *linespec,double_list *p_head,double_list *p_current);
int movelines(char *linespec, double_list *p_head, double_list *p_current);
int parse_linespec(char *linespec, double_list head,
    double_list current, double_list *p_start, double_list *p_end);
```

By using a single function to parse the line specifications, the techniques can be modified without impacting any other function.

6.4.2 Line Editor Program Driver

The line editor program driver initializes the data structure and reads commands from the user. For each command read, it calls a function that performs the operation.

```
main()
{
    /*
     *  A simple text editor.
     */
    char filename[BUFSIZ];
    char buffer[BUFSIZ];
    double_list linelist, currentline;
    bool file_edited, exit_flag;
    int rc;

    init_double_list(&linelist);
    printf("Enter the name of the file to edit: ");
    gets(filename);
    if ((rc = readfile(filename, &linelist)) != 0) {
        printerror(rc);
        exit(1);
    }
    printf("%d lines read.\n", double_length(linelist));
    currentline = nth_double_node(linelist, -1);
    file_edited = FALSE;
    exit_flag = FALSE;
    while (exit_flag == FALSE) {
        printf("cmd: ");
        gets(buffer);
        /*
         *  Implement the following commands:
         *      p   -   print
         *      d   -   delete
         *      i   -   insert
         *      m   -   move
         *      w   -   write
         *      q   -   quit.
         */
        switch (toupper(buffer[0])) {
            case '\0':
                break;
            case 'P':
                rc = printlines(&buffer[1], &linelist, &currentline);
                if (rc)
                    printerror(rc);
                break;
```

```
        case 'D':
            file_edited = TRUE;
            rc = deletelines(&buffer[1], &linelist, &currentline);
            if (rc)
                printerror(rc);
            break;
        case 'I':
            file_edited = TRUE;
            rc = insertlines(&buffer[1], &linelist, &currentline);
            if (rc)
                printerror(rc);
            break;
        case 'M':
            file_edited = TRUE;
            rc = movelines(&buffer[1], &linelist, &currentline);
            if (rc)
                printerror(rc);
            break;
        case 'W':
            if (buffer[1] != '\0')
                strcpy(filename, &buffer[1]);
            rc = writefile(filename, &linelist);
            if (rc != 0)
                printerror(rc);
            else
                printf("%d lines written\n", double_length(linelist));
            file_edited = FALSE;
            break;
        case 'Q':
            /*
             * If text has been modified, can't quit without writing
             * unless you enter q two times in a row.
             */
            if (file_edited == TRUE) {
                printf("File modified. Enter W to save, Q to discard.\n");
                file_edited = FALSE;
            } else
                exit_flag = TRUE;
            break;
        default:
            printerror(E_BADCMD);
            break;
        }
    }
}

printerror(errnum)
int errnum;
```

```
{
    /*
     *  Print error messages to standard output.
     */
    static char *errmsg[] = {
        "io error",
        "out of memory space",
        "invalid line specification",
        "invalid command",
        "error deleting lines"
        };

    if (errnum < 0 || errnum >= MAXERROR) {
        printf("System Error.  Invalid error number: %d\n", errnum);
        return;
    }
    printf("%s\n", errmsg[errnum-1]);
}
```

The program driver has several local variables. **Filename** is used to hold
the string that represents the file to be edited. The user is prompted to enter
the file name when the program begins execution. When the user issues the
write command with no arguments, this is the name of the file that is written. **Buffer** is the command line input buffer. The two **double_list** variables,
linelist and **currentline**, point to the first line and the current line, respectively. If there are no lines, both these variables are **NULL**. **File_edited** is set
to **TRUE** whenever the data has been modified (and is not synchronized with
the corresponding file). This variable is reset whenever the data is written.
Exit_flag is set to **TRUE** when quit has been entered and **rc** is the return
code set by functions that are called by the driver.

The general function of the driver is straightforward. First, the user enters
the name of a file. That file is read (if it exists) and the data is stored in the
list **linelist**. The current line is set to be the last line read. Then a loop is
entered in which the user enters commands. In order to keep the code short,
checks for white space in the input were removed. This means the user must
not enter any extraneous blanks or tabs. Both uppercase and lowercase letters
are recognized for the commands and the appropriate function is called to
perform the operation. In general, the functions that perform the operations
have three arguments: the remainder of the command line (which will indicate
a range of lines), a pointer to the head of the list, and a pointer to the current
line. It is the responsibility of each of those functions to update the **linelist**
and **currentline** variables as necessary.

Errors are handled the same way as in the LISP interpreter. Each function returns either 0, indicating success, or a nonzero error code. If an error code is returned, **printerror()** is called to display the error message.

```
#define E_IO 1
#define E_SPACE 2
#define E_LINES 3
#define E_BADCMD 4
#define E_DELETE 5
#define E_MOVE 6
#define MAXERROR 7
```

In this implementation, only a few error messages are included, but it is obvious how to extend the error handling to support more informative error messages.

6.4.3   User Operations

Not surprisingly, much of the user functions are simply interfaces into primitive list operations.

Reading and Writing Files

Readfile(), **writefile()**, and **writeline()** perform the necessary input and output functions.

```
int readfile(filename, p_L)
char *filename;
double_list *p_L;
{
    /*
     *  Read data from filename and put in the linked list *p_L.
     */
    char buffer[BUFSIZ];
    FILE *fd;

    if ((fd = fopen(filename, "r")) == NULL)
        return 0;

    while (fgets(buffer, BUFSIZ, fd) != NULL) {
        if (string_double_append(p_L, buffer) == ERROR)
            return E_SPACE;
    }
    fclose(fd);
    return 0;
}
```

```
static FILE *outputfd;

int writefile(filename, p_L)
char *filename;
double_list *p_L;
{
    /*
     *  Output the data in *p_L to the output file, filename.
     *  Use the static global variable outputfd to store the output
     *  file descriptor so that it can be used by writeline().
     */
    status rc;

    if ((outputfd = fopen(filename, "w")) == NULL)
        return E_IO;

    rc = double_traverse(*p_L, writeline);
    fclose(outputfd);
    return (rc == ERROR) ? E_IO : 0;
}

status writeline(s)
char *s;
{
    /*
     *  Write a single line of output to outputfd.  Outputfd
     *  must point to a file previously opened with fopen (as
     *  is done in writefile().
     */
    if (fputs(s, outputfd) == EOF)
        return ERROR;

    return OK;
}
```

Readfile() takes a file name and a pointer to a list, reads the data associated with the file, and stores it in the list. If the file cannot be opened, it is assumed that it does not exist, and no error is returned. If the file does exist, then each line is read and appended to the linked list. At the end of input, the file is closed and 0 is returned.

Writefile() uses the list traversal function **double_traverse()**. It first opens the file and stores the file descriptor in a **static** global variable. This makes the file descriptor accessible only to **writefile()** and **writeline()**. Then the traversal function is called with the list as the first parameter and function **writeline()** as the second parameter. Recall that the linked list traversal function calls the function passed as a parameter once for each node in the list.

The data stored in the node is used as an argument to that function. In this application, the data stored in the doubly-linked list are strings. Therefore, **writeline()** outputs its argument to the file and returns **OK**.

Inserting New Lines

Insertlines() inserts new lines into a file. This function prompts the user for the lines to be added and inserts them before the line indicated. The end of user input is indicated by a period (".") on a line by itself.

```
int insertlines(linespec, p_head, p_current)
char *linespec;
double_list *p_head, *p_current;
{
    /*
     *   Insert new lines before the current line.
     */
    double_list newdata, startnode, endnode;
    status rc;
    int cmp, parseerror;
    char buffer[BUFSIZ];

    /*
     *   If the list is empty, no linespec is allowed.
     */
    if (empty_double_list(*p_head) == TRUE) {
        if (strlen(linespec) != 0)
            return E_LINES;
        startnode = endnode = NULL;
    } else {
        /*
         *   If a linespec is given, it better be a single line number.
         */
        parseerror = parse_linespec(linespec, *p_head, *p_current,
                        &startnode,&endnode);
        if (parseerror)
            return parseerror;
        if (startnode != endnode)
            return E_LINES;
    }
    /*
     *   Collect the new lines in newdata. Then "paste" the list before
     *   startnode.
     */
    init_double_list(&newdata);
    do {
        printf("insert>");
```

```
            fgets(buffer, BUFSIZ, stdin);
            cmp = strcmp(buffer, ".\n");
            if (cmp != 0) {
                rc = string_double_append(&newdata, buffer);
                if (rc == ERROR)
                    return E_SPACE;
            }
        } while (cmp != 0) ;
        if (empty_double_list(newdata) == TRUE)
            return 0;

        if (startnode == NULL) {
            /*
             *  Empty list
             */
            *p_head = newdata;
            *p_current = nth_double_node(newdata, -1);
        } else if (PREV(startnode) == NULL) {
            /*
             *  Insert before the first line.
             */
            double_list lastnode = nth_double_node(newdata, -1);
            paste_list(&lastnode, p_head);
            *p_head = newdata;
            *p_current = startnode;
        } else {
            /*
             *  Insert in the middle of the list.
             */
            paste_list(&PREV(startnode), &newdata);
            *p_current = startnode;
        }
        return 0;
    }
```

Since **insertlines()** must be able to insert lines into an empty file, it first checks to see if the file is empty. If it is, no range specification is allowed and **startnode** and **endnode** are both set to **NULL**. If the file is not empty, the range specification is parsed. Since lines can only be added in one place, the range specification must be such that the starting line and the ending line are the same. This means only commands such as **i.** or **i5** are allowed. If the user wanted to be fancy, a full range specification could be entered as in **i1,1** or **i5,6-1**. These latter specifications are valid because the starting line and the ending line are the same.

The **do** loop prompts the user for input and creates a new doubly-linked list, **newdata**, to store the lines entered. The input loop is terminated when the user enters a period on a line by itself. If the user does not enter any input, no further actions are performed. Otherwise, the new data is "pasted" into the current list. There are two cases to be considered. If there are currently no nodes in the list, then **p_head** is set to **newdata** and the current line is set to the last node in the list using the primitive operation **nth_double_node()**. If the data is to be added before the first node in the list, the existing list is added to the end of the newly input data using the **paste_list()** primitive operation and **p_head** is modified to point to the new first node (the **paste_list()** primitive operation inserts its second argument after the node pointed to by the first argument). Otherwise, the new data is inserted into the existing list before **startnode**.

With the assumption that **paste_list()** works as described, inserting one list after the node indicated, the three cases handled by **insertlines()** are (1) inserting into an empty list,

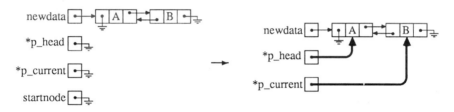

(2) inserting before the first node,

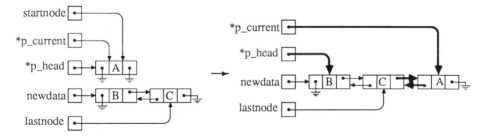

and (3) inserting into the middle of the list.

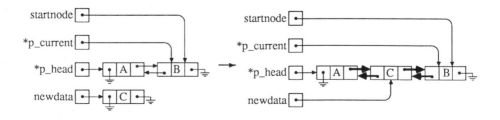

The observant reader may note that it is not possible to insert lines at the very end of the file. This is because lines are always inserted before the current line. A solution to this problem is proposed in the Exercises.

Deleting Lines

Deleting lines from a file is done with **deletelines()**.

```
int deletelines(linespec, p_head, p_current)
char *linespec;
double_list *p_head, *p_current;
{
    /*
     *  Delete some lines (according to linespec) from p_head.
     *  Update p_current to be after last line deleted.
     *  If the last line is deleted, make p_current be before first line.
     */
    double_list startnode, endnode, tmplist;
    double_list new_current;
    int startnumber, endnumber;
    int rc;

    rc = parse_linespec(linespec,*p_head,*p_current,&startnode,&endnode);
    if (rc)
        return rc;

    startnumber = double_node_number(startnode);
    endnumber = double_node_number(endnode);
    if (startnumber > endnumber) {
        tmplist = startnode;
        startnode = endnode;
        endnode = tmplist;
    }
    new_current = nth_relative_double_node(endnode, 1);
    if (new_current == NULL)
        new_current = nth_relative_double_node(startnode, -1);

    cut_list(p_head, &startnode, &endnode);

    *p_current = new_current;
    destroy_double_list(&startnode, free);
    return 0;
}
```

Deletelines() uses **parse_linespec()** to determine the range of lines to be deleted. Note that if there are no lines in the file (something that was a special case for insertion), **parse_linespec()** is expected return an error code. The line that is to be the current line is either the node after the last node deleted (if there is one) or the node before the first node delete. This is set using a call to the primitive operation **nth_relative_double_node()**, which returns a node in the nth position relative to the node passed. If n is negative, then the node will be before (i.e., **PREV** pointers will be used) the passed node. If n is positive, then the node will be after (i.e., **NEXT** pointers will be used) the passed node. Note that a temporary variable is used to store the "new current line." This is because subsequent operations may fail, and if this does occur, the actual current line, **p_current**, should not be modified.

To delete the appropriate nodes from the list, the primitive operation **cut_list()** is used. **Cut_list()** has three arguments: a pointer to the list to be modified, and the nodes that represent the ends of the set to be unlinked (inclusive). This function does not delete the nodes; it unlinks them from the list passed and makes them into a separate list by setting the **PREV** and **NEXT** fields to **NULL** (as appropriate). After the sublist is cut, it can then be destroyed with a call to **destroy_double_list()**.

Moving Lines

Lines are moved about in a text file by using the **move** command which invokes the **movelines()** function.

```
int movelines(linespec, p_head, p_current)
char *linespec;
double_list *p_head, *p_current;
{
    /*
     *  Move lines to after p_current.  Make sure the lines moved
     *  do not include p_current.
     */
    double_list startnode, endnode;
    double_list tmpnode;
    int startnumber, endnumber;
    int rc, currentnumber;
    int tmp;

    rc = parse_linespec(linespec,*p_head,*p_current,&startnode,&endnode);
    if (rc)
        return rc;

    startnumber = double_node_number(startnode);
    endnumber = double_node_number(endnode);
    currentnumber = double_node_number(*p_current);
```

```
    /*
     *   Make sure start < end.
     */
    if (startnumber > endnumber) {
        tmp = startnumber;
        startnumber = endnumber;
        endnumber = tmp;
        tmpnode = startnode;
        startnode = endnode;
        endnode = tmpnode;
    }
    /*
     *   Do not include the current line in the ones being moved.
     */
    if (currentnumber >= startnumber && currentnumber <= endnumber)
        return E_LINES;

    cut_list(p_head, &startnode, &endnode);
    paste_list(&PREV(*p_current), &startnode);
    return 0;
}
```

As with the other functions, **movelines()** uses **parse_linespec()** to determine the range of lines to be moved. It then ensures that **startnode** occurs
before **endnode** by swapping the values if necessary. If the current line is in
the range of lines to be moved, an error is returned. The lines are moved using
the primitive operations **cut_list()** and **paste_list()**.

As with **insertlines()**, it is not possible to move lines to the very end of
the file, because lines are always moved to the point before the current line.
A solution to this problem is proposed in the Exercises.

Printing Lines

Printing a range of lines is done by the **printlines()** function.

```
int printlines(linespec, p_head, p_current)
char *linespec;
double_list *p_head, *p_current;
{
    /*
     *   Print out lines. Direction indicates whether going forward or
     *   backward.
     */
    double_list startnode, endnode;
    int startnumber, endnumber, count, direction;
    int rc;
```

```
    rc = parse_linespec(linespec,*p_head,*p_current,&startnode,&endnode);
    if (rc)
        return rc;

    startnumber = double_node_number(startnode);
    endnumber = double_node_number(endnode);
    direction = (startnumber < endnumber) ? 1 : -1;
    count = (endnumber - startnumber) * direction + 1;
    while (count-- > 0) {
        printf("%d   %s", startnumber, DATA(startnode));
        startnumber += direction;
        startnode = nth_relative_double_node(startnode, direction);
    }
    *p_current = endnode;
    return 0;
}
```

Printlines() calls **parse_linespec()** to determine the range of lines to be printed. The number of nodes that are to be visited is calculated by taking the difference in the line numbers of the start node and the end node of the range and adding 1. Note that the difference is multiplied by the value of **direction**. This is because the lines in a range specification can be in any order. The command **p1,5** is equivalent to **p5,1** except that the values of **startnode** and **endnode** will be reversed. Since **direction** indicates the sign of the difference between the ending line and the starting line, multiplying that difference by **direction** will always yield a positive number.

Printlines() simply loops through that many nodes, printing out their contents. Since **direction** is either +1 or −1, that value is be added to the current line number to determine the next line number. The sign and magnitude of **direction** is used by **nth_relative_double_node()** to get the next node to be printed. **Printlines()** sets the current line pointer to point to the ending node of the range.

6.4.4   Referencing Lines in the Editor

The most difficult part of this line editor is the routines that determine the range of nodes corresponding to a given range specification. A range specification is of the form:

$$numberspec, numberspec$$

where a *numberspec* is an absolute line number, a period (indicating current line), or a dollar sign (indicating the last line) with an optional plus or minus an integer. The comma and second *numberspec* are optional. If no range specification is given, the current line is returned.

Two routines are used to parse a range specification. **Parse_linespec()** takes an entire specification and returns the nodes corresponding to both ends of the range and **parse_number()** performs the actual parsing for a single *numberspec*.

```
int parse_linespec(linespec, head, current, p_start, p_end)
char *linespec;
double_list head, current;
double_list *p_start, *p_end;
{
    /*
     *   Parse linespec (consisting of numberspec,numberspec).
     *   Set p_start to the starting line and p_end to the ending line.
     */
    int rc;
    char *nextnumber;

    if (*linespec == '\0') {
        *p_start = current;
    } else {
        rc = parse_number(linespec, head, current, p_start);
        if (rc)
            return rc;
    }
    nextnumber = strchr(linespec, ',');

    if (nextnumber == NULL) {
        *p_end = *p_start;
    } else {
        rc = parse_number(nextnumber + 1, head, current, p_end);
        if (rc)
            return rc;
    }
    if (*p_start == NULL || *p_end == NULL)
        return E_LINES;
    return 0;
}

parse_number(numberspec, head, current, p_node)
char *numberspec;
double_list head, current;
double_list *p_node;
{
    /*
     *   Parse a single numberspec.
```

```c
 */
char numberbuffer[BUFSIZ], *p_num;
int nodenumber;
int direction;

if (*numberspec == '.') {
    /*
     *   Start with the current line.
     */
    *p_node = current;
    numberspec++;
} else if (*numberspec == '$') {
    /*
     *   Start with the last line.
     */
    *p_node = nth_double_node(head, -1);
    if (*p_node == NULL)
        return E_LINES;
    numberspec++;
} else if (isdigit(*numberspec)) {
    /*
     *   Have a line number.
     */
    p_num = numberbuffer;
    while (isdigit(*numberspec))
        *p_num++ = *numberspec++;
    *p_num = '\0';
    nodenumber = atoi(numberbuffer);
    *p_node = nth_double_node(head, nodenumber);
    if (*p_node == NULL)
        return E_LINES;
} else
    return E_LINES;

/*
 *   Any pluses or minuses?
 */
if (*numberspec == '+') {
    direction = 1;
    numberspec++;
} else if (*numberspec == '-') {
    direction = -1;
    numberspec++;
} else
    direction = 0;

/*
 *   If a digit and previously saw a plus or minus, figure
```

```
     *   offset  from  p_node.
     */
    if (isdigit(*numberspec) && direction != 0) {
        p_num = numberbuffer;
        while (isdigit(*numberspec))
            *p_num++ = *numberspec++;
        *p_num = '\0';
        nodenumber = atoi(numberbuffer) * direction;
        *p_node = nth_relative_double_node(*p_node, nodenumber);
        if (p_node == NULL)
            return E_LINES;
        direction = 0;
    }
    /*
     *   If direction is 0 (meaning no offset or offset was parsed ok)
     *   and at the end of this numberspec, then everything is ok.
     */
    if (direction == 0 && (*numberspec == '\0' || *numberspec == ','))
        return 0;
    else
        return E_LINES;
}
```

There are three input parameters to **parse_linespec**(): the string that is the
specification, the head of the list, and the current line in the list. The output
parameters to this function are **p_start** (a pointer to the node corresponding
to the start of the range) and **p_end** (a pointer to the node corresponding to
the end of the range).

Parse_linespec() first checks if a range specification was given. If not, the
start node is set to the current node. Otherwise, **parse_number**() is called
to determine the start node. Whether an ending range value was given is
determined by the presence of a comma in the range specification. If no
ending value was given, the end node is set to the start node. If a value was
given, **parse_number**() is called again to determine the end node. If either
the starting node or the ending node is equal to **NULL**, an error is indicated.

Parse_number() does the actual determination of the ends of the range.
If the first character of the number specification is a period, the end of the
range is set to the current node. If it is a dollar sign, the end of the range is
set to the last node in the list. If the first character is a digit (0 through 9),
the string representation of the number is copied into another buffer, which is
then converted into an integer value. Note that as the digits of the string are
copied, **numberspec** is being advanced along the input. At the conclusion of
the copying, **numberspec** will point to the character after the last digit. The
number that is entered for a range specification represents an absolute line

number, so the corresponding node is found with a call to **nth_double_node()**.

After the base node is determined, **numberspec** can still contain a plus or minus value. If it does, the number that follows is parsed and the primitive operation **nth_relative_double_node()** is called to find the node relative to the base node.

An error in the number specification has occurred if any of these function calls returns **ERROR**, if either a plus or minus has been entered without a corresponding offset value, or if the character now pointed to by **numberspec** is neither a comma or the end of string marker (a null character).

6.4.5   List Interface Routines for Strings

The only list interface routine required, **string_double_append()**, is left as an exercise.

```
status string_double_append(double_list *p_L, char *buffer);
```

The difference between this function and the other interface routines already discussed is the type of data for which space is to be allocated. In this case, enough memory must be allocated for the entire string, which is given by **strlen(buffer)+1**.

6.4.6   Additional Doubly-Linked List Operations

The coding of the line editor was simplified due to the use of stubs representing primitive list operations. The eight operations that were used and still need to be developed are **double_length()**, **double_traverse()**, **nth_double_node()**, **destroy_double_list()**, **double_node_number()**, **nth_relative_double_node()**, **cut_list()**, and **paste_list()**. Of those, all but the last four have been implemented for the other types of lists (linear linked and circular linked) discussed previously. As such, the actual implementations of those are left as exercises. **Double_node_number()** and **nth_relative_double_node()** are also relatively straightforward, so the implementations of those routines are also left as exercises.

The last two routines, **cut_list()** and **paste_list()**, are used to extract and add sections of a list, respectively. Those routines represent a good example of how to manipulate pointers in a doubly-linked list and hence are discussed here.

Extracting Sections of a List

To cut a section from a list requires three parameters: a node that is not in the section to be extracted and nodes that represent the edges of the sublist to be extracted.

```
void cut_list(p_L, p_start, p_end)
double_list *p_L;
double_list *p_start, *p_end;
{
    /*
     *   Extract the range of nodes *p_start -- *p_end from *p_L.
     */
    double_list start, end;

    start = *p_start;
    end = *p_end;

    if (PREV(start))
        NEXT(PREV(start)) = NEXT(end);
    if (NEXT(end))
        PREV(NEXT(end)) = PREV(start);
    if (*p_L == start)
        *p_L = NEXT(end);
    PREV(start) = NEXT(end) = NULL;
}
```

Cut_list() simply sets the node before ***p_start** to point to the node after ***p_end**. It ensures that both the **PREV** and **NEXT** fields are correctly updated, taking into consideration that they may be **NULL**. It also will reset the list pointer ***p_L** if it points to the first node in the sublist being extracted. The last thing the routine does is modify the ends of the sublist so that it can be accessed as a doubly-linked list.

These steps are illustrated one statement at a time:

Initially

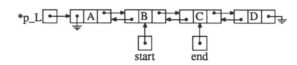

`NEXT(PREV(start)) = NEXT(end);`

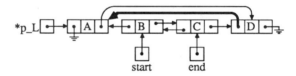

`PREV(NEXT(end)) = PREV(start);`

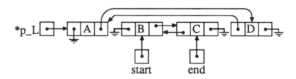

`PREV(start) = NEXT(end) = NULL;`

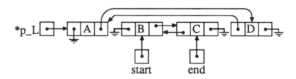

6.4.7   Combining Two Lists

Combining two lists is the inverse of extracting a sublist. This routine takes a source list and inserts it after the specified node in the target list.

```
void paste_list(p_target, p_source)
double_list *p_target;
double_list *p_source;
{
    /*
     *  Take *p_source and put it after *p_target.   Assumes
     *  *p_source is the first node in the list.
     */
    double_list target, source, lastnode;
```

```
    if (empty_double_list(*p_source) == TRUE)
        /*
         *  Nothing  to  do.
         */
        return;

    if (empty_double_list(*p_target) == TRUE)
        *p_target = *p_source;
    else {
        source = *p_source;
        target = *p_target;
        lastnode = nth_double_node(source, -1);
        NEXT(lastnode) = NEXT(target);
        if (NEXT(target) != NULL)
            PREV(NEXT(target)) = lastnode;
        PREV(source) = target;
        NEXT(target) = source;
    }
    *p_source = NULL;
}
```

Paste_list() places the nodes in ***p_source** after ***p_target**. If there are
no nodes in the source list, then the routine returns. If there are no nodes in
the target list, then all that is necessary is to set the target list to point to
the source list. If there are nodes in both lists, the lists are spliced together
by setting the **NEXT** field of the last node in ***p_source** to point to the node
after ***p_target** and setting **NEXT** field of ***p_target** to point to ***p_source**.

```
Initially
```

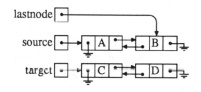

```
NEXT(lastnode)  =  NEXT(target);
PREV(NEXT(target))  =  lastnode;
```

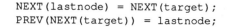

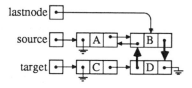

```
PREV(source) = target;
NEXT(target) = source;
```

Note that care must be taken to handle the special case of adding to the end of a list.

6.5   Lists With Header Nodes

A *header* node is a special list node found at the front (head) of the list. It is useful when information other than that found in each node of the list is needed. For example, imagine an application in which the number of items in a list is often calculated. In a standard linked list, the list function *length* has to traverse the entire list every time. However, if the current length is maintained in an additional header node, that information can be obtained very quickly.

6.5.1   Implementation Strategies

There are a few variations in implementations of a list with a header node. Each implementation can be appropriate, depending on the actual use of the linked list.

1. Distinguish the header node from the other nodes on the basis of its value. For example, if the nodes all contain positive integers and it is desired to keep the length in the header, then the header could contain the negative of the length. This is convenient when practical, but sometimes it is difficult (or impossible) to find out-of-range values to use in the header node.

2. Make the nodes of the list able to contain either the application data *or* the header information, using a construct similar to C **union**.

3. Make the header node a different type from the other nodes. For example, the queue implementation in Section 5.11 used a header node containing pointers to the first node and the last node of the list.

Regardless of the method of implementation, maintaining header node information in a general manner is very difficult, because its use is application-dependent. Consider, then, the ramifications of each of the above strategies for lists that are not developed in an application-independent manner. First, it should be noted that header nodes eliminate the recursive nature of linked lists. For example, without a header node, appending a node can be done correctly regardless of which node was passed as the list variable. Now, since header node information may have to be updated, the header node must *always* be passed as the list variable.

Is it safe to assume, then, that the node passed is always the header node? In practice, that assumption is almost always made, simply because one cannot always distinguish between the header node and the data. There is no guarantee that this will actually be true given the basic **list** declaration. It can be enforced, however, if another level of code is placed between the application and the list manipulation functions. This was the technique used in Section 5.11 and will be used again in what follows.

6.5.2 The Empty List

Now that a list contains two types of information, a header node and the list of application data, what comprises an empty list? Is a list empty when there is no header node *and* no data? Or can the empty list consist of just the header node? In practice, either choice can be made. There are times when it is convenient to insist that an empty list contains no nodes at all (including the header). An example of this would be when the header of a list is also contained in another list (a list of lists). In this case, when there is no more data in the list, the header should be deleted. Alternatively, it may be more convenient always to have the header node. In this latter case, the header node can be created when the list is initialized. This simplifies insertion and deletion routines because it is guaranteed that the list will always contain at least one node.

6.6 Sparse Matrices

Certain scientific applications require manipulating very large matrices with one important characteristic: most of the entries are zero. These matrices are called *sparse matrices*. Imagine a square matrix 1000×1000, but containing only 250 nonzero elements. To allocate a million cells when only 250 will be used is very wasteful. In this section, an implementation of sparse matrices is described.

6.6.1   Matrix Organization

The matrix will be organized along rows and columns. Each element will be stored as a member of a row doubly-linked list and a member of a column doubly-linked list. The information stored in each element will be the row number, the column number, and the value stored (as a **generic_ptr**). There will be a header node for each row and for each column that contains an element.

All the row header nodes will be organized into a doubly-linked list with the header nodes stored in ascending row number. The column header nodes will be stored in the same manner. The header nodes will be of the same type as the element nodes because out-of-range values exist for this application. The lower bound for row and column numbers in this implementation will be zero. Therefore, header nodes for each column will have the corresponding column number with the row number being -1. Row header nodes will have the correct row number with the column number being -1. A header for the entire matrix consists of a node with both the row and column number set to -1. Diagrams representing a matrix are of the form

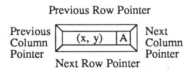

where (x, y) are the row and column numbers and A is a pointer to the data. For the sake of simplicity, data will be shown within the matrix node as opposed to using the actual pointer.

For example, the following diagram represents the matrix structure when all values are 0 except for **matrix[4][1]**, **matrix[4][100]**, **matrix[5][1]**, and **matrix[300][241]** which are set to 10, 20, 30, and 40, respectively.

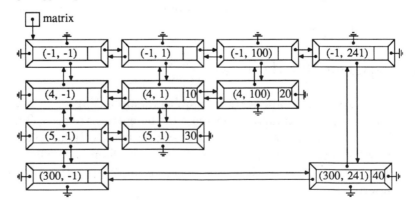

This organization yields the following C structures:

```
typedef struct matrix_node matrix_node, *matrix;

struct matrix_node {
    int row, column;
    generic_ptr datapointer;
    matrix_node *nextrow, *prevrow;
    matrix_node *nextcol, *prevcol;
};

#define ROW(M) ((M)->row)
#define COL(M) ((M)->column)
#define DATA(M) ((M)->datapointer)
#define NEXTROW(M) ((M)->nextrow)
#define PREVROW(M) ((M)->prevrow)
#define NEXTCOL(M) ((M)->nextcol)
#define PREVCOL(M) ((M)->prevcol)
```

Since each node is a member of two doubly-linked lists, there are two sets of next and previous node pointers. This sparse matrix implementation is application-independent because the data stored in the node is a **generic_ptr**.

Since a **generic_ptr** is being used, it is not clear what constitutes a zero value. This is important since zero values should not be stored in the matrix. Therefore, in addition to the standard matrix operations of storing a value and retrieving a value, a *clear value* operation will be introduced. This operation will be equivalent to setting the matrix element to 0 (thereby deleting it). Although this departs from what is viewed as a standard matrix interface, the application programmer can implement a consistent interface to these functions that will take into account the true (application-dependent) "zero" value.

6.6.2 An Interface for Allocating Matrix Nodes

The interface for dynamically allocating and freeing space for nodes of the matrix is almost identical to that discussed in Section 4.2.3. The only difference is that instead of passing only the data value, the row and column numbers are passed as well.

```
status allocate_matrix_node(p_M, row, col, data)
matrix *p_M;
int row, col;
generic_ptr data;
{
```

```
    matrix M = (matrix) malloc(sizeof(matrix_node));

    if (M == NULL)
        return ERROR;

    *p_M = M;
    ROW(M) = row;
    COL(M) = col;
    DATA(M) = data;
    NEXTROW(M) = NULL;
    PREVROW(M) = NULL;
    NEXTCOL(M) = NULL;
    PREVCOL(M) = NULL;
    return OK;
}

void free_matrix_node(p_M)
matrix *p_M;
{
    free(*p_M);
    *p_M = NULL;
}
```

Since the isolated node is not part of any linked list structure, the fields that link it to other nodes are set to **NULL**.

6.6.3   Initializing a Sparse Matrix

Some implementations of sparse matrices may require the programmer to specify the upper bound on rows and columns. The implementation developed here leaves that value open. Therefore, any nonnegative row or column number is considered valid and **init_matrix()** requires no extra arguments.

```
status init_matrix(p_M)
matrix *p_M;
{
    /*
     *  Initialize a matrix by creating the matrix header node [−1,−1].
     */
    if (allocate_matrix_node(p_M, −1, −1, NULL) == ERROR)
        return ERROR;
    return OK;
}
```

To initialize the matrix, all that is required is to create the matrix header node. This node has the row and the column both set to −1. Since there is no data associated with a header node, **NULL** is passed to the node allocation function.

6.6.4   Storing a Value

The general procedure for storing a value in the matrix is to first create the row and column header nodes (if necessary) and then traverse each of those lists to find the appropriate position for the new value. Two sets of auxiliary functions will be used. The first set of functions returns the header node for a particular row or column. If the header node does not exist, these functions will create one, insert it in the header node linked list, and return the new node. There are two functions in this set: one for locating a row header node and one for locating a column header node.

```
#define CREATE_HEADER 0
#define FIND_HEADER 1
status find_row_head(int matrix_opflag, matrix *p_M, int row,
    matrix *p_headnode);
status find_col_head(int matrix_opflag, matrix *p_M, int col,
    matrix *p_headnode);
```

These functions include an operation flag that specifies whether the header node should be created if it does not already exist.

While the first set of functions finds a node with a particular row or column value, the second set of functions finds the node with the row or column value that is less than the passed value. These functions will return the node that matches the passed row or column value if one exists, otherwise they will return the node that is immediately before the row or column value passed. No new nodes are allocated, and there is a separate function for rows and columns:

```
matrix get_previous_row(matrix *p_head, int row);
matrix get_previous_column(matrix *p_head, int col);
```

The function to store a value at a given row and column in the matrix, **matrix_put()**, uses these functions to locate the appropriate position for the new value and then inserts that new node into the row and column linked lists.

```
status matrix_put(p_M, row, col, value)
matrix *p_M;
int row, col;
generic_ptr value;
```

```
{
    /*
     *   p_M[row][col]  =  value
     *      This is done by locating correct position in the column list
     *      and the row list and inserting the new node (containing value)
     *      in the correct position in each of those lists.
     */
    matrix colheader, rowheader;
    matrix colprev, rowprev;
    matrix newnode;

    if (row < 0 || col < 0)
        return ERROR;
    if (allocate_matrix_node(&newnode, row, col, value) == ERROR)
        return ERROR;
    if (find_col_head(CREATE_HEADER, p_M, col, &colheader) == ERROR) {
        free_matrix_node(&newnode);
        return ERROR;
    }
    if (find_row_head(CREATE_HEADER, p_M, row, &rowheader) == ERROR) {
        free_matrix_node(&newnode);
        return ERROR;
    }
    /*
     *   Insert in column list.
     */
    colprev = get_previous_column(&rowheader, col);
    if (COL(colprev) == col) {
        DATA(colprev) = value;
        free_matrix_node(&newnode);
        return OK;
    }
    NEXTCOL(newnode) = NEXTCOL(colprev);
    if (NEXTCOL(newnode) != NULL)
        PREVCOL(NEXTCOL(newnode)) = newnode;
    PREVCOL(newnode) = colprev;
    NEXTCOL(colprev) = newnode;
    /*
     *   Insert in row list.
     */
    rowprev = get_previous_row(&colheader, row);
    NEXTROW(newnode) = NEXTROW(rowprev);
    if (NEXTROW(newnode) != NULL)
        PREVROW(NEXTROW(newnode)) = newnode;
    PREVROW(newnode) = rowprev;
    NEXTROW(rowprev) = newnode;
    return OK;
}
```

First, **matrix_put()** verifies that the desired position for the new value is valid, and, if so, a new node is allocated. The header node for the column linked list is located, as is the header node for the row linked list. Note that these nodes are created in the **find...** functions if they do not already exist. Then, the linked list of nodes that are in the same row as the new node is traversed via a call to **get_previous_column()**. This function locates the node that is in the same row, but in the previous column as the new node. The new node is to be inserted after this node. If a node already exists for this column, however, the data value is set to the new value, the newly allocated node is freed, and the function returns **OK**. Otherwise, the node is added to the linked list of nodes for this row by manipulating the column pointers.

Next, the linked list of nodes that are in the same column as the new node is traversed via a call to **get_previous_row()**. Since it is guaranteed that a node that is in the same column and the same row does not already exist, it is not necessary to check for that condition. The node is added to the linked list of nodes for this column by setting the row pointers.

A small example helps clarify the exactly how the variables in **matrix_put()** are set. Assume a matrix exists as before. When adding a node at position [300,1] with value 83, **colheader** and **rowheader** are set by the **find...** functions:

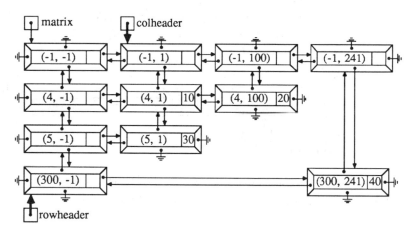

Then the row header is used to find the node in the column before the desired location of the new value:

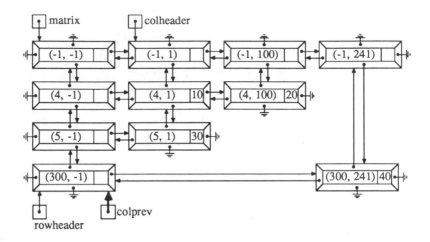

A doubly-linked list insertion operation is performed to add the new node to this linked list:

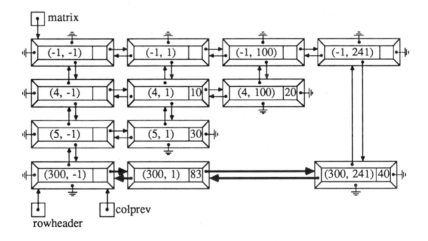

Then, an analogous procedure is used to insert the node in the column linked list. First, the node before the desired location is found:

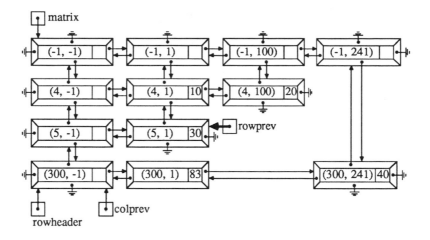

The node is then inserted into the column linked list:

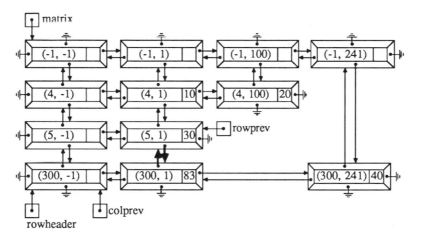

6.6.5   Retrieving a Value

The auxiliary functions described before make retrieving a value from the matrix a simple operation.

```
status matrix_get(p_M, row, col, p_value)
matrix *p_M;
int row, col;
generic_ptr *p_value;
{
    /*
     *  Set *p_value to the value at p_M[row][col].
     */
    matrix colheader;
    matrix rowprev;

    if (row < 0 || col < 0)
        return ERROR;
    if (find_col_head(FIND_HEADER, p_M, col, &colheader) == ERROR)
        return ERROR;
    rowprev = get_previous_row(&colheader, row);
    if (ROW(rowprev) != row)
        return ERROR;
    *p_value = DATA(rowprev);
    return OK;
}
```

Find_col_head() locates, but does not create, the header node of the linked list corresponding to the desired column. If this function returns **ERROR**, the header node does not exist and there are no nodes in the specified column. In this case, **matrix_get()** returns **ERROR**. Otherwise, **get_previous_row()** locates the node that corresponds to the desired row. If the node returned is not the desired row, then, although there are values in the desired column, no value was stored for the desired row/column pair. In this case, **ERROR** is returned. Otherwise, the value is returned via a pointer parameter and the function returns **OK**.

This function could have been written in two ways. The previous implementation uses **find_col_head()** and **get_previous_row()** to locate the node. Alternatively, **find_row_head()** and **get_previous_col()** could have been used.

6.6.6   Clearing a Value

Clearing a value from the matrix is necessary in this implementation because it is not possible for the matrix functions to know what constitutes a "zero" value.

```
status matrix_clear(p_M, row, col)
matrix *p_M;
int row, col;
{
    /*
     * Free the space used by p_M[row][col].  This assumes the
     * application has already freed the space used by the DATA field
     */
    matrix element;
    matrix colheader;

    if (row < 0 || col < 0)
        return ERROR;
    if (find_col_head(FIND_HEADER, p_M, col, &colheader) == ERROR)
        return ERROR;
    element = get_previous_row(&colheader, row);
    if (ROW(element) != row)
        return ERROR;
    NEXTROW(PREVROW(element)) = NEXTROW(element);
    if (NEXTROW(element) != NULL)
        PREVROW(NEXTROW(element)) = PREVROW(element);
    NEXTCOL(PREVCOL(element)) = NEXTCOL(element);
    if (NEXTCOL(element) != NULL)
        PREVCOL(NEXTCOL(element)) = PREVCOL(element);
    free_matrix_node(&element);
    return OK;
}
```

Matrix_clear() uses the same procedure as **matrix_get()** to locate the desired node. When the node is found, it is deleted from both the row linked list and the column linked list.

6.6.7   Auxiliary Functions

The ease in which **matrix_put()**, **matrix_get()**, and **matrix_clear()** were implemented is due to the auxiliary functions for finding/creating header nodes and locating nodes within a linked list.

Finding an Element

There are two routines for finding an element within a linked list. One routine traverses the row pointers and the other the column pointers.

```
matrix get_previous_column(p_head, col)
matrix *p_head;
```

```
int col;
{
    /*
     *   Find  the  existing  column  node  <=  col.
     */
    matrix node;

    for (node = *p_head; COL(node) <= col && NEXTCOL(node) != NULL;
        node = NEXTCOL(node)) ;
    return (COL(node) > col) ? PREVCOL(node) : node;
}

matrix get_previous_row(p_head, row)
matrix *p_head;
int row;
{
    /*
     *   Find  the  existing  row  node  <=  row.
     */
    matrix node;

    for (node = *p_head; ROW(node) <= row && NEXTROW(node) != NULL;
        node = NEXTROW(node)) ;
    return (ROW(node) > row) ? PREVROW(node) : node;
}
```

Get_previous_column() expects a row header node and a column number, and finds the node with the column value that is less than or equal to the desired column. **Get_previous_row()** expects a column header and a row number, and finds the node with the row value that is less than or equal to the desired row. Note that both these functions assume that at least one node will have a value less than the desired value. This is a safe assumption because the header node value is less than any real value. These functions will never return **NULL** since the matrix header node will always exist.

Finding Column/Row Headers

Finding a row or column header is similar to finding any other node in a list except when the header node does not exist. In that case, it will be created if the operation flag, which is passed as a parameter, is appropriately set.

```
status find_col_head(matrix_opflag, p_M, col, p_headnode)
int matrix_opflag;
matrix *p_M;
int col;
```

```
matrix *p_headnode;
{
    /*
     *   Find a specific column header node.  If it doesn't exist,
     *   optionally create it depending on opflag.  If opflag is
     *   FIND_HEADER, return ERROR if it doesn't exist.  If opflag
     *   is CREATE_HEADER, create the header, add it to the linked
     *   list of headers, and return that new node.
     */
    matrix header;

    header = get_previous_column(p_M, col);
    if (COL(header) == col) {
        *p_headnode = header;
        return OK;
    } else if (matrix_opflag == FIND_HEADER) {
        *p_headnode = NULL;
        return ERROR;
    } else {
        matrix newhead;
        if (allocate_matrix_node(&newhead, -1, col, NULL) == ERROR)
            return ERROR;
        NEXTCOL(newhead) = NEXTCOL(header);
        if (NEXTCOL(header) != NULL)
            PREVCOL(NEXTCOL(header)) = newhead;
        PREVCOL(newhead) = header;
        NEXTCOL(header) = newhead;
        *p_headnode = newhead;
        return OK;
    }
    return ERROR;
}


status find_row_head(matrix_opflag, p_M, row, p_headnode)
int matrix_opflag;
matrix *p_M;
int row;
matrix *p_headnode;
{
    /*
     *   Find a specific row header node.  If it doesn't exist,
     *   optionally create it depending on opflag.  If opflag is
     *   FIND_HEADER, return ERROR if it doesn't exist.  If opflag
     *   is CREATE_HEADER, create the header, add it to the linked
     *   list of headers, and return that new node.
     */
    matrix header;
```

```
        header = get_previous_row(p_M, row);
        if (ROW(header) == row) {
            *p_headnode = header;
            return OK;
        } else if (matrix_opflag == FIND_HEADER) {
            *p_headnode = NULL;
            return ERROR;
        } else {
            matrix newhead;
            if (allocate_matrix_node(&newhead, row, -1, NULL) == ERROR)
                return ERROR;
            NEXTROW(newhead) = NEXTROW(header);
            if (NEXTROW(header) != NULL)
                PREVROW(NEXTROW(header)) = newhead;
            PREVROW(newhead) = header;
            NEXTROW(header) = newhead;
            *p_headnode = newhead;
            return OK;
        }
        return ERROR;
}
```

Find_col_head() locates a column header node. A parameter controls the creation of the header node if it does not exist. **Find_row_head()** performs an analogous function for row header nodes. These functions work by first using the appropriate **get_previous...** function to traverse the list consisting of just header nodes to locate the position of the desired header node. If **header**, the node returned by the **get_previous...** function, is the desired node, it is returned via a pointer parameter and the function returns **OK**. Otherwise, if the operation as specified by **matrix_opflag** was to locate (but not create) the header node, **ERROR** is returned.

If the header node does not exist and **matrix_opflag** indicates that it should be created, a new node is allocated and inserted in the header node linked list. The location in which the new node should be placed has already been determined via the call to the **get_previous...** function. The last statement in the function, **return ERROR**, will never be executed since each clause in the **if** statement ends with a **return** statement.

6.6.8   A Driver

A simple driver is given that exercises the three matrix functions. The most interesting part of this driver is the application interface to the matrix functions.

```
main()
{
    matrix M;
    int row, col, value;

    init_matrix(&M);
    while (TRUE) {
        printf("put (row col value)? ");
        scanf("%d %d %d", &row, &col, &value);
        if (row < 0 || col < 0)
            exit(0);
        matrix_put_int(&M, row, col, value);
        printf("get (row col)? ");
        scanf("%d %d", &row, &col);
        if (row < 0 || col < 0)
            exit(0);
        printf("matrix[%d][%d]=", row, col);
        if (matrix_get_int(&M, row, col, &value) == ERROR)
            printf("system error!\n");
        else
            printf("%d\n", value);
    }
}
```

The driver enters an infinite loop in which it prompts the user for a row, column, and value. It adds the value to the sparse matrix at the specified row and column using the interface function **matrix_put_int()**. Then it prompts the user for a row and a column and reports the value found at that location. The loop is exited whenever a negative number is entered for either the row or column.

The interface functions show how **matrix_put()** and **matrix_clear()** can be used together.

```
status matrix_put_int(p_M, row, col, value)
matrix *p_M;
int row, col;
int value;
{
    /*
     *  Store integer values in a sparse matrix.
     */
    int *p_i;

    if (value == 0) {
        if (matrix_get(p_M, row, col, (generic_ptr *) &p_i) != ERROR) {
            matrix_clear(p_M, row, col);
```

```
                free(p_i);
            }
            return OK;
        }

        p_i = (int *) malloc(sizeof(int));
        if (p_i == NULL)
            return ERROR;
        *p_i = value;
        return matrix_put(p_M, row, col, (generic_ptr) p_i);
    }

    status matrix_get_int(p_M, row, col, p_value)
    matrix *p_M;
    int row, col;
    int *p_value;
    {
        /*
         *   Retrieve integer values from a sparse matrix.
         */
        int *p_i;

        if (matrix_get(p_M, row, col, (generic_ptr *) &p_i) == ERROR)
            *p_value = 0;
        else
            *p_value = *p_i;
        return OK;
    }
```

Since **matrix_put_int()** knows what constitutes a zero value, it first checks to see if that is the value stored in the matrix. If so, it gets the previous value and clears out that matrix entry. It is necessary to get the previous value so that the space used by that value can be freed. If the value stored in the matrix is nonzero, **matrix_put()** is called after space is allocated for the new value.

Matrix_get_int() uses **matrix_get()** to get the value from the matrix. If that function returns **ERROR**, no value was stored at the specified location in the matrix. In that case, the value returned to the calling function is zero. Note that this function never returns **ERROR**. This differs from **matrix_get()**, but from this application's point of view, this is a reasonable approach.

6.7   Exercises

1. Eliminate the side effects in **c_cdr()** and **c_cons()** by creating an **expression_copy()** function that creates a duplicate of a LISP expression.

2. Enhance the LISP interpreter by adding the following built-in functions:

(a) **Atomp, listp, nullp.** These functions all take a single lisp object and return **T** or **NIL**. **Atomp** will return **T** if the object is an atom. **Listp** will return **T** if the object is a list. **Nullp** will return **T** if the object is **NIL**. For example:

```
(atomp 'a) ⟹ T
(atomp '(a)) ⟹ NIL
(listp '(a)) ⟹ T
(listp 'a') ⟹ NIL
(nullp '()) ⟹ T
(nullp '(a b)) ⟹ NIL
```

(b) **Equal.** This function has two LISP objects as arguments and returns **T** if they are equal. For example,

```
(equal '(a (b c) d) '(a (b c) d)) ⟹ T
(equal '(a (b c) d) '(d a (b c)) ⟹ NIL
(equal 'a 'a) ⟹ T
```

(c) **Setq.** This function is the LISP equivalent of an assignment statement. It has two arguments, an atom and a LISP object. The second argument is evaluated and assigned as the value of the atom that is the first argument. The function returns the second argument. With this modification, evaluating atoms should yield the value which was assigned using **setq**. For example,

```
(setq a '(a b c)) ⟹ (A B C))
a ⟹ (QUOTE (A B C))
b ⟹ error (no value assigned)
(setq b (cons 'a '(b))) ⟹ (A B)
b ⟹ (A B)
```

Note that **T** and **NIL** are special atoms and it is an error to assign values to them. Note that in writing this you must also modify the interpreter to print the correct value of the atoms.

(d) **Cond.** This is the LISP conditional function, analogous to the **if-else** construct in C. Arguments to this function are lists containing pairs of expressions. The first expression in each pair is the condition test. The condition tests are evaluated in order until one is found that does not evaluate to **NIL**. Then, the second expression in that pair (corresponding to the action) is evaluated, and **cond**

returns its value. If all of the first expressions evaluate to NIL,
cond returns NIL. For example,

```
(setq a '(a b c)) ⟹ (A B C)
(setq d nil) ⟹ NIL
(cond ((listp a) (cons 'b a)) (t '(b))) ⟹ (B A B C)
(cond ((listp d) (cons 'b d)) (t '(b))) ⟹ (B)
```

Note that since **t** evaluates to **T** its action will always be executed
provided none of the previous condition tests return a non-**NIL**
value.

(e) **Defun.** This function lets you define your own functions. The
first argument is the function name (an atom), followed by a list
of argument names, followed by the function body. **Defun** returns
function name. For example,

```
(defun combine (one two)
(cons one (cons two ())))
```

defines function **combine** which has two arguments, and **cons**es a
the first argment to a list containing the second argument. After
the function is defined, it can be used in subsequent code to be
interpreted.

```
(combine 'a 'b) ⟹ (A B)
(combine '(a) '(b)) ⟹ ((A) (B))
```

Note that function parameters are call-by-value. That is, they contain copies of the variables that are passed as parameters.

```
(defun makeb (x) (setq x 'b)) ⟹ MAKEB
(setq a a) ⟹ A
(makeb a) ⟹ B
a ⟹ A
```

3. Write the following functions in LISP for the enhanced interpreter:

(a) **Member.** This function has two arguments a list and another LISP
object. It returns **T** if the LISP object is a member of the list. For
example,

```
(member '(a (b c) d) 'a) ⟹ T
(member '(a (b c) d) 'b) ⟹ NIL
(member '(a (b c) d) '(b c)) ⟹ T
```

(b) **Reverse.** This function expects a list as an argument and returns the list with the elements reversed. For example,

```
(reverse '(a b c d)) ⟹ '(d c b a)
(reverse '(a (b c) d) ⟹ '(d (b c) a)
```

4. Add integer atoms to the LISP interpreter. Integer atoms evaluate to themselves. Also add the built-in mathematical functions, +, −, *, and /, and the predicate function **integerp** which return **T** if its argument is an integer atom.

5. Write a LISP interpreter using linear linked lists.

6. Why do **cut_list()** and **paste_list()** copy their pointer parameters to auxiliary variables before performing the linked list manipulation?

7. Write **double_append()**, which has two arguments: a pointer to a doubly-linked list, and a data item. This function should append a node containing the data item to the end of the list. This function is similar in nature to **append()** in Section 4.2.4.

8. Since it is not possible to insert lines at the end of the file using the insert command, add an **append** command to the simple line editor that adds lines after the current line.

9. Since it is not possible to move lines to the end of the file using the **move** command, add a command that moves lines after the current line.

10. As an alternative to the multiplicity of commands to handle inserting/moving data before and after lines, consider creating a new line number, **0**. With this dummy line number, lines can be appended at any point in the file. Rewrite the simple editor to include this new line number. Before making any changes in the code, consider the impact this new line number will have on the current line. Implement a consistent scheme for maintaining the current line pointer.

11. Implement the function **string_double_append()** described in Section 6.4.5.

12. Implement the doubly-linked list primitives described in Section 6.4.6:

(a)   `int double_length(double_list L);`

This function returns the number of nodes in list **L**. The assumption can be made that the node passed is the first in the list (i.e., only the **NEXT** pointers need be traversed).

(b) `status double_traverse(double_list L, status (*p_func_f)());`

This function is similar in function to **traverse()** for linear linked lists. ***P_func_f()** should be called with each the **DATA** field of each node in the list **L**. If **p_func_f()** returns **ERROR**, **double_traverse()** returns **ERROR**. Otherwise, **OK** is returned.

(c) `void destroy_double_list(double_list *p_L, void (*p_func_f)());`

This function deletes every node in the list ***p_L** and if **p_func_f()** is non-**NULL**, it is called with the **DATA** field of each node. This function is the doubly-linked list counterpart to **destroy()**.

(d) `int double_node_number(double_list L);`

This function returns the node number of **L** relative to the beginning of the list (the first node is number 1). If the list is empty, 0 should be returned.

(e) `double_list nth_double_node(double_list L, int n);`

This function returns the nth node in a list. The first node in the list is node number 1. If **n** is -1, this function should return the last node in the list. If **n** is greater than the number of nodes in the list, **NULL** should be returned.

(f) `double_list nth_relative_double_node(double_list L, int n);`

This function returns the nth node relative to **L**. In **n** is 0, **L** is returned. If **n** is greater than 0, **n NEXT** pointers are traversed. If **n** is less than 0, **n PREV** pointers are traversed. If either end of the list is reached, **NULL** is returned.

13. Modify the sparse matrix implementation of Section 6.6 to work with arbitrary indices. It should possible to store a value at matrix$[-100][-299]$, for example. Can you develop an implementation that does not require declaring the lower bound of the array in the call to **init_matrix()**?

14. The **matrix_clear()** deletes nodes from both the row linked list and the column linked list, but it does not delete the corresponding header node. Modify **matrix_clear()** to delete the header node (either row or column or both) if the node deleted is the last one in the linked list.

15. Consider the following related modifications to the sparse matrix program driver and library routines.

   (a) Modify the *driver* program (not the sparse matrix routines) so that the nonzero matrix entries are displayed each time through the loop. You may want to arbitrarily decide on an upper bound for the number of rows and columns.

   (b) Create additional sparse matrix routines that call an application-defined function for each row/column that contains values. The following functions would be appropriate:

```
status traverse_matrix(matrix *p_M, status (*p_func_f)());
status traverse_column(matrix_node *p_M, int column,
                status (*p_func_f)());
status traverse_row(matrix_node *p_M, int row,
                status (*p_func_f)());
```

   These functions should call **(*p_func_f)()** with three parameters: the row number, the column number, and a pointer to the data stored at that position of the matrix. The functions should return immediately if **(*p_func_f)()** returns **ERROR**.

CHAPTER
SEVEN

TREES AND
GRAPHS

Many times, data is not linear. When data is hierarchical, *trees* can be used for the internal representation. When the data relationships are cyclic or strongly interconnected, *graphs* may be more appropriate. This chapter describes these data structures.

7.1   Tree and Graph Concepts

A graph is a set of points (called vertices or nodes) together with a set of connections (called edges, links, arcs, or branches). The links in a graph can be either one-way or two-way. If the links are one-way, the graph is called *directed*.

An *undirected* graph is comprised of two-way links. Typically, when drawing undirected graphs, the arrowheads are not shown.

238

A tree is a graph in which there is exactly one path between any pair of nodes. Any of the following graphs are also trees:

The most common kind of tree used in computer science applications is a rooted ordered tree. In this kind of tree, there is one node, called the *root*, that has no links entering it. All other nodes in the tree have exactly one link entering. The links are one-way (although two-way links are sometimes used), and every node in the tree can be reached by traversing links starting from the root. Furthermore, there are no cycles in the tree. Nodes that can be reached by traversing a single link from a given node are called the *children* of that node. Each child may be the root of its own subtree. Nodes that have no children are called *leaves* of the tree.

A tree is ordered in the sense that trees with transposed children are considered distinct. Furthermore, when a rooted tree is drawn, the directed nature of the links is implicit, so arrowheads are usually omitted. The following trees are all distinct.

7.2 Binary Trees

A binary tree is a tree where each node in the tree has 0, 1, or 2 children.

Given the way a binary tree is drawn, children are often referred to as the "left child" or the "right child." Note, as exemplified in the previous diagram, there is no requirement that a left child exist if a right child exists. Furthermore, although the following looks suspiciously like a linked list, it is a binary tree structure.

The *depth* of a binary tree is defined as the maximum number of links traversed to get from the root to any leaf. A *balanced* binary tree is one in which the distance from the root of any subtree to its leaves differs by at most 1.

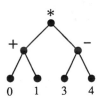

7.2.1   Traversing a Binary Tree

A binary tree is used to impose a hierarchy or an order on data. Therefore, the order in which the data is retrieved from the tree is important. Suppose, for example, the following expression tree[1] was created:

There are several ways in which this tree can be traversed, each producing very different results. The most common methods are preorder, inorder, postorder, and level (breadth-first) traversal.

Preorder Traversal

With preorder traversal, the order of visitation of nodes is "root, left, right." That is, first visit the node at the root of any subtree, then visit its left child,

---

[1]An expression tree is a tree in which the interior nodes contain operators and the leaves contain operands.

and then visit its right child. Of course, any child may itself be the root of a subtree, so this traversal is inherently recursive. The general algorithm is

```
procedure PREORDER(T)
visit T
if there is a left child PREORDER(left child(T))
if there is a right child PREORDER(right child(T))
```

By applying this algorithm to the previous expression tree, the nodes are visited in the following order: *** + 0 1 − 3 4**. This expression is the prefix notation for the mathematical expression **(0 + 1) * (3 − 4)**.

Inorder Traversal

With inorder traversal, the order of visitation of nodes is "left, root, right." As with preorder traversal, the algorithm is recursive:

```
procedure INORDER(T)
if there is a left child INORDER(left child(T))
visit T
if there is a right child INORDER(right child(T))
```

Applying this visitation algorithm to the above expression tree yields: **0 + 1 * 3 − 4** which is mathematical infix notation without the parentheses.

Postorder Traversal

It should be obvious by this time that the order traversals refer to at what point the root node is visited. Extrapolating this knowledge to postorder traversal indicates that the order of visitation should be "left, right, root."

```
procedure POSTORDER(T)
if there is a left child POSTORDER(left child(T))
if there is a right child POSTORDER(right child(T))
visit T
```

This visitation algorithm yields **0 1 + 3 4 − *** when applied to the previous tree. This result is the postfix notation for the mathematical expression **(0 + 1) * (3 − 4)**.

Level Traversal

The level traversal is significantly different from the other traversal algorithms. In the level traversal, the order that nodes are visited is based on their distance from the root node. First, the root node is visited. Then, all those nodes that are of distance 1 to the root are visited. And then, those nodes of distance 2 are visited. Successively farther nodes are visited until all the nodes in the tree have been visited.

Since the standard binary representation of a tree does not allow for direct determination of all nodes on the same level, a queue must be used to maintain that information. By adding the children of the node being visited to the end of the queue, each level will be traversed before going on to the next.

```
add the root node to the queue
while the queue is not empty
    remove a node, T, from the queue
    visit T
    add T's children (if any) to the queue
```

Applying this algorithm to the previous expression tree yields * + − 0 1 3 4, which does not correspond to any usual mathematical notation (level traversal is not normally used with expression trees).

7.2.2   C Representation of Binary Trees

A tree is made up of nodes that contain two pointers: one to the left subtree, and one to the right subtree. This is embodied in a single C structure:

```
typedef struct tree_node tree_node, *tree;

struct tree_node {
    generic_ptr datapointer;
    tree left;
    tree right;
};

#define DATA(T)   ((T)->datapointer)
#define LEFT(T)   ((T)->left)
#define RIGHT(T)  ((T)->right)

typedef enum { PREORDER, INORDER, POSTORDER } ORDER;
```

The previous expression tree would be represented as[2]

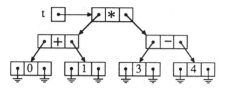

Preprocessor macros are included to make the final code more readable. The enumerated type **ORDER** is used for the tree traversal functions to indicate the order in which the nodes should be visited.

As with the previous implementations, special functions are used for managing memory for the nodes in a tree. Since this set of functions is almost identical to the one previously described (see Section 4.2.3), they are presented without discussion.

```
status allocate tree node(p_T, data)
tree *p_T;
generic_ptr data;
{
    /*
     *  Allocate a tree_node and initialize the DATA field with data.
     */
    tree T = (tree) malloc(sizeof(tree_node));

    if (T == NULL)
        return ERROR;
    *p_T = T;
    DATA(T) = data;
    LEFT(T) = NULL;
    RIGHT(T) = NULL;
    return OK;
}

void free_tree_node(p_T)
tree *p_T;
{
    /*
     *  Reclaim the space used by the tree_node.
     */
    free(*p_T);
    *p_T = NULL;
}
```

---

[2]For simplicity, the data is shown as being part of the tree node instead of being pointed to by the node.

7.2.3   Primitive Operations on Binary Trees

Without making assumptions about the sort of data stored in a node in a tree, there are few primitive operations that can be developed. Some functions can be considered basic to any binary tree structure. These functions are initializing a tree, testing for emptiness, creating a new nonempty tree, destroying a tree, and traversing a tree.

Initializing a Tree

When a variable of type **tree** is declared, it contains no specific value. Therefore, it should be initialized. This is done with a call to **init_tree()**.

```
status init_tree(p_T)
tree *p_T;
{
    /*
     *   Initialize  a  tree  to  empty.
     */
    *p_T = NULL;
    return OK;
}
```

This function initializes its parameter to **NULL**, which indicates that the tree is empty.

Status of a Tree

With trees, the determination of whether a tree is empty is done with a comparison of the tree variable to **NULL**.

```
bool empty_tree(T)
tree T;
{
    /*
     *   Return  TRUE  if  T  is  empty,  otherwise  return  FALSE.
     */
    return (T == NULL) ? TRUE : FALSE;
}
```

Creating a New Nonempty Tree

A new nonempty tree is created by taking an existing empty tree and making it the parent of at most two other trees.

```
status make_root(p_T, data, left, right)
tree *p_T;
generic_ptr data;
tree left;
tree right;
{
    /*
     *  Allocate a new node and make that the root of a tree.
     */
    if (empty_tree(*p_T) == FALSE)
        return ERROR;

    if (allocate_tree_node(p_T, data) == ERROR)
        return ERROR;

    LEFT(*p_T) = left;
    RIGHT(*p_T) = right;
    return OK;
}
```

Make_root() has four arguments: a pointer to the tree to be modified, the data to be stored at the root of the tree, and the left and right subtrees. If the tree to be created is actually a leaf, the pointers to the left and right subtrees will be **NULL**.

This functions first verifies that the tree passed is indeed empty. If it is not, **ERROR** is returned. Otherwise, a new **tree_node** is allocated, the data is copied into the node, and the left and right subtree pointers are initialized.

Destroying a Tree

To destroy a tree, it is necessary to visit every node in the tree and recover the space used by that node and the data within the node.

```
void destroy_tree(p_T, p_func_f)
tree *p_T;
void (*p_func_f)();
{
    /*
     *  Delete an entire tree (uses a postorder traversal), calling
     *  p_func_f with the DATA stored at each node.
     */
    if (empty_tree(*p_T) == FALSE) {
        destroy_tree(&LEFT(*p_T), p_func_f);
        destroy_tree(&RIGHT(*p_T), p_func_f);
        if (p_func_f != NULL)
            (*p_func_f)(DATA(*p_T));
```

```
            free_tree_node(p_T);
    }
}
```

Since the application programmer must handle memory management for the data stored within each node, the second parameter to **destroy_tree()** is a function to be called for that purpose. **Destroy_tree()** does a postorder traversal of the tree. When the root node is "visited," the passed function is called with the data stored in the node as an argument, and the root **tree_node** is deleted.

Traversing a Tree

Four methods for traversing a tree were described before. Three of those methods (preorder, inorder, and postorder traversals) are described here.

```
status traverse_tree(T, p_func_f, order)
tree T;
status (*p_func_f)();
ORDER order;
{
    /*
     *   Traverse a tree in preorder, postorder, or inorder.
     */
    switch (order) {
        case PREORDER: return preorder_traverse(T, p_func_f);
        case INORDER: return inorder_traverse(T, p_func_f);
        case POSTORDER: return postorder_traverse(T, p_func_f);
    }
    return ERROR;
}

static status preorder_traverse(T, p_func_f)
tree T;
status (*p_func_f)();
{
    /*
     *   Traverse a tree in preorder, calling p_func_f() with the
     *   DATA stored in each node visited.
     */
    status rc;

    if (empty_tree(T) == TRUE)
        return OK;
    rc = (*p_func_f)(DATA(T));
    if (rc == OK)
```

```
            rc = preorder_traverse(LEFT(T), p_func_f);
        if (rc == OK)
            rc = preorder_traverse(RIGHT(T), p_func_f);
        return rc;
}

static status inorder_traverse(T, p_func_f)
tree T;
status (*p_func_f)();
{
    /*
     *  Traverse a tree in inorder, calling p_func_f() with the
     *  DATA stored in each node visited.
     */
    status rc;

    if (empty_tree(T) == TRUE)
        return OK;
    rc = inorder_traverse(LEFT(T), p_func_f);
    if (rc == OK)
        rc = (*p_func_f)(DATA(T), p_func_f);
    if (rc == OK)
        rc = inorder_traverse(RIGHT(T), p_func_f);
    return rc;
}

static status postorder_traverse(T, p_func_f)
tree T;
status (*p_func_f)();
{
    /*
     *  Traverse a tree in post-order calling p_func_f() with the
     *  DATA stored in each node visited.
     */
    status rc;

    if (empty_tree(T) == TRUE)
        return OK;
    rc = postorder_traverse(LEFT(T), p_func_f);
    if (rc == OK)
        rc = postorder_traverse(RIGHT(T), p_func_f);
    if (rc == OK)
        rc = (*p_func_f)(DATA(T));
    return rc;
}
```

The application-programmer interface to this set of routines is through **tra-verse_tree()**. This function verifies that the desired order of traversal is valid and then calls the appropriate traversal function.

7.3   Application: Expression Evaluator

In Section 5.6, an algorithm was described in which postfix expressions could be evaluated. This algorithm used a stack, and with a single left-to-right scan of the input, a result could be obtained. A limitation of this method, however, is that an expression can be evaluated only once. In this section, a program is developed that can evaluate postfix expressions over several sets of values for the variables that make up the expressions.

The program to be developed should allow the user to enter an expression containing constants and variables. For the sake of simplicity, constants will be limited to single-digit values (0-9), the variables will be limited to **A**, **B**, and **C**, and the expressions must be entered in postfix notation (see Section 5.6 for a review of postfix notation). After the expression is entered, the user should be able to enter sets of values for **A**, **B**, and **C** for which the expression will be evaluated. It is not necessary for the user to be able to enter multiple expressions in a single run of the program.

Some sample program interaction would be[3]

Enter the expression (postfix notation): A B 5 + *
Expression is: A B 5 + *
Enter values for A B C: 4 1 0
Expression value is 24
Are there more values (y or n)? y
Enter values for A B C: 1 4 0
Expression value is 9
Are there more values (y or n)? n
End of program.

7.3.1   Expression Evaluator Design

In order to evaluate an expression multiple times, it must be represented in a form that will not change when evaluated. A binary expression tree provides that form. Recall that in a binary expression tree, the operators are stored in the internal nodes, with the operands stored at the leaves. For example, the expression **5 * 7 + 3 − 2** would be represented as

---

[3]Program output is shown in boldface.

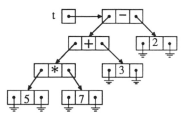

whereas the expression **5 * (7 + 3) − 2** would be represented as

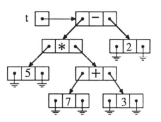

Evaluating these expressions involves a single tree traversal. Since traversing a tree does not modify it, expressions can be evaluated multiple times.

The basic form for the overall program is

```
read a postfix expression and create the tree
print the tree
read a set of values
evaluate the expression for that set
```

It is logical to implement each of these steps using a separate function. The requirements placed on these functions, and hence the function prototypes, can be defined before the functions are actually written.

```
status read_expr(tree *p_T);
status print_expr(tree T);
int read_symbols(symbol_table *p_symtab);
status eval_expr(tree T, symbol_table symtab, int *p_value);
```

Read_expr() will read from standard input an expression in postfix form and return that expression in an expression tree pointed to by its argument. **Print_expr()** will display an expression in postfix form on standard output. **Eval_expr()** will take the expression tree and the symbol table and return the value of the expression in **p_value**. **Read_symbols()** will read the variable values from standard input and store them in a symbol table.

The symbol table routines are simplified by the fact that in this implementation, the only valid variables are A, B, and C. Hence, a symbol table and functions that operate on the symbol table can be prototyped:

```
typedef struct symbol_table {
    int A, B, C;
} symbol_table;

void set_symbol(symbol_table *p_symtab, char sym, int value);
int get_symbol(symbol_table symtab, char sym);
```

The coding of these functions is left to the reader. Note that **get_symbol()** has two arguments: the symbol table, and the symbol name whose value should be retrieved. If the symbol name is one of **A**, **B**, or **C**, the corresponding value from the symbol table should be returned. If it is not one of those names, then 0 should be returned.

Implementing the User Interface

Assuming that the functions corresponding to the previous prototypes already exist, a program driver can be developed.

```
main()
{
    /*
     *   Read a postfix expression and evaluate it for sets of variables.
     */
    int result;
    tree T;
    symbol_table symtab;
    char yn;

    printf("Enter the expression (postfix notation): ");
    if (read_expr(&T) == ERROR) {
        fprintf(stderr, "Error reading expression.\n");
        exit(-1);
    }

    printf("Expression is: ");
    print_expr(T);

    do {
        read_symbols(&symtab);
        eval_expr(T, symtab, &result);
        printf("Expression value is %d\n", result);
        printf("Are there more values (y or n)? ");
        scanf(" %c", &yn);
    } while (yn == 'y' || yn == 'Y');
```

```
        printf("End of program.\n");
    }
```

The program driver only deviates from the form given before by the introduction of a loop. The **do** loop is used to obtain the sets of values for the variables to be used when evaluating the expression. Each time through the loop, a single set is read in (via **read_symbols()**) and the expression is evaluated. The user is then asked if there is another set to be read. Entering anything other than "y" means that there are no further values to be substituted.

7.3.2 Storing Data in the Tree

There are three types of data items that have to be stored in the expression tree: operators, variable names, and constants.

```
typedef enum { OPERATOR, CONSTANT, VARIABLE } NodeType;
typedef enum { PLUS, MINUS, TIMES, DIVIDE } Operator;
typedef struct exprnode {
    NodeType nodetype;
    union {
        Operator optype;
        char symbolname;
        int constvalue;
    } nodevalue;
} exprnode;

#define TYPE(n) ((n)->nodetype)
#define OP_VALUE(n) ((n)->nodevalue.optype)
#define SYM_VALUE(n) ((n)->nodevalue.symbolname)
#define CON_VALUE(n) ((n)->nodevalue.constvalue)
```

The actual character that makes up the operator (e.g., $+$, $-$, ...) is not stored in the node. Instead, the internal representation of the operators is based on an enumerated type, **Operator**.

The data stored in each tree node is an **exprnode**. Since this structure must be able to hold any one of three types of values, a C **union** is used. The type of data stored in the **exprnode** at any given time is indicated by the enumerated type **NodeType**.

The interface for allocating expression nodes uses a different function for each "type" of data that could be stored in the node.

```
exprnode *allocate_constexpr(value)
int value;
{
```

```
        exprnode *p_expr = (exprnode *) malloc(sizeof(exprnode));

        if (p_expr != NULL) {
            TYPE(p_expr) = CONSTANT;
            CON_VALUE(p_expr) = value;
        }
        return p_expr;
    }

exprnode *allocate_symbolexpr(value)
char value;
{
        exprnode *p_expr = (exprnode *) malloc(sizeof(exprnode));

        if (p_expr != NULL) {
            TYPE(p_expr) = VARIABLE;
            SYM_VALUE(p_expr) = value;
        }
        return p_expr;
    }

exprnode *allocate_operatorexpr(value)
Operator value;
{
        exprnode *p_expr = (exprnode *) malloc(sizeof(exprnode));

        if (p_expr != NULL) {
            TYPE(p_expr) = OPERATOR;
            OP_VALUE(p_expr) = value;
        }
        return p_expr;
    }
```

Each of these routines has a single argument, the value to be stored in the
node. The expression node is allocated, the type is set appropriately, and
the value is copied. The function returns a pointer to the newly allocated
expression node or **NULL** if the dynamic memory allocation function fails.

7.3.3   Reading Expressions

There are many techniques that could be used for reading the input expression.
A lexical analyzer function **gettoken()**, similar to those developed in Sections
5.6.3 and 6.2.7, can be used. Since the requirements of the program simplify
the input by making each token a single character, the returned token value
will be an **int** that must be typecast to a character whenever a variable or an
operator is indicated by the token type:

```
typedef enum { OPERATOR_T, VARIABLE_T, CONSTANT_T, EOL_T } inputtype;

typedef struct tokendata {
    inputtype tokentype;
    int tokenvalue;
} tokendata;

tokendata *gettoken();

#define ERROR_CHECK(var)  if (var == ERROR) return ERROR;

status read_expr(p_T)
tree *p_T;
{
    /*
     *  Read a postfix expression and create an expression tree.
     *  A minimal amount of error checking is done.  If input is
     *  malformed, it will be caught, but the exact error is not
     *  described.
     */
    stack S;
    tree tmptree, rightchild, leftchild;
    exprnode *p_expr;
    status rc;
    tokendata *p_token;

    init_stack(&S);

    while (TRUE) {
        p_token = gettoken();
        switch (p_token->tokentype) {
            case EOL_T:
                rc = pop_tree(&S, p_T);
                ERROR_CHECK(rc);
                return OK;
            case CONSTANT_T:
            case VARIABLE_T:
                if (p_token->tokentype == CONSTANT_T) {
                    char buffer[2];
                    buffer[0] = (char) p_token->tokenvalue;
                    buffer[1] = '\0';
                    p_expr = allocate_constexpr(atoi(buffer));
                } else
                    p_expr = allocate_symbolexpr(p_token->tokenvalue);
                if (p_expr == NULL)
                    return ERROR;
                rc = init_tree(&tmptree);
                ERROR_CHECK(rc);
                rc = make_root(&tmptree,(generic_ptr)p_expr,NULL,NULL);
```

```
                    ERROR_CHECK(rc);
                    rc = push_tree(&S, tmptree);
                    ERROR_CHECK(rc);
                    break;
                case OPERATOR_T:
                    switch (p_token->tokenvalue) {
                        case '+':
                            p_expr = allocate_operatorexpr(PLUS);
                            break;
                        case '-':
                            p_expr = allocate_operatorexpr(MINUS);
                            break;
                        case '*':
                            p_expr = allocate_operatorexpr(TIMES);
                            break;
                        case '/':
                            p_expr = allocate_operatorexpr(DIVIDE);
                            break;
                        default:
                            return ERROR;
                    }
                    if (p_expr == NULL)
                        return ERROR;
                    rc = pop_tree(&S, &rightchild);
                    ERROR_CHECK(rc);
                    rc = pop_tree(&S, &leftchild);
                    ERROR_CHECK(rc);
                    rc = init_tree(&tmptree);
                    ERROR_CHECK(rc);
                    rc = make_root(&tmptree, (generic_ptr) p_expr,
                                    leftchild, rightchild);
                    ERROR_CHECK(rc);
                    rc = push_tree(&S, tmptree);
                    ERROR_CHECK(rc);
                    break;
            default:
                return ERROR;
        }
    }
    /* can't get here */
    return OK;
}
```

Read_expr() uses a stack to store parts of the tree as it is being created. When
a digit or a character (representing a constant or a variable, respectively) is
read, the appropriate **exprnode** is allocated and a tree containing a single
node is created. This tree is then pushed onto the stack.

When an operator is encountered, an operator **exprnode** is allocated and a tree is created. However, the tree is created so that the root of the tree is the operator and the left and right subtrees consist of the top two trees on the stack. Since all the operators that are implemented require two arguments, the stack is popped twice to get those arguments and the resulting expression tree is pushed back onto the stack. After the final symbol is processed, the stack will contain the root of the tree representing the entire expression.

Given **A 5 + B *** (which is postfix notation for $A + 5 * B$), the state for each input token at the bottom of the **while** loop is shown in the following sequence:

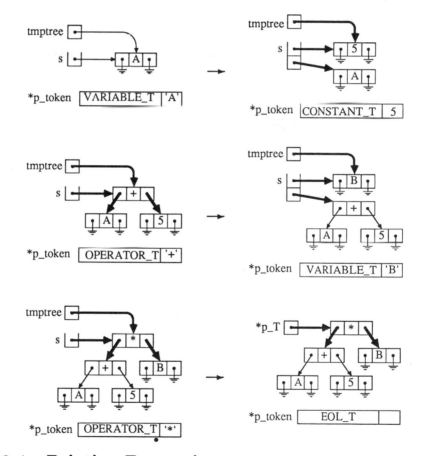

7.3.4 Printing Expressions

Printing the expression tree involves performing a postorder traversal, printing the data at each node as it is visited.

```
status print_expr(T)
tree T;
{
    /*
     *   Print an expression tree.
     */
    traverse_tree(T, print_exprnode, POSTORDER);
    putchar('\n');
    return OK;
}

status print_exprnode(p_expr)
exprnode *p_expr;
{
    /*
     *   Write the contents of an expression node to standard output.
     */
    char c;

    switch (TYPE(p_expr)) {
        case OPERATOR:
            switch (OP_VALUE(p_expr)) {
                case PLUS: c = '+'; break;
                case MINUS: c = '-'; break;
                case TIMES: c = '*'; break;
                case DIVIDE: c = '/'; break;
            }
            printf("%c ", c);
            break;
        case CONSTANT:
            printf("%d", CON_VALUE(p_expr));
            break;
        case VARIABLE:
            printf("%c ", SYM_VALUE(p_expr));
            break;
    }
    return OK;
}
```

7.3.5   Evaluating Expressions

The evaluation function recursively evaluates each subtree to determine the
value of the entire expression tree.

```
status eval_expr(T, symtab, p_value)
tree T;
symbol_table symtab;
```

```
int *p_value;
{
    /*
     *   Evaluate an expression tree.  Return the value in *p_value.
     *   If the root is an:
     *       integer node:  return that value.
     *       variable node:  return the value of that variable.
     *       operator node:  evaluate left and right subtrees,
     *                         apply the operator, and return that value.
     */
    status rc;
    exprnode *p_expr;
    int left_value, right_value;

    if (empty_tree(T) == TRUE)
        *p_value = 0;
    else {
        p_expr = (exprnode *) DATA(T);
        switch (TYPE(p_expr)) {
            case CONSTANT:
                *p_value = CON_VALUE(p_expr);
                break;
            case VARIABLE:
                *p_value = get_symbol(symtab, SYM_VALUE(p_expr));
                break;
            case OPERATOR:
                rc = eval_expr(LEFT(T), symtab, &left_value);
                ERROR_CHECK(rc);
                rc = eval_expr(RIGHT(T), symtab, &right_value);
                ERROR_CHECK(rc);
                switch (OP_VALUE(p_expr)) {
                    case PLUS:
                        *p_value = left_value + right_value;
                        break;
                    case MINUS:
                        *p_value = left_value - right_value;
                        break;
                    case TIMES:
                        *p_value = left_value * right_value;
                        break;
                    case DIVIDE:
                        if (right_value == 0)
                            return ERROR;
                        *p_value = left_value / right_value;
                }
                break;
        }
    }
}
```

```
        return OK;
}
```

Eval_expr() has three arguments: the expression tree, the symbol table to use in evaluating variables, and a pointer in which to return the expression value. If the tree is empty, the expression value is 0. Otherwise, if the root node in the tree is a constant node, the constant value is returned. If the root node is a variable node, the value is retrieved from the symbol table. If the root node is an operator node, the left and right subtrees are recursively evaluated to retrieve the operands. The operator is then applied to the operands and that value is returned.

7.3.6   The Lexical Analyzer

The lexical analyzer for the expression evaluator is a simplified version of the ones developed earlier because (1) only one line of input will be read and (2) each token is a single character.

```
tokendata *gettoken()
{
    /*
     *   Return an input token.  Anything that is not a digit
     *   or a operator is considered a variable.
     */
    static tokendata token;
    static char buffer[BUFSIZ], *bufptr;

    if (bufptr == 0) {
        if ((bufptr = gets(buffer)) == NULL) {
            /*
             *   Treat end-of-file as though it were end-of-line.
             */
            buffer[0] = '\0';
            bufptr = buffer;
        }
    }
    while (*bufptr != '\0' && isspace(*bufptr))
        bufptr++;
    if (*bufptr == '\0')
        token.tokentype = EOL_T;
    else if (isdigit(*bufptr))
        token.tokentype = CONSTANT_T;
    else if (isoperator(*bufptr))
        token.tokentype = OPERATOR_T;
    else
```

```
            token.tokentype = VARIABLE_T;
        token.tokenvalue = toupper(*bufptr);
        bufptr++;
        return &token;
}

isoperator(c)
char c;
{
    return (c == '*' || c == '/' || c == '+' || c == '-');
}
```

Stack Interface Routines

The interface routines for accessing the stack should seem familiar. They are
of the same form as those presented in Chapter 5.

```
status push_tree(p_S, T)
stack *p_S;
tree T;
{
    tree *p_T = (tree *) malloc(sizeof(tree));

    if (p_T == NULL)
        return ERROR;
    *p_T = T;
    if (push(p_S, (generic_ptr) p_T) == ERROR) {
        free(p_T);
        return ERROR;
    }
    return OK;
}

status pop_tree(p_S, p_T)
stack *p_S;
tree *p_T;
{
    tree *ptr;

    if (pop(p_S, (generic_ptr *) &ptr) == ERROR)
        return ERROR;

    *p_T = *ptr;
    free(ptr);
    return OK;
}
```

Push_tree() has two arguments: a pointer to the stack, and the **tree** data to
be pushed onto the stack. It dynamically allocates a new **tree** structure and
copies the existing data. The newly allocated space is what is stored on the
stack. If the dynamic allocation function **malloc()**, or **push()** fail, **ERROR** is
returned.

Pop_tree() performs the inverse operation. It has two arguments: a pointer
to the stack, and a pointer to the location at which the data that is retrieved
should be stored. If the pop operation is successful, the data is copied to that
location and the dynamically allocated space that was returned by **pop()** is
freed.

7.4   Heaps

A heap is an ordered, balanced binary tree in which the value of the node
at the root of any subtree is less than or equal to the value of either of its
children. This inherent ordering implies that only valued items may be placed
in the heap. Note, furthermore, that there is no implied relationship between
siblings. That is, the following two trees are both heaps:

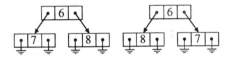

In a balanced tree, the distance (number of links traversed) between the root
of the tree and any leaf node will differ by only one. Due to this limitation,
the following tree is not a heap:

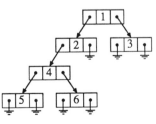

7.4.1   Heap Implementation

Unlike a generalized binary tree, a heap can be implemented either using
pointers (as before) or using an array. The ability to use an array is achieved
by virtue of the balanced nature of the heap. The array implementation scheme
is deceptively simple:

Let the root of any subtree be at position i in the array. The left child will then be at position $2i$ and the right child will be at position $2i + 1$.

If the first index of the array is considered to be one, then the tree is organized as follows (the value at each node is the array index):

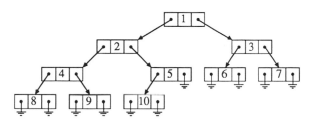

Holes in the array must be avoided, so as new elements are added, they are always added at the end of the array. If the value of the new element is less than its parent, the new element must be swapped with its parent. This swapping procedure continues between the new element and its parent until no more swaps are needed or it is at the root of the tree. It is not necessary to compare the new element (or a swapped parent) with any other elements in the heap, since it is already known that the value of that parent of any subtree is less than the value of any of the elements in the subtree.

The hole left by deleting an arbitrary item in the heap can be filled by taking the last element in the array and moving it. Then that newly shifted element must be compared with its children and swapped with the smaller of the two. This swapping procedure continues between the shifted element and its children until no more swaps occur or a leaf is reached.

The algorithms used to insert and delete items ensure that the heap property is maintained. They apply regardless of whether the implementation is array-based or a tree-based. An array-based implementation may be more desirable due to the ease of locating both *parents* and children. Locating the parents in a tree-based implementation requires that nodes have pointers to their parents as well as to their children.

7.4.2   C Representation of a Heap

Representing a heap using an array implies a bound on the number of elements. As opposed to using a statically declared array, a dynamically allocated array can be used. Its size will be limited by the amount of contiguous space available to the program at run time. This decision makes it difficult to determine the conditions under which the program will fail, but also allows for more flexibility.

By using dynamic arrays, the representation of a heap is very similar to that of a stack in Section 5.5.

```
#define HEAPINCREMENT  128

typedef struct {
    generic_ptr *base;
    int nextelement;
    int heapsize;
} heap;
```

An integer is used to index the array (as opposed to pointer references used in Section 5.5) as it makes the implementations of the insertion and deletion algorithms more easily understood.

7.4.3   Primitive Operations on Heaps

There are four primitive operations on heaps that will be considered here: initialization, testing for emptiness, insertion, and deletion.

Initializing and Status of a Heap

Initializing a heap requires allocating the initial space to be used.

```
status init_heap(p_H)
heap *p_H;
{
    /*
     *   Initialize a heap by allocating the array.
     */
    p_H->base = (generic_ptr *)malloc(HEAPINCREMENT*sizeof(generic_ptr));

    if (p_H->base == NULL)
        return ERROR;

    p_H->nextelement = 0;
    p_H->heapsize = HEAPINCREMENT;
    return OK;
}

bool empty_heap(p_H)
heap *p_H;
{
```

```
        /*
         *   Return TRUE if p_H is an empty heap.
         */
        return (p_H->nextelement == 0) ? TRUE : FALSE;
}
```

Init_heap() allocates the space for the heap. It also sets the variable indicating the index of the next available element to 0. Although the algorithms for updating a heap require that the first index of the heap be 1, C requires that the first index be 0. Therefore, the insertion and deletion routines will have to add to the actual index when implementing the algorithms.

Since a heap is empty when **nextelement** is equal to 0, **empty_heap()** returns the results of the comparison of that field with 0.

Inserting an Item

Since **generic_ptr**'s are used to maintain data in the heap, inserting a new item requires that a comparison function be passed as a parameter.

```
status heap_insert(p_H, data, p_cmp_f)
heap *p_H;
generic_ptr data;
int (*p_cmp_f)();
{
        /*
         *   Insert data into p_H.  p_cmp_f() is a comparison function that
         *   returns a value less than 0 if its first argument is less than
         *   its second, 0 if the arguments are equal.  Otherwise, p_cmp_f()
         *   returns a value greater than 0.
         *
         *   The data is inserted in the heap by placing it at the end and
         *   using siftup() to find its proper position.
         */
        if (p_H->nextelement == p_H->heapsize) {
                /*
                 *   Not enough space in the array, so more must be allocated.
                 */
                generic_ptr *newbase = (generic_ptr *) realloc(p_H->base,
                    (p_H->heapsize+HEAPINCREMENT)*sizeof(generic_ptr));
                if (newbase == NULL)
                        return ERROR;
                p_H->base = newbase;
                p_H->heapsize += HEAPINCREMENT;
        }
        p_H->base[p_H->nextelement] = data;
        siftup(p_H, p_H->nextelement, p_cmp_f);
```

```
        p_H->nextelement++;
        return OK;
}

static void siftup(p_H, element, p_cmp_f)
heap *p_H;
int element;
int (*p_cmp_f)();
{
    /*
     *   p_H is a heap except for element.  Find the correct place for
     *   element by swapping it with its parent if necessary.  If a swap
     *   is made, p_H is a heap except for the parent's position, so
     *   call siftup() recursively.
     */
    int parent;
    int cmp_result;
    generic_ptr tmpvalue;

    if (element == 0)
        return;

    parent = (element - 1) / 2;
    cmp_result = (*p_cmp_f)(p_H->base[element], p_H->base[parent]);
    if (cmp_result >= 0)
        return;

    tmpvalue = p_H->base[element];
    p_H->base[element] = p_H->base[parent];
    p_H->base[parent] = tmpvalue;
    siftup(p_H, parent, p_cmp_f);
    return;
}
```

Heap_insert() first ensures that there is enough space in the array for the new item. If there is not enough space, a larger block of memory is allocated and the data is copied into the new space (by the function **realloc()**). The new item is added at the end of the array, and **siftup()** is called to find the correct location for that item.

Siftup() compares the element with its parent and swaps the data if necessary. If the data is swapped, the parent (which is now the new data) must be checked with its parent to make sure that their relative ordering is correct. This is done with a recursive call. Note that the determination of the parent index is slightly different from that of the algorithm described before. This is because the heap starts at position 0, not position 1.

With an initial heap (shown in both "tree" and array format):

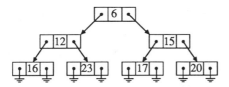

the **siftup()** operation to insert a 9 is given by the following trace (the shaded blocks represent the elements being compared):

6	12	15	16	23	17	20	9
6	12	15	9	23	17	20	16
6	9	15	12	23	17	20	16

Deleting an Item

As with lists, there are at least two types of deletion functions possible: delete based on position in the array or delete based on value. Since deletion based on position in the array is the more general of the two methods, that function will be developed.

```
status heap_delete(p_H, element, p_data, p_cmp_f)
heap *p_H;
int element;
generic_ptr *p_data;
int (*p_cmp_f)();
{
    /*
     *  Delete element from p_H.  Store the data from the deleted node in
     *  p_data.  p_cmp_f() is a comparison function that returns a value less
     *  than 0 if its first argument is less than its second, 0 if the
     *  arguments are equal.  Otherwise, p_cmp_f() returns a value greater than 0.
     *
     *  The data is deleted by placing the last element in its place and
     *  using siftdown() to find its proper position.
     */
    if (element >= p_H->nextelement)
        return ERROR;

    *p_data = p_H->base[element];
    p_H->nextelement--;
    if (element != p_H->nextelement) {
        p_H->base[element] = p_H->base[p_H->nextelement];
        siftdown(p_H, element, p_cmp_f);
    }
    return OK;
```

```
}
static void siftdown(p_H, parent, p_cmp_f)
heap *p_H;
int parent;
int (*p_cmp_f)();
{
    /*
     *  p_H is a heap except for parent.  Find the correct place for parent
     *  by swapping it with the smaller of its children.  If a swap is
     *  made, p_H is a heap except for the child's position, so call
     *  siftdown() recursively.
     */
    int leftchild, rightchild, swapelement;
    int leftcmp, rightcmp, leftrightcmp;
    generic_ptr tmpvalue;

    leftchild = 2 * parent + 1;
    rightchild = leftchild + 1;

    if (leftchild >= p_H->nextelement)
        /*
         *  No children.
         */
        return;

    leftcmp = (*p_cmp_f)(p_H->base[parent], p_H->base[leftchild]);
    if (rightchild >= p_H->nextelement) {
        /*
         *  No right child.
         */
        if (leftcmp > 0) {
            tmpvalue = p_H->base[parent];
            p_H->base[parent] = p_H->base[leftchild];
            p_H->base[leftchild] = tmpvalue;
        }
        return;
    }
    rightcmp = (*p_cmp_f)(p_H->base[parent], p_H->base[rightchild]);
    if (leftcmp > 0 || rightcmp > 0) {
        /*
         *  Two children.  Swap with the smaller child.
         */
        leftrightcmp = (*p_cmp_f)(p_H->base[leftchild],
                                  p_H->base[rightchild]);
        swapelement = (leftrightcmp < 0) ? leftchild : rightchild;
        tmpvalue = p_H->base[parent];
        p_H->base[parent] = p_H->base[swapelement];
        p_H->base[swapelement] = tmpvalue;
```

```
        siftdown(p_H, swapelement, p_cmp_f);
    }
    return;
}
```

Delete_heap() first checks to see if the element to be deleted is a valid index into the current heap. If it is not, **ERROR** is returned. Otherwise, the data is copied out of the element. The special case of deleting the last element is considered by comparing the index of the element to be deleted with the index of the last valid element. If the deleted element is not the last, the last element's data is copied into the hole. That location then represents the only spot where (potentially) the heap property is not maintained. Since it was previously known that the element now in that spot was lower down in the heap, its correct location is determined by calling **siftdown()**.

Siftdown() locates the correct position for the data in the index passed by comparing it with its children. First, the indices of the left and right child are determined. The equation for the location of the left child is different from that in the algorithm because the heap starts at position 0, not position 1. A quick check shows that the equation correctly locates position 0's children at positions 1 and 2 and 1's children at 3 and 4, etc.

There are three cases to consider in locating the correct position for the data. If the index of the left child is greater than the number of elements in the heap, there are no children. In this case, the element is in its correct position.

If there is a left child, but the index of the right child is greater than the number of elements, there is only one child. In this case, the value at the parent is compared with the left child. The data will be swapped if the value at the parent is greater than the value at the child. Note that since there is only one child to the **parent**, its child can have no children, as that would violate the rules governing heaps. Therefore, there is no need to recursively call **siftdown()**. However, in the last case, when there are two children, if a swap is necessary, the parent will be swapped with the smaller of the two children and **siftdown()** will be called recursively.

6	16	15	12	23	17	20	
6	12	15	16	23	17	20	

7.5 Application: Job Scheduler

In Section 5.9, an operating system was simulated. A simple queue was used so that the jobs entering the operating system were executed on a "first-come, first-served" basis. Most operating systems, however, have some concept of priority associated with each job. Jobs of the same priority may be executed on a "first-come, first-served" basis, but those with higher priority will be executed before ones with a lower priority.

Although the scheduling algorithm seemed adequate at the time, perhaps a "first-come, first-served" algorithm is not ideal. It may seem fair to each individual, but what about the job requiring only 1 unit of CPU time that was submitted after the job requiring 80 units. Perhaps from an overall system point of view it is better to give jobs requiring less CPU time a higher priority. One way to verify this is to modify the job scheduling strategy in the operating system simulation program and compare the average time jobs wait in the queue. The goal is to shorten the average time a job waits in the queue.

7.5.1   Priority Queues

The concept of priority is embodied in the *priority queue* data structure. In a priority queue, as items are added, they are automatically positioned appropriately, depending on their relative priority to items already in the queue. Items are always deleted from the front of a priority queue.

A priority queue can be implemented in many ways. One such way is to add a comparison function to the queue implementation developed in Chapter 5. The comparison function would be used to compare items in the linked list so that the new item could be inserted in the correct position. One problem with this technique is that inserting new items can take a long time. The advantage of using a special header node for queues, which was developed in Section 5.11, would be negated, since it possible that every node in the list would have to be compared against the new item.

An alternative implementation is to implement a priority queue as a heap. Since a heap is a balanced binary tree, at most $\log(n)$ nodes will have to be visited when a new item is inserted. Of course, to delete an item will require $\log(n)$ nodes to be visited as well. Deletion from the linked list implementation of a priority queue would not require visiting any other nodes. Nonetheless, since the number of deletions will always equal the number of insertions, the heap implementation will be more efficient.

Implementing Priority Queues

There are four primitive operations associated with a queue, and hence a priority queue: *init_queue*, *empty_queue*, *qadd*, and *qremove*.

```
typedef heap queue;
```

```
#define init_queue(p_Q)   init_heap(p_Q)
#define empty_queue(p_Q) empty_heap(p_Q)
#define qadd(p_Q, data, p_cmp_f) heap_insert(p_Q, data, p_cmp_f)
#define qremove(p_Q, p_data, p_cmp_f) heap_delete(p_Q, 0, p_data, p_cmp_f)
```

As is obvious, the implementation of priority queues is primarily an interface to the heap functions. It was deliberately chosen not to rename the queue functions to ease the integration into the existing program.

7.5.2 Modifying the Simulation Program

The modifications to the simulation program presented in Section 5.9 are quite minor. All that is needed is to add an extra argument, the comparison function, to calls to **qadd()** and **qremove()**. Since these calls to these routines are isolated in the interface routines, only two routines have to be modified (although the entire program must be recompiled with the priority queue definitions) — **qadd_job()** and **qremove()**.

```
typedef struct {
    int basetime;
    int elapsedtime;
    int runtime;
} job;

status qadd_job(p_Q, base, elapse, run)
queue *p_Q;
int base, elapse, run;
{
    job *p_j = (job *) malloc(sizeof(job));

    if (p_j == NULL)
        return ERROR;

    p_j->basetime = base;
    p_j->elapsedtime = elapse;
    p_j->runtime = run;

    if (qadd(p_Q, (generic_ptr) p_j, cmp_runtime) == ERROR) {
        free(p_j);
        return ERROR;
    }
    return OK;
}

status qremove_job(p_Q, p_base, p_elapse, p_run)
queue *p_Q;
```

```
int *p_base, *p_elapse, *p_run;
{
    job *p_j;

    if (qremove(p_Q, (generic_ptr *) &p_j, cmp_runtime) == ERROR)
        return ERROR;

    *p_base = p_j->basetime;
    *p_elapse = p_j->elapsedtime;
    *p_run = p_j->runtime;
    free(p_j);
    return OK;
}

static int cmp_runtime(p_job1, p_job2)
job *p_job1, *p_job2;
{
    return p_job1->runtime - p_job2->runtime;
}
```

These functions are identical to those presented in Section 5.9 except that
these include the extra reference to function **cmp_runtime()**. This function
has two arguments, pointers to **job**s, and returns a negative number if the run
time remaining on the first job is less than that remaining on the second, zero
if there are equal run times, and a positive number otherwise. This function
is called by the heap functions **siftup()** and **siftdown()** to perform the data
comparisons.

7.5.3   Simulation Results

One run of the simulation using the "smallest job first" scheduling strategy
showed an average time in the queue of 25.01 time units. Comparing this to
the results in Section 5.9.5 shows a significant decrease in the time waiting in
the queue. To determine whether these results are reliable, one must average
the results of many runs of the program.

After doing this, it will be seen that the "smallest job first" strategy *does*
provide significantly better system throughput as measured by the average
time a job waits in the queue. In fact, it can be proven that this strategy
is the optimal scheduling strategy. Unfortunately, it may be realistic only in
a simulation environment and not in practice. In practice, it will be found
that some jobs that were submitted *never* ran. These jobs sat in the queue
waiting their turn which never arrived. This happens because jobs that were
subsequently submitted had smaller run times. A solution to this problem is

proposed in the Exercises.

7.6 N-ary Trees

The binary tree structure is quite powerful and can be used to represent many different types of data. However, it is not appropriate for all applications. Suppose, for example, the C conditional expression,

$$\textbf{(condition) ? (expr1) : (expr2)}$$

were to be represented using an expression tree. One way of viewing the conditional expression is as a ternary operator. That is, there are *three* operands. Since a binary expression tree only allows each operator to have at most two operands, it could not represent the conditional expression. One solution would be to create a tree in which each node could have an arbitrary number of children. This type of tree is called an *N-ary tree*.

N-ary trees are a superset of binary trees. Graphically, an N-ary tree can be viewed as:

However, the method in which the tree is represented inside a program may be different. To say that each node in the tree has "left," "right," and "middle" pointers allows one to implement a "ternary" tree (pictured above), but does not allow for arbitrary trees.

One solution is to have an array of children pointers stored at each node. Of course, an array is a static object. Were a dynamically allocated array to be used, the bookkeeping at each node might tend to make the programming quite confusing. The obvious alternative is to have a linked list of children stored in each parent node. Given the linked list functions developed in Chapter 4, the previous tree could be represented as:

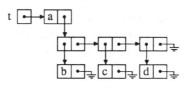

However, this storage method is somewhat redundant (see Exercise 14). A more efficient method of storage for N-ary trees is using a CHILD–SIBLING

technique. As opposed to having a node point directly to all its children, it
points to only the first child. Furthermore, each node points to its siblings
(i.e., the parent's other children). The CHILD–SIBLING technique allows one
to use a binary tree to represent the data. Given tree node, **T**, **LEFT(T)** will
point to the first child and **RIGHT(T)** will point to the first of **T**'s siblings.
Using this representation, the previous tree becomes:

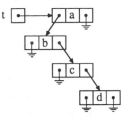

It is often convenient to show such trees with the right pointers drawn horizontally, thus pictorially preserving the original structure:

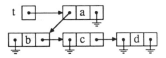

7.6.1   C Representation of N-ary Trees

Since N-ary trees can be represented using binary trees, binary tree functions
can be used. Although it makes no sense to do a postorder traversal of an N-ary
tree, it is reasonable to use functions such as **empty_tree()** and **make_root()**.
One should keep in mind, however, that the **LEFT** pointer is the first child
and the **RIGHT** pointer is a sibling.

One way to help maintain this view is to introduce some "syntactic sugar."
As opposed to using the macros **LEFT** and **RIGHT**, new macros are defined:

```
#define FIRST_CHILD(T) LEFT(T)
#define SIBLING(T) RIGHT(T)
```

and the calling semantics (i.e., the way in which the function is viewed) of
make_root() should be changed. In particular, **make_root()** has four parameters, two of which are pointers to the first child and pointers to the node's
sibling.

7.7 Application: Four-in-a-Row Game

Four-in-a-row is a game similar to tic-tac-toe, but somewhat more complex. The game is played on a 6 × 6 grid, and the object is to get four consecutive pieces in a row (horizontally, vertically, or diagonally) or in a square. In the general game, pieces can be added anywhere on the board. For the game developed in this section, however, play is limited to spaces along the bottom of the board or spaces immediately above occupied spaces.

7.7.1 Game Trees

The game tree approach to a two player game uses an N-ary tree to represent different board configurations. The root of the tree is the starting board configuration and the immediate children are configurations that are obtainable from the parent in a single move. By generating a tree of the possible sequences of move and countermoves, the computer can determine the ramifications of a given line of play. Each move by a single player is called a *half-move* or *ply*. The number of ply examined corresponds to the depth of the tree.

Most games have a discrete outcome (win, lose, or draw). If the game is simple enough, like tic-tac-toe, the computer can create a complete game tree that contains all lines of play pursued to their ultimate outcome. A complete game tree in essence "solves" the game. It shows whether either player has a strategy that can force a win (or a draw).

The Minimax Technique

Since the computer may not have enough time or memory to follow paths in the tree all the way to the end of the game, it must come up with a way to choose a move based on incomplete information. Suppose, for example, the computer can look ahead two plies (i.e., it can examine its opponent's possible countermove to its pending move). The computer should make the move that leaves its opponent the weakest possible reply. In order to make such a determination, the computer needs a way of determining which of a set of configuration is the best.

This can done using a *static evaluation function*. This function (sometimes called a *heuristic function*) takes a fixed board position and returns a number indicating to what extent either player appears to have an advantage. The assumption will be made that a large value means that player one has an advantage, and a small value (negative) indicates that player two has an advantage.

In order to choose a move, the computer generates as large a tree as it can. It then applies the heuristic function to each of the leaves. If a set of leaves with a common parent represents possible moves by player one, the parent is assigned the maximum of their values. This corresponds to the best move to make from that position.

Conversely, if a set of leaves represent possible moves by player two, the parent is assigned the minimum of their values, because player two will want to make the move that looks worst for player one. Values are propagated up the tree in using this minimum-maximum technique. If the computer is player one, then it will pick the move that has the greatest value.

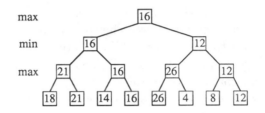

If the computer is player two, then it will pick the move that has the smallest value.

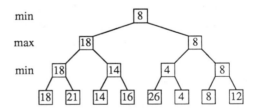

This technique is based on the assumption that the opponent will always make what appears to the computer as his best possible move. Although this has some drawbacks (e.g., the computer will not "lay traps" that it would know to avoid), it has proven to be the best strategy.

7.7.2   Program Design

It is possible to write the game program without explicitly storing the game tree. Nodes could be evaluated recursively as they are generated, thereby using the "tree" of recursive calls to implicitly maintain the game tree structure. However, the tree will be explicitly generated to allow it to be displayed, so that the computer's play can be analyzed and the heuristic modified accordingly.

At the highest level, the program performs three operations. The player's move is read and applied to the game board. The resulting game board represents the root of the game tree that is generated and evaluated to determine the computer's move. The three important pieces of this program, therefore, are (1) the representation of the game board, (2) the generation/evaluation of the game tree, and (3) soliciting user input.

7.7.3 The Game Board

Since a board configuration, or state, will be stored at each node in the game tree, the structure of the board is developed first.

```
#define BOARD_SIZE 8
#define BOARD_MIN 1
#define BOARD_MAX 6

typedef char board[BOARD_SIZE][BOARD_SIZE];

typedef struct {
    int value;
    board brd;
} state;

#define BOARD(p_S) (((state *) (p_S))->brd)
#define VALUE(p_S) (((state *) (p_S))->value)

typedef char player;
#define COMPUTER 'O'
#define PLAYER 'X'
#define OPEN '-'
#define FILLED '+'

#define WIN 1000
```

Although the board is 6 × 6, the array representing the board is declared to be 8 × 8. The playable area is the 6 × 6 square represented by the array indices **BOARD_MIN** and **BOARD_MAX**. The nonplayable area of the board will be discussed later.

As the game tree is developed, each node will contain a board configuration. That board configuration, along with its associated heuristic value, represent the game state. Furthermore, since there are two players in the game, the computer and the "player," the preprocessor #defines are created to indicate their respective board markings. The **OPEN** value to indicates that a space is available. The **FILLED** value is used for the border around the board.

```
void initialize_board(b)
```

```
board b;
{
    int i, j, last;

    /*
     *  Initialize game board b by making all slots OPEN except for the
     *  nonplayable boarder around the playing area which is initialized
     *  to FILLED.
     */
    for (i = BOARD_MIN; i <= BOARD_MAX; i++)
        for (j = BOARD_MIN; j <= BOARD_MAX; j++)
            b[i][j] = OPEN;
    last = BOARD_SIZE - 1;
    for (i = 0; i < BOARD_SIZE; i++)
        b[0][i] = b[last][i] = b[i][0] = b[i][last] = FILLED;
}

void print_board(b)
board b;
{
    /*
     *  Output the game board.
     */
    int i, j;

    printf("   ");
    for (i = BOARD_MIN; i <= BOARD_MAX; i++)
        printf("%d", i);
    for (i = BOARD_MIN; i <= BOARD_MAX; i++) {
        printf("\n%d ", i);
        for (j = BOARD_MIN; j <= BOARD_MAX; j++)
            putchar(b[i][j]);
    }
    putchar('\n');
}

bool valid_move(b, i, j)
board b;
int i, j;
{
    /*
     *  Return TRUE if b[i][j] is a valid move.  A move is valid if the
     *  desired slot is empty, and the slot "below" it is filled.
     */
    if (i < BOARD_MIN || i > BOARD_MAX || j < BOARD_MIN || j > BOARD_MAX)
        return FALSE;
    if (b[i][j] == OPEN && b[i+1][j] != OPEN)
        return TRUE;
```

```
    else
        return FALSE;
}

void set_board(b, i, j, who)
board b;
int i, j;
player who;
{
    b[i][j] = who;
}
```

Initialize_board() marks the playing area of the board as **OPEN** and the boundary as **FILLED**. Print_board() displays the playing area of the board on standard output along with row and column labels. Valid_move() determines whether the passed row and column represent a valid move.

For a move to be valid, the indices passed must be between **BOARD_MIN** and **BOARD MAX**, the space must be open, and the space below the current space must *not* be open. Since there is a filled-in row below the playing area, there is no need to explicitly check for the bottom row condition. This technique of avoiding multiple conditionals can help reduce the amount of time spent executing the function by eliminating special cases. Although the amount of time is insignificant in a single function call, were the function to be called repeatedly, the savings in time can be appreciable.

7.7.4 Generating a Game Tree

In order to build the game tree, the program must be able to make moves for either player (itself and the user). Since trees are recursively defined structures, the function that builds the tree is best developed using recursion.

```
state *make_move(p_T, depth, ply, p_eval_f, p_thisply_f, p_nextply_f)
tree *p_T;
int depth;
player ply;
int (*p_eval_f)(), (*p_thisply_f)(), (*p_nextply_f)();
{
    /*
     *  Advance a ply in game tree p_T.  Current depth is depth, ply
     *  indicates whose turn, p_eval_f() is a static evaluation function,
     *  and p_thisply_f() and p_nextply_f() are greater than or less than
     *  functions (depending upon the ply).
     */
    static int thinkcount = 0;
```

```
state *p_currentstate, *p_nextstate;
tree tmptree, childtree;
state tmpstate;
int i, j, value;

p_currentstate = (state *) DATA(*p_T);
if (depth == 0 || have_winner(BOARD(p_currentstate)) == TRUE) {
    VALUE(p_currentstate) = (*p_eval_f)(BOARD(p_currentstate));
    return NULL;
}

/*
 *  Childtree is the root of the tree representing moves from the
 *  current configuration (i.e. child nodes of passed tree node).
 */
init_tree(&childtree);
/*
 *  Evaluate each possible valid move.
 */
for (i = BOARD_MIN; i <= BOARD_MAX; i++) {
    for (j = BOARD_MIN; j <= BOARD_MAX; j++) {
        if (valid_move(BOARD(p_currentstate), i, j) == TRUE) {
            if (++thinkcount % 250 == 0) {
                printf("Thinking...\n");
                thinkcount = 0;
            }
            copy_board(BOARD(&tmpstate), BOARD(p_currentstate));
            set_board(BOARD(&tmpstate), i, j, ply);
            init_tree(&tmptree);
            /*
             *  Make move and use new board configuration as the root
             *  of a new game tree.
             */
            if (make_state_root(&tmptree,tmpstate,NULL,NULL) == ERROR)
                return NULL;
            make_move(&tmptree, depth-1, other_player(ply),
                    p_eval_f, p_nextply_f, p_thisply_f);
            if (empty_tree(childtree)) {
                /*
                 *  First move on this ply (i.e. first child).
                 */
                childtree = tmptree;
                p_nextstate = (state *) DATA(tmptree);
                value = VALUE(p_nextstate);
            } else {
                /*
                 *  Subsequent move on this ply so make new tree a sibling.
                 */
```

```
                        SIBLING(tmptree) = childtree;
                        childtree = tmptree;
                        /*
                         *  Determine best move so far.
                         */
                        if ((*p_thisply_f)(VALUE(DATA(tmptree)), value)) {
                            value = VALUE(DATA(tmptree));
                            p_nextstate = (state *) DATA(tmptree);
                        }
                    }
                } /* if (valid...) */
            } /* for (j...) */
        } /* for (i...) */

        FIRST_CHILD(*p_T) = childtree;
        VALUE(p_currentstate) = value;
        return p_nextstate;
}


player other_player(who)
player who;
{
    return (who == COMPUTER) ? PLAYER : COMPUTER;
}
```

Make_move() is passed a pointer to the node of the game tree that represents the current state, the depth of the tree (number of moves) still to be generated, the player whose move should be generated, a pointer to the heuristic function, and pointers to min and max functions. **P_thisply_f()** performs either a less-than or greater-than operation depending on the level in the tree. In each recursive call to **make_move()**, that function and **p_nextply_f()** are swapped so that the appropriate minimum or maximum value is calculated. **Make_move()** returns a pointer to the state that represents the best move.

In this function, the first calculation is the base case for the recursion. If the **depth** is 0 or a winner has been found, the current board is evaluated. Since no next move is generated in the base case, **NULL** is returned. The recursive case examines each possible valid move that could be made from the initial state.

Make_move() is always called with a newly generated root node. In each recursive call, the **depth** is decremented, the player is set to the "other player," and the min and max functions (represented by **p_thisply_f()** and **p_nextply_f()**) are swapped. Upon return from the recursive call, **tmptree** will be a fully generated tree that represents a single child of the board configuration (tree) passed as a parameter. If it is not the first child, it is compared

using the appropriate minimum or maximum function to the previously minimum (or maximum, depending upon the ply) valued state. If the child state
represents a better move, it is recorded in **value** and **p_nextstate**. When all
the valid moves have been considered, the tree of children is set to be the child
of the passed tree and the value of the current state is set correspondingly.

The tree generation and evaluation can potentially involve long periods
involving no user feedback. The **static** variable **thinkcount** is used to provide
occasional feedback. It controls the printing of messages to reassure the user
that the computer is indeed performing *some* operation and has not locked
up.

7.7.5   The Heuristic Function

Any number of heuristic functions can be used. Obviously, the better the
heuristic function, the better the computer will play the game. In general,
however, the "smarter" the heuristic, the longer it will take to evaluate a
configuration. This may require placing a limit on the depth of the search.
The function developed here represents a reasonably complex heuristic.

```
#define ABS(i)  (((i) < 0) ? (-i) : (i))

int eval(b)
board b;
{
    /*
     *  A static evaluation function.  Use determine_value() to get a value
     *  for each possible move and return the sum.
     */
    int i, j, thisvalue, valuesum;

    valuesum = 0;
    for (i = BOARD_MIN; i <= BOARD_MAX; i++)
        for (j = BOARD_MIN; j <= BOARD_MAX; j++) {
            thisvalue = determine_value(b, i, j);
            if (ABS(thisvalue) == WIN) {
                return thisvalue;
            }
            valuesum += thisvalue;
        }
    return valuesum;
}

int determine_value(b, i, j)
board b;
int i, j;
```

```
{
    /*
     *  Determine the heuristic value of making move b[i][j] by giving a
     *  "point" for consecutive pieces up, down, left, right, or diagonal.
     *  Also give a points for having pieces in a square.
     */
#define HORIZ_LT 0
#define HORIZ_RT 1
#define VERT_UP 2
#define VERT_DN 3
#define DIAG_UPLT 4
#define DIAG_UPRT 5
#define DIAG_DNLT 6
#define DIAG_DNRT 7
#define SQAR_UPLT 8
#define SQAR_UPRT 9
#define SQAR_DNLT 10
#define SQAR_DNRT 11
    int value[12];
    int sum;
    int k;

    if (b[i][j] == OPEN)
        return 0;

    for (k = 0; k < 12; k++)
        value[k] = 1;

    for (k = 1; k <= 3; k++) {
        if (b[i+k][j] == b[i][j])
            value[VERT_UP]++;
        else if (b[i+k][j] != OPEN)
            value[VERT_UP] = -10;

        if (b[i-k][j] == b[i][j])
            value[VERT_DN]++;
        else if (b[i-k][j] != OPEN)
            value[VERT_DN] = -10;

        if (b[i][j+k] == b[i][j])
            value[HORIZ_LT]++;
        else if (b[i][j+k] != OPEN)
            value[HORIZ_LT] = -10;

        if (b[i][j-k] == b[i][j])
            value[HORIZ_RT]++;
        else if (b[i][j-k] != OPEN)
            value[HORIZ_RT] = -10;
```

```
        if (b[i+k][j+k] == b[i][j])
            value[DIAG_DNRT]++;
        else if (b[i+k][j+k] != OPEN)
            value[DIAG_DNRT] = -10;

        if (b[i+k][j-k] == b[i][j])
            value[DIAG_DNLT]++;
        else if (b[i+k][j-k] != OPEN)
            value[DIAG_DNLT] = -10;

        if (b[i-k][j+k] == b[i][j])
            value[DIAG_UPRT]++;
        else if (b[i+k][j+k] != OPEN)
            value[DIAG_UPRT] = -10;

        if (b[i-k][j-k] == b[i][j])
            value[DIAG_UPLT]++;
        else if (b[i+k][j-k] != OPEN)
            value[DIAG_UPLT] = -10;
    }

    if (b[i+1][j] == b[i][j]) {
        value[SQAR_DNRT]++;
        value[SQAR_DNLT]++;
    } else if (b[i+1][j] != OPEN) {
        value[SQAR_DNRT] = -10;
        value[SQAR_DNLT] = -10;
    }

    if (b[i-1][j] == b[i][j]) {
        value[SQAR_UPRT]++;
        value[SQAR_UPLT]++;
    } else if (b[i-1][j] != OPEN) {
        value[SQAR_UPRT] = -10;
        value[SQAR_UPLT] = -10;
    }

    if (b[i][j+1] == b[i][j]) {
        value[SQAR_DNRT]++;
        value[SQAR_UPRT]++;
    } else if (b[i][j+1] != OPEN) {
        value[SQAR_DNRT] = -10;
        value[SQAR_UPRT] = -10;
    }

    if (b[i][j-1] == b[i][j]) {
        value[SQAR_DNLT]++;
        value[SQAR_UPLT]++;
```

```
        } else if (b[i][j-1] != OPEN) {
            value[SQAR_DNLT] = -10;
            value[SQAR_UPLT] = -10;
        }

        if (b[i+1][j+1] == b[i][j])
            value[SQAR_DNRT]++;
        else if (b[i+1][j+1] != OPEN)
            value[SQAR_DNRT] = -10;

        if (b[i+1][j-1] == b[i][j])
            value[SQAR_DNLT]++;
        else if (b[i+1][j-1] != OPEN)
            value[SQAR_DNLT] = -10;

        if (b[i-1][j+1] == b[i][j])
            value[SQAR_UPRT]++;
        else if (b[i-1][j+1] != OPEN)
            value[SQAR_UPRT] = -10;

        if (b[i-1][j-1] == b[i][j])
            value[SQAR_UPLT]++;
        else if (b[i-1][j-1] != OPEN)
            value[SQAR_UPLT] = -10;

        /*
         *  The value for this move is the sum of the points.  If any move yields
         *  four points, then there is a win in that direction, so immediately
         *  exit the loop.
         */
        for (sum = k = 0; value[k] != 4 && k < 12; k++)
            if (value[k] > 0)
                sum += value[k];

        if (k < 12)
            sum = WIN;

        return (b[i][j] == COMPUTER) ? -sum : sum;
}

bool have_winner(b)
board b;
{
    /*
     *  Return TRUE if the configuration of b is a winning configuration for
     *  either player.  Return FALSE otherwise.
     */
    int i, j, value;
```

```
        for (i = BOARD_MIN; i <= BOARD_MAX; i++)
            for (j = BOARD_MIN; j <= BOARD_MAX; j++)
                if (b[i][j] != OPEN) {
                    value = determine_value(b, i, j);
                    if (ABS(value) == WIN)
                        return TRUE;
                }
        return FALSE;
}
```

Eval() examines each possible position on the board in turn and calls **determine_value()** to calculate how much that position contributes to a winning configuration. The values returned by **determine_value()** are summed. If **determine_value()** returns a value indicating a winning configuration, then the **WIN** value is returned instead of the sum.

Determine_value() calculates the number of consecutive symbols in any one of 12 winning chains. The calculations always assume that the position passed represents the first of the symbols in the chain. The chains that are evaluated are vertical, moving up and moving down; horizontal, moving left and moving right; any one of four diagonals; and a square with the passed position in any of the four corners.

The entry in the **value** array is initialized to one indicating that at least one symbol has been found. Then the other three positions (for each possible winning chain) are checked. If the symbol matches the starting symbol, then the **value** is incremented. If a filled space blocks the chain, then the **value** is set to a negative number and is not included in calculating the overall contribution. If any of the values reach 4, then four consecutive symbols have been found, indicating a win. The function will return a negative value for the computers turn and a positive number otherwise.

Note that **determine_value()** returns a special value when a winning configuration has been achieved using a given location. That function can be used, therefore, to determine if there exists a winning configuration anywhere on the board. **Have_winner()** provides the interface for that purpose.

7.7.6   The User Interface

The program driver performs board initialization and prompts the user for the desired depth of the tree. Then a loop is entered in which the board is displayed, the user's move is applied, and the computer's move is calculated.

```
main()
{
```

```
        /*
         *  A simple four-in-a-row game.
         */
        tree T;
        state currentstate, *p_nextstate;
        int depth;

        initialize_board(BOARD(&currentstate));
        do {
            printf("Enter game tree depth: ");
            scanf("%d", &depth);
        } while (depth < 1) ;
        print_board(BOARD(&currentstate));

        while (get_move(BOARD(&currentstate), PLAYER) != 0) {
            print_board(BOARD(&currentstate));
            if (have_winner(BOARD(&currentstate)) == TRUE) {
                printf("You win.\n");
                exit(0);
            }
            printf("Calculating my move...\n");
            init_tree(&T);
            if (make_state_root(&T, currentstate, NULL, NULL) == ERROR) {
                printf("Memory allocation error in main().\n");
                exit(-1);
            }
            p_nextstate = make_move(&T,depth,COMPUTER,eval,less,greater);
            if (p_nextstate == NULL) {
                printf("Memory allocation error in move().\n");
                exit(-1);
            }
            printf("Board is now:\n");
            print_board(BOARD(p_nextstate));
            printf("Minimax value is %d\n", VALUE(p_nextstate));
            if (have_winner(BOARD(p_nextstate)) == TRUE) {
                printf("I win.\n");
                exit(0);
            } else if (VALUE(p_nextstate) == WIN) {
                printf("I concede.\n");
                exit(0);
            }
            copy_board(BOARD(&currentstate), BOARD(p_nextstate));
            destroy_tree(&T, free);
        }
}

int get_move(b, who)
board b;
```

```
player who;
{
    int row, col;

    while (1) {
        printf("Enter row col of your move (0 0 to quit): ");
        scanf("%d%d", &row, &col);
        if (row == 0  &&  col == 0)
            return 0;
        if (valid_move(b, row, col) == TRUE) {
            set_board(b, row, col, who);
            return 1;
        }
        printf("Invalid move.\n");
    }
}
int greater(i, j)
int i, j;
{
    return i > j;
}

int less(i, j)
int i, j;
{
    return i < j;
}
```

After the user enters his move, the program calculates whether he has just
won. If not, a new game tree is created and **make_move()** is called. An
error check is prudent here, because the number of nodes in the tree increases
exponentially with its depth.

The computer also checks to see if a winner exists after its move. If not,
it checks to see if the value of the board configuration is such that there is no
way the computer could win. If that is the case, it concedes gracefully.

7.8   Graphs

In mathematics, a graph is viewed as a set of vertices and a set of (possibly
directed) edges: $G = (V, E)$. Vertices can be referenced by their number and
edges by the vertices they connect. Vertices A and B are said to be **adjacent**
if there is an edge between them. If by traversing a set of edges vertex B can
be reached from vertex A, there is said to be a **path** between those vertices.
Recall that there need not be a path between all pairs of vertices.

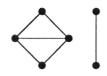

Such a graph is called *unconnected*. Note also the *cycle* containing vertices $0 - 1 - 2$. A cycle is a path containing a minimum of two vertices (for directed graphs) or three vertices (for undirected graphs) such that the last vertex is adjacent to the first.

7.8.1 Graph Primitive Operations

There are several different ways in which the abstract data type *graph* can be represented in C. Two of those methods will be discussed in detail. At this stage, however, all that need be considered is the interface to the data type. For simplicity, vertices will be integers beginning with 0 and a graph will be created by specifying the number of vertices and the type of graph: directed or undirected. It will also be assumed that there exists an **edge** type that represents a connection between two vertices. Associated with each edge out of a given vertex will be the vertex number of the adjacent vertex (given by the preprocessor macro **VERTEX(e)**) and a "cost" (greater than 0) of traversing the edge (given by the preprocessor macro **WEIGHT(e)**).

```
typedef enum { directed, undirected } graph_type;
typedef int vertex;
typedef /* implementation-specific */ edge;
typedef /* implementation-specific */ graph;
#define WEIGHT(e)   /* implementation-specific */
#define VERTEX(e)   /* implementation-specific */
#define UNUSED_WEIGHT (32767)

status init_graph(graph *p_G, int vertex_cnt, graph_type type);
void destroy_graph(graph *p_G);
status add_edge(graph G, vertex vertex1, vertex vertex2, int weight);
status delete_edge(graph G, vertex vertex1, vertex vertex2);
bool isadjacent(graph G, vertex vertex1, vertex vertex2);
void graph_size(graph G, int *p_vertex_cnt, int *p_edge_cnt);
edge *edge_iterator(graph G, vertex vertex_number, edge *p_last_return);
```

The **typedef** statements for **edge** and **graph** are not syntactically correct. They are included, however, to stress the fact that their actual definition is dependent on how the graph is implemented (as are the preprocessor macros **WEIGHT** and **VERTEX**). A discussion of **UNUSED_WEIGHT** is deferred until Section 7.10.

The primitive operations are all dependent on the implementation details of the graph data type. However, since graphs are being implemented as abstract data types, the interfaces to these routines can be defined. **Init_graph()** initializes the graph (either directed or undirected, depending upon **type**) with **vertex_cnt** vertices numbered 0 to **vertex_cnt−1**, while **destroy_graph()** recovers the space used by a graph. **Add_edge()** and **delete_edge()** are used for adding and deleting edges between two vertices (respectively). **Isadjacent()** returns **TRUE** if there is an edge connecting **vertex1** and **vertex2**. **Graph_size()** returns the number of vertices and the number of edges in a graph. Lastly, **edge_iterator()** successively returns each edge out of **vertex_number**.

It may seem as though traversing the graph should be a primitive operation, but it can in fact be developed independently of the graph implementation details.

7.9   Graph Algorithm: Traversing a Graph

As with trees, there is more than one way of traversing graphs. Two methods are depth-first traversal and breadth-first traversal. Depth-first traversal is analogous to inorder traversal for trees, and breadth-first traversal is analogous to the level traversal for trees. For example, with the graph:

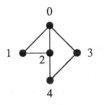

A depth-first traversal starting with vertex 0 would have vertices visited in order: 0 1 2 4 3. In a breadth-first traversal starting with the same vertex, vertices would be visited: 0 1 2 3 4.

With the tree implementations for depth-first and level traversals as examples, developing routines for traversing a graph should be quite straightforward. However, since graphs are more general than trees, some assumptions made for trees do not apply. With trees, it was guaranteed that there was a single edge into a given vertex. With graphs, that restriction is removed. To avoid "visiting" a vertex multiple times (i.e., recursion without a base case), some special bookkeeping has to be performed. It becomes necessary to maintain a record of the vertices that have been visited. Before "visiting" a vertex, it is ensured that it has not previously been visited.

```
typedef enum { DEPTH_FIRST, BREADTH_FIRST } searchorder;
status traverse_graph(G, order, p_func_f)
graph G;
searchorder order;
status (*p_func_f)();
{
    /*
     *   Traverse a graph, either breadth-first or depth-first.
     */
    status rc;
    bool *visited;
    int vertex_cnt, edge_cnt;
    int i;

    graph_size(G, &vertex_cnt, &edge_cnt);
    visited = (bool *) malloc(vertex_cnt * sizeof(bool));
    if (visited == NULL)
        return ERROR;

    for (i = 0; i < vertex_cnt; i++)
        visited[i] = FALSE;

    for (rc = OK, i = 0; i < vertex_cnt && rc == OK; i++) {
        if (visited[i] == FALSE) {
            switch (order) {
                case DEPTH_FIRST:
                    rc = depth_first_search(G, i, visited, p_func_f);
                    break;
                case BREADTH_FIRST:
                    rc = breadth_first_search(G, i, visited, p_func_f);
                    break;
            }
        }
    }
    free(visited);
    return rc;
}
```

Traverse_graph() implements the two types of graph traversals described
before. It allocates and initializes the **visited** array that maintains the record
of vertices visited. The appropriate traversal is performed via a function call.
Note that the depth-first (or breadth-first) traversal routine is called from
inside a **for** loop. Since the graph may be unconnected, it is necessary to
ensure that all vertices are visited using this loop. This is also true for directed
graphs (even if they are connected), since an edge into a vertex does not imply
an edge out of the vertex.

Depth-First Traversal

The depth-first traversal (sometimes called a depth-first search) of a graph simply loops over the edges of the vertex passed as an argument and performs a depth-first search beginning with the adjacent vertices.

```
status depth_first_search(G, vertex_number, visited, p_func_f)
graph G;
vertex vertex_number;
bool visited[];
status (*p_func_f)();
{
    /*
     *  Perform a depth—first search on G (starting with vertex_number).
     *  Call (*p_func_f)() at each vertex.  Use the visited array to
     *  keep track of the vertices that have been visited.
     */
    edge *p_edge;
    status rc;

    visited[vertex_number] = TRUE;
    if ((*p_func_f)(vertex_number) == ERROR)
        return ERROR;

    p_edge = NULL;
    while ( (p_edge = edge_iterator(G, vertex_number, p_edge)) != NULL)
        if (visited[VERTEX(p_edge)] == FALSE)
            rc = depth_first_search(G,VERTEX(p_edge),visited,p_func_f);
            if (rc == ERROR)
                return ERROR;
    return OK;
}
```

The assumption is made that the vertex passed as a parameter has not been visited. The "visitation" function **p_func_f()** is called and the vertex is marked as visited. Then the adjacent vertices are visited (provided that they have not already been visited) via a recursive call.

The implementation of **breadth_first_search()** is left as an exercise.

7.10   Graph Implementation: Adjacency Matrix

One common way to implement graphs is to use an *adjacency matrix*. An adjacency matrix **m** is a $v \times v$ array of weights (where v is the number of vertices, and the weight is the "cost" of traversing the edge). If vertex $v1$ is connected to vertex $v2$ with weight w, then $\mathbf{m}[\mathbf{v1}][\mathbf{v2}]$ will be set to w. In an undirected graph, if **m[v1][v2]** is set to w, then it follows that **m[v2][v1]** will also be set to w. In a directed graph, this will not necessarily be the case.

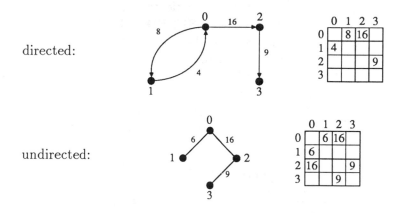

7.10.1   C Representation

Since the graph can contain an arbitrary number of vertices, the C **graph** structure must allow for dynamically allocating the matrix.

```
typedef int vertex;

typedef struct {
    int weight;
    vertex vertex_number;
} edge;
#define UNUSED_WEIGHT (32767)
#define WEIGHT(p_e) ((p_e)->weight)
#define VERTEX(p_e) ((p_e)->vertex_number)

typedef enum { directed, undirected } graph_type;

typedef struct {
    graph_type type;
    int number_of_vertices;
    edge **matrix;
} graph_header, *graph;
```

An edge is defined to contain the weight and the vertex number of the "other vertex". Since an edge can only be found from a given vertex, the "other vertex" construct supplies complete information. If it were possible to reference edges as independent entities (without first requiring a vertex), then it would be necessary to store references to both vertices. In this case, it is not needed.

Since a cell will exist in the adjacency matrix for every possible combination
of vertices, a construct is needed to indicate that there is no edge between
particular pairs of vertices. The **UNUSED_WEIGHT** value will be used
to specify a weight in the cells of the adjacency matrix where there is no
edge. In this case, it was chosen to set the value to a large number. This
places the requirement on **add_edge()** that the weight specified be less than
UNUSED_WEIGHT. Alternatively, zero could have been used for this value.

The **graph** itself is actually a pointer to a structure containing the type of
graph, the number of vertices, and the adjacency matrix.

7.10.2   Primitive Operations

Initializing a Graph

The are primarily two ways to dynamically allocate a two-dimensional array in
C: allocate a single large block and write access functions, or mimic the scheme
used when multidimensional arrays are used and use the existing array access
constructs. To use the existing array access constructs, one must allocate an
array of pointers and set each to point to a one-dimensional array.

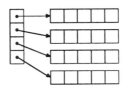

```
status init_graph(p_G, vertex_cnt, type)
graph *p_G;
int vertex_cnt;
graph_type type;
{
    /*
     *   Initialize a graph structure.  Allocate the graph header node
     *   and the adjacency matrix.  Allocate one dimension of the matrix
     *   as vertex_cnt pointers to edges.  Then allocate the actual
     *   matrix in one big chunk, setting the rows to point to the
     *   correct offsets.
     */
    graph G;
    int i, j;

    G = (graph) malloc(sizeof(graph_header));
    if (G == NULL)
```

```
            return ERROR;

    G->number_of_vertices = vertex_cnt;
    G->type = type;

    G->matrix = (edge **) malloc(vertex_cnt * sizeof(edge *));
    if (G->matrix == NULL) {
        free(G);
        return ERROR;
    }
    G->matrix[0] = (edge *) malloc(vertex_cnt*vertex_cnt*sizeof(edge));
    if (G->matrix[0] == NULL) {
        free(G->matrix);
        free(G);
        return ERROR;
    }

    for (i = 1; i < vertex_cnt; i++)
        G->matrix[i] = G->matrix[0] + vertex_cnt * i;

    for (i = 0; i < vertex_cnt; i++) {
        for (j = 0; j < vertex_cnt; j++) {
            G->matrix[i][j].weight = UNUSED_WEIGHT;
            G->matrix[i][j].vertex_number = j;
        }
    }
    *p_G = G;
    return OK;
}
```

First, **init_graph()** allocates the graph header node and populates its fields from the passed parameters. Then the array of pointers is allocated. The **vertex_cnt** one-dimensional arrays (of size **vertex_cnt**) are allocated in a single chunk and the pointer elements of **G->matrix** are initialized. These will point to the start of subarrays every **vertex_cnt** cells.

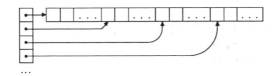

The edges are then initialized to be unused and to indicate the "other vertex." The "other vertex" number is defined to be the second index. This specifies that the vertex from which the edge will emanate is the first index and the vertex in which the edge terminates is the second index.

Destroying a Graph

To reclaim the space used by the graph, the three dynamically allocated blocks
of memory allocated in **init-graph()** are freed.

```
void destroy_graph(p_G)
graph *p_G;
{
    /*
     *   Delete an entire graph.
     */
    free((*p_G)->matrix[0]);
    free((*p_G)->matrix);
    free(*p_G);
    *p_G = NULL;
}
```

Adding an Edge

Most of the work in adding an edge is in verifying that the parameters are
valid.

```
status add_edge(G, vertex1, vertex2, weight)
graph G;
vertex vertex1, vertex2;
int weight;
{
    /*
     *   Add an edge.  If the graph is undirected, fill in both
     *   cells in the matrix.
     */
    if (vertex1 < 0 || vertex1 >= G->number_of_vertices)
        return ERROR;
    if (vertex2 < 0 || vertex2 >= G->number_of_vertices)
        return ERROR;
    if (weight <= 0 || weight >= UNUSED_WEIGHT)
        return ERROR;

    G->matrix[vertex1][vertex2].weight = weight;
    if (G->type == undirected)
        G->matrix[vertex2][vertex1].weight = weight;

    return OK;
}
```

Note that if the graph is undirected, then two cells of the matrix are set
to **weight**. Although this information is redundant for undirected graphs,

the resulting code is simplified. Techniques for removing this redundancy are
described in Section 7.13.

Deleting an Edge

To delete an edge, the weight is set to the value **UNUSED_WEIGHT**.

```
status delete_edge(G, vertex1, vertex2)
graph G;
vertex vertex1, vertex2;
{
    /*
     *   Delete an edge.  If the graph is undirected, reset
     *   both cells in the matrix.
     */
    if (vertex1 < 0 || vertex1 >= G->number_of_vertices)
        return ERROR;
    if (vertex2 < 0 || vertex2 >= G->number_of_vertices)
        return ERROR;

    G->matrix[vertex1][vertex2].weight = UNUSED_WEIGHT;
    if (G->type == undirected)
        G->matrix[vertex2][vertex1].weight = UNUSED_WEIGHT;
    return OK;
}
```

Testing for Adjacency

Two vertices are adjacent if there is an edge connecting them.

```
bool isadjacent(G, vertex1, vertex2)
graph G;
vertex vertex1, vertex2;
{
    /*
     *   Return TRUE if there is an edge from vertex1 to vertex2.
     */
    if (vertex1 < 0 || vertex1 >= G->number_of_vertices)
        return FALSE;
    if (vertex2 < 0 || vertex2 >= G->number_of_vertices)
        return FALSE;

    return (G->matrix[vertex1][vertex2].weight==UNUSED_WEIGHT)?FALSE:TRUE;
}
```

If there is an error in the parameters to this function, **FALSE** is returned. Otherwise, the weight of the edge between the specified vertices is compared to **UNUSED_WEIGHT**. If it they are equal, then there is no edge between the 2 vertices and **FALSE** is returned. Otherwise, **TRUE** is returned.

Determining Graph Size

The size of a graph is given by the number of vertices and the number of edges. This information is returned by **graph_size()**.

```
void graph_size(G, p_vertex_cnt, p_edge_cnt)
graph G;
int *p_vertex_cnt;
int *p_edge_cnt;
{
    /*
     *   Return the number of vertices in p_vertex_cnt and the number of
     *   edges in p_edge_cnt.
     */
    int i, j, edges;

    *p_vertex_cnt = G->number_of_vertices;

    edges = 0;
    for (i = 0; i < G->number_of_vertices; i++)
        for (j = 0; j < G->number_of_vertices; j++)
            if (G->matrix[i][j].weight != UNUSED_WEIGHT)
                edges++;
    if (G->type == undirected)
        edges /= 2;
    *p_edge_cnt = edges;
}
```

The number of vertices is stored in the **graph** structure. The number of edges is given by the number of cells in the adjacency matrix that are not **UNUSED_WEIGHT**. If the graph is undirected, this number is divided by two (since each edge in an undirected graph is represented by two cells in the adjacency matrix).

Edge Iterator

The iteration over the edges emanating from a given vertex is done with **edge_iterator()**.

```
edge *edge_iterator(G, vertex_number, p_last_return)
```

```
graph G;
vertex vertex_number;
edge *p_last_return;
{
    /*
     *   Return all the edges out of vertex_number in turn.
     *   To start, p_last_return should be NULL.   In subsequent
     *   calls, it should be what was returned in the previous call.
     *   When there are no more edges, NULL is returned.
     */
    vertex other_vertex;

    if (vertex_number < 0 || vertex_number >= G->number_of_vertices)
        return NULL;

    if (p_last_return == NULL)
        other_vertex = 0;
    else
        other_vertex = VERTEX(p_last_return) + 1;

    for ( ; other_vertex < G->number_of_vertices; other_vertex++)
        if (G->matrix[vertex_number][other_vertex].weight!=UNUSED_WEIGHT)
            return &G->matrix[vertex_number][other_vertex];
    return NULL;
}
```

The edge iterator is similar in function to iterators described in previous chapters. It requires that the value that was last returned by the function be passed as a parameter. To initialize the iterator, **NULL** should be passed as the "last value returned." The **for** loop in this function finds the first existing edge after the one that was last returned. This is done by searching the matrix sequentially for a value in the **vertex_number** row of the array that is not **UNUSED_WEIGHT**. A pointer to that cell (if found) is returned.

This function implicitly orders the edges leaving a vertex. However, since the concept of a graph does not imply any particular ordering, the ordering given by this function is as good as any. Moreover, no application should build a dependency on the ordering since a different implementation of the graph abstract data type is free to order the edges as is convenient.

7.11   Graph Algorithm: The Shortest-Path Problem

Outside the realm of mathematics, both the vertices and edges of a graph often have associated information. For example, graphs are often used to analyze computer networks. Vertices can represent computers, and edges (most likely undirected) can represent connections. Associated with each connection (edge) in a network is the cost of traversing that edge. Ideally, in a network, a message going from computer A to computer B will follow the least expensive path. In general, it is not more difficult to determine the shortest path between a source vertex and all other vertices than between a pair of vertices. Finding those paths is called the "single-source shortest-path" problem.

Dijkstra developed an algorithm for solving the single-source shortest-path problem that partitions the vertices into two sets: **S**, containing those to which a shortest path is already known, and **T**, containing all others. Vertices in set **T** have associated with them the distance (based on the weight associated with the edge) from a vertex in set **S**. Initially, only the source vertex is in **S**. To add a new vertex to **S**, the vertex in **T** with the smallest distance is removed. When this new vertex is added to **S**, the vertices adjacent to it become closer to a vertex in **S**, so the associated distances must be updated.

By assuming the starting vertex is vertex i, the algorithm can be stated as follows:

1. Initialize the set **S** to contain vertex i.

2. Initialize an array, **distance**, to contain infinite values, except for **distance**[i], which is set to 0. Set distance[j] (where j is a vertex adjacent to i) to the weight of the edge between the two vertices. This represents the shortest known distances to vertices in **S**.

3. Until the shortest distance to all vertices is found, do:

   3.1 Select vertex **v** such that **distance**[v] is smallest of all vertices not in **S**.

   3.2 Add **v** to **S**.

   3.3 For each vertex **w** adjacent to **v**, set **distance**[w] to the smaller of **distance**[w] and **distance**[v] + **weight**(v,w).

Since the shortest path to one vertex is found each time through the loop, the statements inside the loop will be executed $n - 1$ times, where n is the number of vertices. Statement 3.3, which updates the known distances between the two sets of vertices, ensures that the distance maintained is always the smallest possible distance. **Distance**[w] represents the distance from vertex **w** to the **known** vertices. **Distance**[v] + **weight**(v,w) represents the distance from **w** to **v** (the vertex being added to **S**). By choosing the smaller of these values, the distance from **w** to any vertex in **S** is minimized.

To be sure of the correctness of the algorithm, it must be certain that when the path to vertex **v** is determined, no shorter path can exist. To verify this, suppose that a shorter path, through vertex **w** did exist.

Were this the case, then before **v** could be picked to be added to **S**, **w** would be chosen (in step 3.1), since its distance to **S** must be smaller (i.e., distance[w] < distance[v]). Since the updating of the distances always minimizes the distance to **S**, the assumption is incorrect and hence the algorithm is valid.

To help illustrate this algorithm, consider the following graph:

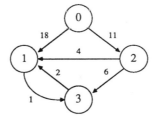

Associated with each vertex is the vertex number and the distance to **S** (which is shaded). Specifying 0 as the initial vertex yields the shortest path as follows:

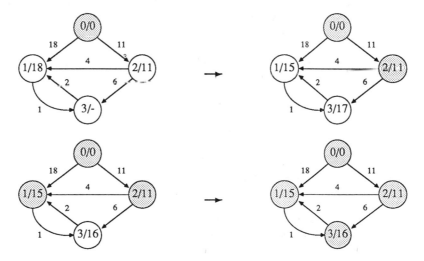

Algorithms such as this, where at each step one immediately performs what appears to be the best choice, are called *greedy* algorithms.

7.11.1   C Implementation

For the implementation of Dijkstra's Algorithm, one must consider how to represent the set of vertices to which the shortest path is known and the distance of the other vertices to that set. The set can be represented using a boolean array and the distances using an integer array (each containing one element for each vertex). The algorithm can be implemented without regard for the actual graph implementation.

```
status single_source_shortest_path(G, source_vertex, distance)
graph G;
int source_vertex;
int distance[];
{
    /*
     *   Use Dijkstra's Algorithm to find the single source-shortest path.
     */
    bool *path_found;
    edge *p_edge;
    int vertex_cnt, edge_cnt;
    int close_vertex;
    int i;

    graph_size(G, &vertex_cnt, &edge_cnt);
    path_found = (bool *) malloc(vertex_cnt * sizeof(bool));
    if (path_found == NULL)
        return ERROR;
    /*
     *   Initialize the path_found and distance arrays to include only
     *   the source_vertex.
     */
    for (i = 0; i < vertex_cnt; i++) {
        path_found[i] = FALSE;
        distance[i] = UNUSED_WEIGHT;
    }
    path_found[source_vertex] = TRUE;
    distance[source_vertex] = 0;

    /*
     *   Update the distance array to contain the weight of edges
     *   out of source_vertex
     */
    p_edge = NULL;
```

```
    while ( (p_edge = edge_iterator(G, source_vertex, p_edge)) != NULL)
        distance[VERTEX(p_edge)] = WEIGHT(p_edge);
    /*
     *  For all remaining vertices, find the one with the smallest
     *  distance and add it to path_found.
     */
    for (i = 1; i < vertex_cnt; i++) {
        close_vertex = get_closest(distance, path_found, vertex_cnt);
        if (close_vertex == -1)
            /*
             *  This should never be true.
             */
            return ERROR;
        path_found[close_vertex] = TRUE;
        adjust_distance(G, distance, path_found, close_vertex);
    }
    return OK;
}

int get_closest(distance, path_found, vertex_cnt)
int distance[];
bool path_found[];
int vertex_cnt;
{
    /*
     *  Return the index that represents the smallest distance of
     *  those with path_found[] equal to FALSE.
     */
    int closest_vertex = -1;
    int closest_distance = UNUSED_WEIGHT; /* a big number */
    int i;

    for (i = 0; i < vertex_cnt; i++) {
        if (path_found[i] == FALSE && distance[i] < closest_distance) {
            closest_vertex = i;
            closest_distance = distance[i];
        }
    }
    return closest_vertex;
}

void adjust_distance(G, distance, path_found, base_vertex)
graph G;
int distance[];
bool path_found[];
int base_vertex;
{
    /*
```

```
 *   Update the distance of the vertices adjacent to base_vertex if
 *     the new distance is less than the current distance.
 */
int new_distance;
edge *p_edge;

p_edge = NULL;
while ( (p_edge = edge_iterator(G, base_vertex, p_edge)) != NULL)
    if (path_found[VERTEX(p_edge)] == FALSE) {
        new_distance = distance[base_vertex] + WEIGHT(p_edge);
        if (new_distance < distance[VERTEX(p_edge)])
            distance[VERTEX(p_edge)] = new_distance;
    }
}
```

The size of the graph is determined via a call to the primitive operation **graph_size()**. If there is an error allocating space for the auxiliary arrays, **single_source_shortest_path()** returns ERROR. When the **distance** array is initialized, it is set to **UNUSED_WEIGHT**, which will be larger than any valid weight of an edge. The **for** loop is then executed, which, on each pass through, adds a vertex to the **path_found** set. **Get_closest()** is used to find the vertex whose **distance** is smallest and **adjust_distance()** is used to update the distance of the adjacent vertices.

7.12   Graph Implementation: Adjacency Lists

Each node in an *adjacency list* represents an edge from one vertex to another. Instead of using a single list to represent all the edges, an array of adjacency lists can be used, where *list[i]* represents the edges (and, hence, adjacent vertices) emanating from vertex *i*. Since edges have associated weights, each node in an adjacency list contains two types of information: the weight of the edge, and the number of the adjacent vertex.

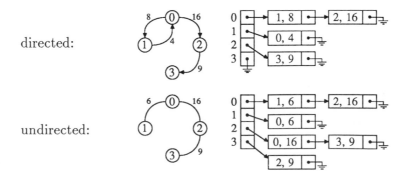

7.12.1   C Representation

Since the graph can contain an arbitrary number of vertices, the C **graph** structure must allow for dynamically allocating the array of adjacency lists.

```
typedef int vertex;
typedef node edge;

typedef struct {
    int weight;
    vertex vertex_number;
} edge_data;
#define UNUSED_WEIGHT (32767)
#define WEIGHT(p_e) ( ((edge_data *)DATA(p_e))->weight )
#define VERTEX(p_e) ( ((edge_data *)DATA(p_e))->vertex_number )

typedef enum { directed, undirected } graph_type;

typedef struct {
    graph type type;
    int number_of_vertices;
    list *edge_list;
} graph_header, *graph;
```

Since each node in an adjacency list represents an edge, **edge** is defined to be a **node** (which was defined in Chapter 4). The data stored in an edge is the weight and the vertex number of the "other vertex." As with the adjacency matrix implementation, edges can only be found from a given vertex; hence, only one vertex has to be stored.

Since adjacency lists contain nodes only where there are edges (unlike the adjacency matrix implementation), the **UNUSED_WEIGHT** construct is not explicitly needed. It is included as part of the implementation so that the interface to the graph abstract data type remains consistent.

7.12.2   Primitive Operations

The primitive operations for adjacency lists all follow the same general form: first the parameters are validated, then list primitive operations are used on the appropriate adjacency list to perform the desired graph operation.

Initializing a Graph

Initializing a graph involves allocating the array of adjacency lists and initializing the lists via calls to **init_list()**.

```
status init_graph(p_G, vertex_cnt, type)
graph *p_G;
int vertex_cnt;
graph_type type;
{
    /*
     *   Initialize a graph structure.  Allocate the graph header node
     *   and the adjacency matrix.  Allocate vertex_cnt lists and
     *   initialize the lists.
     */
    graph G;
    int i, j;

    G = (graph) malloc(sizeof(graph_header));
    if (G == NULL)
        return ERROR;

    G->number_of_vertices = vertex_cnt;
    G->type = type;

    G->edge_list = (list *) malloc(vertex_cnt * sizeof(list));
    if (G->edge_list == NULL) {
        free(G);
        return ERROR;
    }
    for (i = 0; i < vertex_cnt; i++) {
        if (init_list(&G->edge_list[i]) == ERROR) {
            free(G->edge_list);
            free(G);
            return ERROR;
        }
    }

    *p_G = G;
    return OK;
}
```

This function checks the return code from **init_list()**, and if it indicates that an error has occurred, all the space that has been allocated is freed and **ERROR** is returned.

Destroying a Graph

Reclaiming the space used by the graph is done by destroying the adjacency lists, the adjacency list array, and the **graph** structure.

```
void destroy_graph(p_G)
```

```
graph *p_G;
{
    /*
     *  Delete an entire graph by destroying the lists and then
     *  deallocating edge_list and the graph_header.
     */
    int i;

    for (i = 0; i < (*p_G)->number_of_vertices; i++)
        destroy_list(& (*p_G)->edge_list[i], free);

    free((*p_G)->edge_list);
    free(*p_G);
    *p_G = NULL;
}
```

Adding an Edge

The list interface routine **edge_append()** is used to add an edge to the appropriate adjacency list(s).

```
status add_edge(G, vertex1, vertex2, weight)
graph G;
vertex vertex1, vertex2;
int weight;
{
    /*
     *  Add an edge between vertex1 and vertex2 with weight.
     *  If the graph is undirected, place an identical edge
     *  between vertex2 and vertex1.
     */
    if (vertex1 < 0 || vertex1 >= G->number_of_vertices)
        return ERROR;
    if (vertex2 < 0 || vertex2 >= G->number_of_vertices)
        return ERROR;
    if (weight <= 0 || weight >= UNUSED_WEIGHT)
        return ERROR;

    if (edge_append(&G->edge_list[vertex1], vertex2, weight) == ERROR)
        return ERROR;
    if (G->type == undirected)
        if (edge_append(&G->edge_list[vertex2], vertex1, weight) == ERROR)
            return ERROR;

    return OK;
}
```

```
status edge_append(p_L, vertex_number, weight)
list *p_L;
vertex vertex_number;
int weight;
{
    /*
     *   Allocate and append an edge_data node to a list.
     */
    edge_data *p_edgedata = (edge_data *)malloc(sizeof(edge_data));

    if (p_edgedata == NULL)
        return ERROR;

    p_edgedata->weight = weight;
    p_edgedata->vertex_number = vertex_number;
    if (append(p_L, (generic_ptr) p_edgedata) == ERROR) {
        free(p_edgedata);
        return ERROR;
    }
    return OK;
}
```

If the graph is undirected, then nodes are appended to two lists.

Deleting an Edge

Deleting an edge requires removing a node from either one or two lists, depending on whether the graph is directed or undirected.

```
status delete_edge(G, vertex1, vertex2)
graph G;
vertex vertex1, vertex2;
{
    /*
     *   Delete the edge between vertex1 and vertex2.  If the
     *   graph is undirected, delete the edge between vertex2 and
     *   vertex1.
     */
    list L;
    edge_data e;
    status rc;

    if (vertex1 < 0 || vertex1 >= G->number_of_vertices)
        return ERROR;
    if (vertex2 < 0 || vertex2 >= G->number_of_vertices)
        return ERROR;
```

```
        e.vertex_number = vertex2;
        rc=find_key(G->edge_list[vertex1],(generic_ptr)&e,cmp_vertex,&L);
        if (rc == ERROR)
            return ERROR;
        delete_node(&G->edge_list[vertex1], L);
        if (G->type == undirected) {
            e.vertex_number = vertex1;
            rc=find_key(G->edge_list[vertex2],(generic_ptr)&e,cmp_vertex,&L);
            if (rc == ERROR)
                return ERROR;
            delete_node(&G->edge_list[vertex1], L);
        }
        return OK;
}

int cmp_vertex(p_edge1, p_edge2)
edge_data *p_edge1, *p_edge2;
{
        return p_edge1->vertex_number - p_edge2->vertex_number;
}
```

To delete a node from a list, the list primitive operations **find_key()** and **delete_node()** are used. **Find_key()** returns a pointer to a node (via a parameter) whose **DATA** field matches the key passed. To compare the **DATA**, a pointer to a comparison function must be passed. For graphs, the comparison function, **cmp_vertex()**, returns 0 when the **vertex_number** field matches. When the correct node is found, **delete_node()** is called to delete it from the list.

Testing for Adjacency

Vertex1 is adjacent to **vertex2** if there is a node in the adjacency list corresponding to **vertex1** containing **vertex2**. The list primitive operation **find_key()** is used to search the list.

```
bool isadjacent(G, vertex1, vertex2)
graph G;
vertex vertex1, vertex2;
{
        /*
         *   Return TRUE if there is an edge from vertex1 to vertex2.
         */
        list L;
        edge_data e;
        status rc;
```

```
        if (vertex1 < 0 || vertex1 >= G->number_of_vertices)
            return FALSE;
        if (vertex2 < 0 || vertex2 >= G->number_of_vertices)
            return FALSE;

        e.vertex_number = vertex2;
        rc = find_key(G->edge_list[vertex1],(generic_ptr)&e,cmp_vertex,&L);
        return (rc == OK) ? TRUE : FALSE;
}
```

Determining Graph Size

The size of a graph is given by the number of vertices and the number of edges. This information is returned by **graph_size**().

```
    void graph_size(G, p_vertex_cnt, p_edge_cnt)
    graph G;
    int *p_vertex_cnt;
    int *p_edge_cnt;
    {
        /*
         *   Return the number of vertices in p_vertex_cnt and the number of
         *   edges in p_edge_cnt.
         */
        int i, edges;

        *p_vertex_cnt = G->number_of_vertices;

        edges = 0;
        for (i = 0; i < G->number_of_vertices; i++)
            edges += length(G->edge_list[i]);

        if (G->type == undirected)
            edges /= 2;
        *p_edge_cnt = edges;
    }
```

The number of vertices is stored in the **graph** structure. The number of edges out of each vertex is given by the length of the corresponding adjacency list. To get the total number of edges, the number of edges out of each vertex is summed. If the graph is undirected, this number is divided by 2 (since each edge in an undirected graph is represented by a node on two adjacency lists).

Edge Iterator

Iterating over the edges emanating from a given vertex is done by iterating over the corresponding adjacency list.

```
edge *edge_iterator(G, vertex_number, p_last_return)
graph G;
vertex vertex_number;
edge *p_last_return;
{
    /*
     *   Return all the edges out of vertex_number in
     *   turn.  To start p_last_return should be NULL.
     *   In subsequent calls, it should be what was returned
     *   in the previous call.  When there are no more edges,
     *   NULL is returned.
     */

    if (vertex_number < 0 || vertex_number >= G->number_of_vertices)
        return NULL;

    return list_iterator(G->edge_list[vertex_number],p_last_return);
}
```

7.13   Alternate Graph Implementations

The adjacency matrix and adjacency list structures described before are not the only methods through which graphs can be represented. Several variations on those structures, as well as some different types of structures, might prove more appropriate, depending on the application and environment in which the graph programs will be used. Since graphs were implemented as an abstract data type, it should be possible to use any of the structures to be described simply by rewriting the primitive operations appropriately.

Removal of Redundant Data

If it is known that the graph is undirected, only half of the adjacency matrix contains useful information; the other half contains a duplicate of the first half. In fact, less than half of the matrix is needed because no vertex can have an edge to itself.

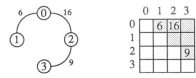

Therefore, the implementation need only allocate half as much space for the matrix. Of course, the primitive operations become slightly more complex as tests must be made to ensure that the correct half of the matrix is accessed.

Similar reasoning can be applied to the adjacency list facility to eliminate half of the nodes.

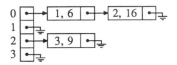

However, the logic to find all adjacent edges for the elements in the "second half" of the vertices is more difficult since only the "first half" of the vertices is explicitly stored.

List of Adjacency Lists

The adjacency list implementation used an array of lists to represent the connectivity information in the graph. A more flexible technique is to use a list of lists. In this way, lists (representing a vertex number) have to be allocated only when there is an edge out of (or in to) the vertex.

Sparse Matrices

An adjacency matrix represents all possible edges in a graph. In practice, it may be the case that only a small subset of those edges actually exists. This leaves many of the cells in the adjacency matrix unused. A sparse matrix implementation would save a considerable amount of space by not allocating space for the unused cells.

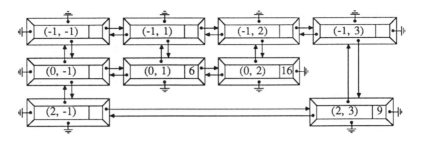

This representation is actually very similar to the "list of adjacency lists" representation. For graphs with a large number of vertices, this technique allows for access as easily as can be done with arrays with the savings in space of linked lists.

7.14 Exercises

1. Modify the expression evaluator so that it can accept an arbitrary number of variables. It should assume that anything in the expression input matching the syntax of a C variable is a variable.

2. Modify the expression evaluator to accept unary minus (represented as ~) and positive exponentiation (represented as ^).

3. (a) Write a print-tree routine that prints binary trees in a simple graphical form.

   (b) Enhance the program so that it can also print n-ary trees stored as binary trees.

4. Modify the expression evaluator to evaluate preorder expressions.

5. (a) Implement a postfix-to-prefix translator using an intermediate tree representation.

   (b) Implement a prefix-to-infix translator. Be sure to add any necessary parentheses.

6. Write a generic function to do level-order (breadth-first) traversal for binary trees.

7. Change the computation of the priority of jobs in the operating system simulation such that as jobs sit in the queue for longer times, their priority becomes higher. How does this effect overall system throughput? *Hint:* When performing priority comparisons, subtract a small value from the run time for each 15 time units the job has been in the queue without running.

8. Draw the complete game tree for tic-tac-toe (you may omit isomorphic boards). Is it possible for player one to force a win? Is it possible for player two to force a draw?

9. Approximately how large would the complete game tree be for chess? Assuming that a node can be generated in 1 nanosecond, how long would it take to generate the entire tree?

10. Which of the following games do you think would be easy for computers to play: checkers, backgammon, bridge, poker? Would it be possible to generate the complete game tree for checkers or backgammon? How can the computer effectively deal with randomness (e.g., dice in backgammon) or incomplete knowledge (e.g., not knowing the opponent's cards in poker?

11. (Difficult.) Write a program to play checkers.

12. (Very difficult.) Write a program to play backgammon.

13. (Difficult.) Write a program to play five-card draw poker. Should your program bluff?

14. **(a)** Exactly why is it more efficient to store N-ary trees as binary trees instead of data pointer/child list? Can you quantify the difference?

   (b) Imagine that trees are stored using LISP. Is it more efficient to store the tree on page 271 as (a ((b nil) (c nil) (d nil))) or (a (b nil (c nil (d nil nil))) nil)? Explain.

15. Generalize the expression evaluator to use N-ary expressions.

16. If the four-in-a-row game is run on a PC, the computer runs out of memory if the depth of the tree is greater than about 4. This is because the amount of data that is stored in each tree node is so large. Modify the program so that the data to be stored in the tree is not the entire board, but only the move required to reach that node from its parent.

Approximately how much space is saved per node? What effect does that have on the depth of the tree?

17. Modify the four-in-a-row game so that the game board can grow dynamically to any size. How does this change the game? What can you say about a forced win if the game is changed to five in a row or n in a row?

18. The code in the heuristic function for the four-in-a-row game seems rather repetitive. A looping construct with a better organized data structure (for the computation of the heuristic) would help reduce the amount of code. Rewrite that function using a more succinct structure.

19. Can you write a better heuristic for the four-in-a-row game?

20. Can you use the game tree method to "solve" the four-in-a-row game?

21. Remove the constraint that play is limited to the bottom or squares on top of others. How does this affect the nature of the game tree and the computer's ability to play?

22. Modify the four-in-a-row game to omit explicit storage of the game tree, but rather to propagate minimax values through the "tree" or recursive calls. Does this speed up the program?

23. If you are using a PC without virtual memory, modify the four-in-a-row game so that if the computer runs out of memory, it makes the best decision it can based on the number of boards it was able to allocate.

24. Modify the game so that the user specifies how many boards the computer should consider, not the depth of the tree.

25. Alpha-beta pruning can be used to cut down on the size of a game tree. The idea is that once one child of a node has been evaluated, it is often possible to make determinations about other children based on the value of a single grandchild. For example, in the case shown below, we know the node at level 2 will be at least 3, and the ? node at level 1 will be at most 2. Therefore, the chosen line of play will not be in the second branch, and it is unnecessary to evaluate the ? nodes at level 0. Modify the game program to use this strategy. Does this speed up play?

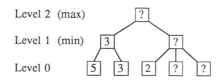

26. In the game just implemented, the computer does not necessarily immediately seize on a win. If two paths lead to a win, they both have the same minimax value regardless of their lengths. Modify the program so that the computer forces a win as quickly as possible whenever it can.

27. Modify the game so that, in addition to the minimax value, the predicted path of moves in the game tree leading to the leaf whose value was propagated is printed.

28. Implement the graph function **breadth_first_search()**, which visits the vertices of a graph as described in Section 7.9.

29. For graphs, if one were to assume that **int**s are 16-bit values and to set **UNUSED_WEIGHT** to the largest value, Dijkstra's Algorithm can be coded directly from the pseudocode (as was done in Section 7.11.1). Since that algorithm involves adding weights, it is conceivable that integer overflow can occur. Give an example showing the circumstances in which integer overflow can occur and propose a solution to this problem.

CHAPTER
EIGHT

SETS, SEARCHING, AND SORTING

There are basically two aspects of computer programming. One is data organization, or, as it is more commonly called, data structures. Thus far, this book has been about data structures and the techniques and algorithms used to access them. The other part of computer programming involves choosing the appropriate algorithm to solve the problem. Data structures and algorithms are inseparably linked. Once one has developed a firm base in the programming techniques required to represent information, it is logical to proceed to a more theoretical study of ways to manipulate it. This chapter introduces this important aspect of problem solving.

8.1   Formal Analysis of Algorithmic Complexity

An algorithm is a sequence of steps whose purpose is to solve a problem. Since there is usually more than one way to solve a problem, it is typical to find that several different algorithms can be used. The choice of which algorithm to use depends on many things. The three most important criteria for judging an algorithm are performance requirements, memory requirements, and programming requirements. Since programming requirements are difficult to analyze precisely, complexity theory concentrates on performance and memory requirements. Specifically, it is used to help determine how the resource requirements of an algorithm grow in relation to the size of the data set being manipulated. Performance requirements are usually more critical than memory requirements; hence, in general, it is not necessary to worry about memory requirements unless they grow faster than performance requirements. In this chapter, algorithms are analyzed only on the basis of performance requirements (run-time efficiency).

Based on an algorithm written in pseudocode, it is impossible to determine the exact resource requirements of a real implementation. This is because certain variable factors such as the language and hardware being used are unknown. Although this may seem to imply that it is better to specify an algorithm in a high-level language and perform actual measurements, that is incorrect. If a specific implementation of the algorithm is studied, general conclusions about the the algorithm may be invalid. Hence, *algorithms* should be compared at the pseudocode stage.

8.1.1   O-Notation

O notation (pronounced *big Oh*) is a categorization scheme that allows measuring such properties as performance requirements or memory requirements in a general fashion. The algorithmic complexity can be determined without implementation-dependent factors based on the size of the input n.[1] This is done by eliminating constant factors in the analysis of the algorithm. It is these constant values that differ between implementations.

Specifically, a function $g(n)$ is $O(f(n))$ if there exist positive constants c and i, such that $g(n) < c \times f(n)$ for all values of $n > i$. That is, for all sufficiently large amounts of input data $(n > i)$, $g(n)$ will grow no more than a constant factor faster than $f(n)$. A function that is $O(f(n))$ is often referred to as being "order f(n)." Some examples help clarify this point:

$g(n)$	$O(f(n))$
20	$O(1)$
$\frac{1}{2}n^2 + 3$	$O(n^2)$
$500n^2 - 17$	$O(n^2)$
$n^3 + n^2 - 1$	$O(n^3)$

Note that the exact constant values do not matter and that the relationship $g(n) < c \times f(n)$ may not hold for some small input sizes. Since the purpose of

---

[1]For the remainder of this chapter, the size of the input will always be assumed to be n.

O notation is to compare algorithms in a general fashion, the anomalies that appear for small input sizes are ignored.

8.1.2 Classes of Algorithms

Important classes of algorithms are those that require constant time ($O(1)$), logarithmic time ($O(\log n)$), linear time ($O(n)$), polynomial time ($O(n^k)$ for fixed $k > 1$), and exponential time ($O(k^n)$ for fixed $k > 1$). Many algorithms are $O(n \log(n))$, which is nearly as fast as $O(n)$.

Algorithms that run in constant time will solve the problem in the same amount of time without regard to input size. For polynomial algorithms, resource requirements grow faster than data size, but the relative proportion remains fixed. For example, if an algorithm is n^2, increasing the data size 10 percent will always incur a 21 percent increase in resources. Exponential algorithms such as $O(k^n)$, $O(n^n)$, and $O(n!)$ are, in many cases, all but worthless. Increases in data size require ever larger increases in resources, thus making the algorithm impractical regardless of any possible technological advance.

8.1.3 Limitations of O-notation

O notation has two basic limitations: it contains no consideration of programming effort, and it masks potentially important constants. As an example of the latter limitation, imagine two algorithms, one using $500,000n^2$ time and the other n^3 time. The first algorithm is $O(n^2)$, which implies that it will take less time than the other algorithm, which is $O(n^3)$. However, the second algorithm will run faster for data sets with less than 500,000 elements, and thus probably would be faster for many real applications.

With these factors in mind, these techniques of algorithmic analysis will be applied to the discussion to follow.

8.2 Sets and Searching

A set is an abstract data type that maintains a collection of objects. Each object within a set is unique. That is, it is not possible for a set of integers to hold four copies of the number 2. Unlike lists, there is a finite set of operations that can be performed on sets. The most basic of these operations are item insertion, test for membership and item deletion. Based on these operations, new operations can be developed to perform more powerful set manipulations, such as set intersection and set union. Furthermore, if the "universe" of objects to be included in the set is known, a set complement function can be developed.

The reader has already been exposed to sets in this book. Section 4.3 described a program in which two polynomials were to be added. The algorithm used for adding the polynomials was to traverse one list of terms and see if the other list contained a term with the same degree. If it did, then that item was deleted from the list. Although certain generalities that were made (in particular, multiple terms with the same degree could be added to the list) prohibit calling the list a true set, it is clear that the list was indeed an implementation of a set.

In this section, some general implementations of sets will considered. Only the more common set operators, *init_set*, *set_insert*, and *member*, will be implemented, with the other operators, *set_delete*, *set_union*, and *set_intersection*, left as exercises. The specifications of the first three primitive operations are

```
status init_set(set *p_S, int size);
status set_insert(set *p_S, int element);
bool set_member(set *p_S, int element);
```

Init_set() creates a set containing **size** elements. The set is initially set to empty. **Set_insert()** inserts an item into the set. If the item is not in the universe of allowed values, an error is returned. **Set_member()** returns **TRUE** if the specified item is in the set. **FALSE** is returned if the item is not in the set (or the universe of allowed values).

8.2.1   Bit-Vector Representation

Up to this point, great effort has been made to develop abstract data types that are independent of the type of data that they maintain. Sometimes, however, the data to be represented can easily be mapped to a small set of integer values. If this is feasible, then it is convenient to represent it with a boolean array, or "bit vector." In a bit-vector, if element i is present in the set, **set**[i] is set to **TRUE**. In a bit vector representation, insertion, deletion, and membership can be performed in constant time. Intersection and union can be performed in time linearly proportional to the universe of the set. When practical, this is the most convenient, and efficient, method to use.

C Implementation of Bit Vectors

One method of representing bit vectors is to simply use an array of integers and use the integer passed as an index into the array. Certainly, every programmer should be able to implement sets in that fashion with minimal effort. Consider, however, how much memory would be wasted if a set containing 10,000 items were needed.

Assuming that integers are made up of 16 bits (this is *not* a safe assumption from an implementation point of view, but it is good enough for analysis), then 10,000 times 16 bits are needed. When an integer is added to the set, the corresponding array element is set to 1. This changes 1onebit. Fifteen bits in each integer are not used. Thus, this method of implementation wastes 150,000 bits, which is not inconsequential when working on a computer with a small amount of memory.

A better implementation would be to use as many bits as possible in each array element. This can be done with bit operators in C. The first step is to allocate as many bits as are needed to contain the entire "universe" of values. C, however, does not allocate bits; it allocates bytes. How many bits are in a byte? In fact, this information can vary between computers. A safe assumption is that there are eight bits are in a byte and that a **char** variable is a single byte. Therefore, a C definition of a set contains two fields: the size of the universe of values, and a pointer to the sequence of bits.

```
#define BYTESIZE 8

typedef char byte;

typedef struct {
    int setsize;
    byte *bytestream;
} set;
```

Function **init_set()** determines the number of bytes that have to be allocated, and then initializes the set to be empty.

```
status init_set(p_S, size)
set *p_S;
int size;
{
    /*
     *   Initialize a set containing size elements to be empty.
     *   This set implementation uses a bit vector.
     */
    int numbytes, i;

    numbytes = (size + BYTESIZE - 1) / BYTESIZE;
    p_S->bytestream = (char *) malloc(numbytes);
    if (p_S->bytestream == NULL)
        return ERROR;
```

```
        p_S->setsize = numbytes * BYTESIZE;
        for (i = 0; i < p_S->setsize; i++)
            p_S->bytestream[i] = 0;
        return OK;
    }
```

The **for** loop that initializes the bytes that were allocated to 0 takes advantage of pointer arithmetic and the fact that bytes are just characters. Since the member **bytestream** is a pointer to a character, setting **bytestream[i]** to **0** will reset the values of all the bits of the character at once. This may seem implementation-dependent, but it is not. The only implementation-dependent aspect of this routine is encapsulated in **BYTESIZE**.

When an item is inserted into the set, the appropriate bit should be set to 1. This is done by finding the bit within the byte that corresponds to the item being inserted.

```
    static byte bit[BYTESIZE] = { 0x01, 0x02, 0x04, 0x08,
                                  0x10, 0x20, 0x40, 0x80 };

    status set_insert(p_S, element)
    set *p_S;
    int element;
    {
        /*
         *  Set the bit corresponding to element.  This indicates
         *  that element is a member of the set.
         */
        if (element < 0 || element >= p_S->setsize)
            return ERROR;
        p_S->bytestream[element / BYTESIZE ] |= bit[element % BYTESIZE];
    }
```

Dividing the element number by the number of bits in a byte (using integer division) yields the correct byte. By using modulo arithmetic, the correct bit within the byte is obtained. The array **bit** contains values with the corresponding bit set. That is, all bits are 0 except for bit 0 in **bit[0]**, bit 1 in **bit[1]**, etc. By performing a bit-wise "or" with a value containing a 1 in the appropriate bit, the bit within the set that corresponds to **element** will be set to 1.

The test for membership uses the same sort of operation:

```
    bool set_member(p_S, element)
    set *p_S;
    int element;
```

```
{
    /*
     *   Return TRUE if element is a member of the set.
     */
    if (element < 0 || element >= p_S->setsize)
        return FALSE;
    return (p_S->bytestream[element/BYTESIZE ] & bit[element%BYTESIZE])
            ? TRUE : FALSE;
}
```

Note how simple these functions are. They perform a very simple operation made somewhat more complex due to the packing of bytes. This represents a trade-off between space and ease of programming. Since the programming is only slightly more complex and yet yields a considerable savings in space, it is worth pursuing. However, even with using all the bits within each byte, the bit-vector method can be wasteful. Since space must be allocated for the entire universe of values regardless of how many values are actually stored at any given time, it is quite possible that much of the space will be wasted anyway.

8.2.2 Sequential Set Representation

Another way to maintain sets is to use a sequential representation. Either an array or a linked list can be used to represent a set. Since arrays can grow dynamically, as was shown in Section 5.5, they are perhaps the ideal structure to use. There are two reasons for not using arrays: there will not be enough contiguous memory to allocate the array, and deletion of elements will leave holes. The second reason is not valid. Since the sets that are being represented here are not ordered, the hole can be filled in $O(1)$ time by using the last element of the array (finding the item to be deleted is an $O(n)$ operation anyway).

Both representations allow set insertion in constant time[2] and membership/deletion in time $O(n)$, where n is the number of elements in the set. Set elements do not have to be premapped to integers with either representation, so the set routines will be redesigned to work with data of type **generic_ptr**.

The use of linked lists for sets should be fairly obvious, and is left as an exercise. The use of an array to manage the set is very similar to the use of dynamic arrays for stacks described in Section 5.5. An implementation is described here that is based on the work done in that section.

---

[2]This is based on the assumption that if an item is already in the set, it will not be inserted again (i.e., this is a multiset).

There are three items of "bookkeeping" information needed for dynamic arrays: the base of the array, the size of the array, and the first element that is available for use. This information is what defines a set:

```
typedef struct {
    generic_ptr *base;
    generic_ptr *free;
    int universe_size;
} set;
```

```
#define MINIMUM_INCREMENT 100
```

When initializing the set, a suggested size for the set is given, although it is not necessary with this representation.

```
#define MAX(a,b)    (((a) > (b)) ? (a) : (b))

status init_set(p_S, size)
set *p_S;
int size;
{
    /*
     *  Initialize a set of size elements.   This set implementation
     *  uses a dynamic array.
     */
    p_S->universe_size = MAX(size, MINIMUM_INCREMENT);
    p_S->base = (generic_ptr *) malloc(p_S->universe_size *
                        sizeof(generic_ptr));
    if (p_S->base == NULL)
        return ERROR;
    p_S->free = p_S->base;
    return OK;
}
```

Init_set() allocates space for the set, but only uses the size that is passed as an argument as a suggestion. It will always allocate a minimum of **MINIMUM_INCREMENT** elements so as to try to avoid excessive calls for allocating (and reallocating) space. This minimum value is not as important in the initial allocation as it is when new items are inserted, which increase the size of the existing universe of values.

```
#define member_count(p_S) ((p_S)->free - (p_S)->base)

status set_insert(p_S, element)
set *p_S;
```

```
    generic_ptr element;
    {
        /*
         *  Insert element into the set.  The dynamic array should
         *  grow if needed.
         */
        if (p_S->universe_size == member_count(p_S)) {
            generic_ptr *newset = (generic_ptr *) realloc(p_S->base,
                (p_S->universe_size+MINIMUM_INCREMENT)*sizeof(generic_ptr *));
            if (newset == NULL)
                return ERROR;
            p_S->base = newset;
            p_S->free = p_S->base + p_S->universe_size;
            p_S->universe_size += MINIMUM_INCREMENT;
        }
        *p_S->free = element;
        p_S->free++;
        return OK;
    }
```

The type of element expected by **set_insert()** has been changed to reflect the added power this set representation brings. If the element being added will increase the size of the universe of values to be greater than was initially allocated, **set_insert()** uses **realloc()** to allocate more space and copy the existing values into the newly allocated space. When the statement after the **if** statement is reached, there will always be enough space in the array to hold at least one more item. Therefore, the new item is added at the first free position, and **p_S->free** is incremented to point to the next available position in the array.

It is important to understand the implication of implementing sequential sets in this manner. Although using dynamic arrays greatly increases the generality of sets, it does have an impact on the actual run time. If one goes under the assumption that the initial guess at the size of the array is always correct, then the insertion operation will be performed in linear time. However, if it becomes necessary to reallocate the array and copy the values, determining the run time is not as simple; after every 100 $O(1)$-time insertions (assuming no deletions), the implementation may perform an insertion in $O(n)$ time. The ramification of this is that an implementation can have an impact on the actual run time of the algorithm.

Regardless of the issues in set insertion, determining membership is always an $O(n)$ operation.

```
    bool set_member(p_S, element, p_cmp_f)
    set *p_S;
```

```
generic_ptr element;
int (*p_cmp_f)();
{
    /*
     *   Determine if element is in the set (using the passed comparison
     *   function p_cmp_f()).  Search the set sequentially.
     */
    generic_ptr *item;

    for (item = p_S->base; item < p_S->free; item++) {
        if ((*p_cmp_f)(*item, element) == 0)
            return TRUE;
    }
    return FALSE;
}
```

8.2.3 Binary Structures

Choosing an appropriate implementation for sets depends on the type of data
to be stored in the set and the type of operations that will be used predom-
inantly. If the set is to contain a finite number of integers, the bit-vector
representation is ideal — insertion, deletion, and test for membership can all
be done in $O(1)$ time. The flexibility of using the sequential structures allows
for insertion in $O(1)$ time, but deletion and membership tests are performed
in $O(n)$ time.

   If there will be significantly more membership tests than insertions, it is
desirable to reduce the amount of time required by that operation (perhaps
at the expense of the other operations). By ordering the items within the set,
this can be accomplished.

Sorted Arrays

If, for the most part, the data being stored in the set will not change much,
the efficiency of membership tests can be increased by using a sorted array.
To insert new items into the set, a comparison function must be used that will
indicate an ordering between two elements. If the set is sorted in ascending
order, then items are shifted up until the correct location is found for the new
element:

```
set setindex to the index of the last element in the set
    or to -1 if the set is empty
loop:
    if setindex < 0
```

```
        exit loop
    if (newelement < set[setindex])
        set[setindex+1] = set[setindex]
    else
        exit loop
    decrement setindex
endloop
set[setindex+1] = newelement
```

The control loop of this algorithm will cause items to be shifted up in the array, until the base of the array has been reached, or until the element in the array is less than the new item. When the loop is exited, the new element is placed after the last item against which it was compared. Since the potential exists for this loop to be executed n times, this is an $O(n)$ algorithm.

The C implementation of this algorithm looks slightly different only because pointers to the array elements were used as opposed to indices:

```c
#define member_count(p_S) ((p_S)->free - (p_S)->base)

status set_insert(p_S, newelement, p_cmp_f)
set *p_S;
generic_ptr newelement;
int (*p_cmp_f)();
{
    /*
     *  Insert the item in the set, but keep the set sorted.  This
     *  is done by starting at the end of the array and shifting
     *  elements up until the correct place is found for the new
     *  element.
     */
    generic_ptr *element;

    if (p_S->universe_size == member_count(p_S)) {
        generic_ptr *newset = (generic_ptr *) realloc(p_S->base,
            (p_S->universe_size+MINIMUM_INCREMENT)*sizeof(generic_ptr *));
        if (newset == NULL)
            return ERROR;
        p_S->base = newset;
        p_S->free = p_S->base + p_S->universe_size;
        p_S->universe_size += MINIMUM_INCREMENT;
    }
    for (element = p_S->free - 1; element >= p_S->base; element--)
        if ((*p_cmp_f)(newelement, *element) < 0)
            *(element + 1) = *element;
        else
```

```
        break;
    *(element + 1) = newelement;
    p_S->free++;
    return OK;
}
```

The **for** loop sets **element** to point to the last element of the set (note that the set member **free** always points to the next *available* position). As long as the element falls within the array, the comparison function is called. If the function returns a value less than 0, **newelement** is less than the current element, so the current element is shifted up in the array. **Element** is decremented in the loop expression. When the loop is exited, **element** points to the position 1 less than where the new element belongs, so the new element is copied into **element+1**. For example, inserting 8 into the set containing (1, 5, 16) uses the following sequence of operations:

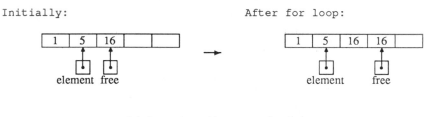

```
*(element + 1) = newelement;
p_S->free++;
```

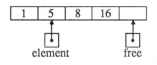

Since the array is now sorted, a binary search can be used to locate an element within the array. The binary search can be implemented using a tail recursive algorithm, with the ends of the sorted array (i.e., the upper and lower indices) and a search key as parameters.

```
if upper < lower
    return -1
if x equals the middle element
    return the index of the middle element
if x > the middle element
    return Search(upper half of the array)
else
    return Search(lower half of the array)
```

The first condition determines if the array is empty. If it is empty, the element cannot be found, so -1 is returned. Otherwise, the algorithm determines which half of the array will contain x by comparing it to the middle element. If x is greater than the middle element, and it is in the array, it will be found in the upper half. If x is less than the middle element, and it is in the array, it will be found in the lower half. Note that the special case of x matching the middle element must explicitly be considered.

In analyzing the amount of time required by this algorithm, the following observations are made: the conditions ("if's") are all $O(1)$ operations, and all the work is done in the recursive calls. Since each recursive call searches an array half the size of the original, the following calculation is made:

$$T(n) = c + T(n/2)$$

That is, the time of the algorithm for input of size n is equal to some constant number and the amount of time required by the algorithm for input of size $n/2$. The closed form for this formula is $\log(n)$. Therefore, the binary search algorithm finds a solution in $O(\log(n))$ time.

The C implementation of this algorithm eliminates the tail recursion with the observation that at an given time, only one section of the array is actually a candidate for containing the new element. By setting the upper and lower indices appropriately, the tail recursion can be eliminated in favor of a loop.

```c
bool set_member(p_S, element, p_cmp_f)
set *p_S;
generic_ptr element;
int (*p_cmp_f)();
{
    /*
     *  Determine whether element is in the set using a binary search.
     */
    generic_ptr *p_upper, *p_lower, *p_middle;
    int cmp;

    p_upper = p_S->free - 1;
    p_lower = p_S->base;
    while (p_upper >= p_lower) {
        p_middle = p_lower + (p_upper - p_lower) / 2;
        cmp = (*p_cmp_f)(element, *p_middle);
        if (cmp == 0)
            return TRUE;
        else if (cmp > 0)
            p_lower = p_middle + 1;
        else
            p_upper = p_middle - 1;
```

```
    }
    return FALSE;
}
```

In the following example, the shaded section of the array represents the elements being searched as the element with value 34 is located.

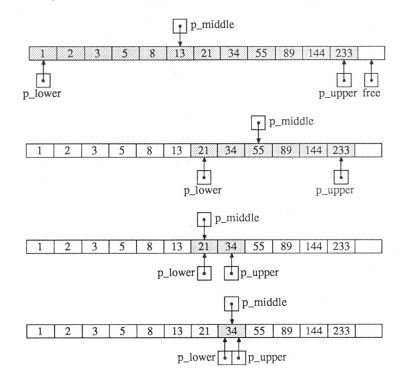

Binary Search Trees

If the data within the set is not static, then the $O(n)$ insertion and deletion algorithms may begin to have a strong impact on the run time of the array set implementation. An alternative is to use a binary search tree where the first element inserted is placed at the root of the tree, and as new items are inserted, their position in the tree depends on their relative value to the root. Smaller elements are placed in the left subtree, and larger elements are placed in the right subtree. If the left (or right) subtree already contains data, then the correct position is found by recursively invoking the insertion procedure.

```
let pS be the root of the tree
if pS is an empty tree
```

```
    make the new element the root of the tree
else if value(new element) < value(pS)
    insert into the subtree, LEFT(pS)
else
    insert into the subtree, RIGHT(pS)
```

The insertion algorithm traverses the left and right pointers of the tree and will insert the new element as a leaf. If the values of inserted elements arrive in random order, the average tree will be balanced. The depth of a balanced binary tree is $\log(n)$; hence, the insertion algorithm is a $O(\log(n))$ algorithm. However, if the values of inserted elements do not arrive in random order, the tree will be imbalanced. At worst, the elements will arrive in sorted order and the tree will be a linear chain. In this case, the insertion algorithm degrades to $O(n)$.[3]

The implementation of **set_insert()** using binary search trees builds on the foundations laid in Chapter 7.

```
typedef tree set;

init_set(p_S)
set *p_S;
{
    init_tree(p_S);
}

status set_insert(p_S, element, p_cmp_f)
set *p_S;
generic_ptr element;
int (*p_cmp_f)();
{
    /*
     *   Insert element into the binary search tree.  All elements
     *   to the left of a root are smaller.  All elements to the
     *   right of a root are bigger.
     */
    tree T;
    int cmp;

    if (empty_tree(*p_S) == TRUE) {
        make_tree(&T, element, NULL, NULL);
        if (T == NULL)
```

---

[3]It is often desirable to expend some additional effort of constant order ($O(1)$) to preserve the balance of the tree. Two popular methods of doing this are AVL trees and 2-3 trees.

```
            return ERROR;
        *p_S = T;
        return OK;
    } else {
        cmp = ((*p_cmp_f)(element, DATA(*p_S)));
        if (cmp < 0)
            return set_insert(&LEFT(*p_S), element, p_cmp_f);
        else if (p_cmp_result > 0)
            return set_insert(&RIGHT(*p_S), element, p_cmp_f);
        else
            return OK;
    }
}
```

With the tree:

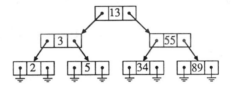

inserting 20 will cause recursive calls to **set_insert()** with ***p_S** referencing nodes containing 13, 55, and 34. The new element will be inserted as the left child of the node containing 34.

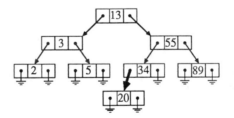

The algorithm for determining whether an element is in the set is actually very similar to the algorithm used with sorted arrays. In both algorithms, half of the elements are eliminated with each comparison. With the tree implementation, however, the elements are eliminated by traversing either the left or right subtrees.

```
bool set_member(p_S, element, p_cmp_f)
set *p_S;
generic_ptr element;
int (*p_cmp_f)();
{
```

```
        /*
         *   Return TRUE if element is in the binary search tree.
         */
        int cmp;

        if (empty_tree(*p_S) == TRUE)
            return FALSE;

        cmp = (*p_cmp_f)(element, DATA(*p_S));
        if (cmp == 0)
            return TRUE;
        else if (cmp < 0)
            return set_member(&LEFT(*p_S), element, p_cmp_f);
        else
            return set_member(&RIGHT(*p_S), element, p_cmp_f);
    }
```

Unlike the sorted array approach to sets, however, careful thought must be given to how an item is deleted. If it is deleted from the middle of an array, the only option is to shift all the elements above it down one position to fill the hole. Consider, however, what must be done if an element is deleted from the middle of the tree. In this case, the various subtrees must be combined so as to maintain the sorted nature of the tree.

The following algorithm gives the steps required to merge the subtrees of the deleted node. It is assumed that the node to be deleted has already been found.

```
if there is no left subtree
    return the right subtree
otherwise
    find the rightmost node in the left subtree
    make the right subtree the right child of the node found
    return the left subtree
```

The implementation of this algorithm is slightly more complex, since it must find the node to be deleted such that the parent of that node is correctly modified to reference the new subtree.

```
    status set_delete(p_S, key, p_cmp_f, p_match)
    set *p_S;
    generic_ptr key;
    int (*p_cmp_f)();
    generic_ptr *p_match;
```

```
{
    /*
     *   Delete an element from a binary search tree.
     *   If deleting an interior node, make the rightmost node
     *   in the left subtree the root of the right subtree.
     */
    tree left, right;
    int cmp;

    if (empty_tree(*p_S) == TRUE)
        return ERROR;

    cmp = (*p_cmp_f)(key, DATA(*p_S));
    if (cmp < 0)
        return set_delete(&LEFT(*p_S), key, p_cmp_f, p_match);
    else if (cmp > 0)
        return set_delete(&RIGHT(*p_S), key, p_cmp_f, p_match);

    *p_match = DATA(*p_S);
    left = LEFT(*p_S);
    right = RIGHT(*p_S);
    free_tree_node(p_S);
    if (left == NULL)
        *p_S = right;
    else {
        tree rightmost = left;
        while (RIGHT(rightmost) != NULL)
            rightmost = RIGHT(rightmost);
        RIGHT(rightmost) = right;
        *p_S = left;
    }
    return OK;
}
```

Set_delete() uses a procedure similar to set_member() to locate the element to be deleted. By using recursive calls, the set pointer, *p_S, will be set to the left or right subtree field of the parent of the node to be deleted. Hence, when the node is found, modifying the parent is accomplished by modifying *p_S.

Once the node to be deleted is found, the data value is copied into a pointer parameter and the subtrees are combined. Note that if the right subtree is **NULL**, traversing to a leaf and then setting its child pointer to the right subtree is unnecessary. The check for a **NULL** right subtree can be included and may, in practice, save a little time. However, since the deletion algorithm is $O(\log(n))$ (average case) regardless of that condition, it was not included.

The algorithm used by **set_delete()** when deleting the root node (for example) is shown in the following diagrams:

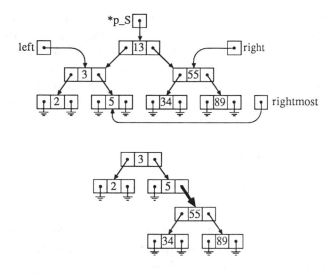

8.2.4 Hashing

A hash function maps a set of arbitrary values into a finite set of integers. Hash functions can be used to implement basic set operations that could potentially run in constant time. Developing a good hash function, however, requires some prior knowledge of the nature of the set to be represented.

Suppose it is known that approximately n members out of some universe of values will be used. An array could hold those values, except that an array is indexed by integers. Some method is needed to convert members of the universe of values to integer values from 0 to $n - 1$. The ideal method, or hash function, would be to map each of those n different members to a different integer representing an index into an array (hash table). A simple hash function for arbitrary integers may return the integer modulo the size of the hash table (n). A hash function for strings may add the integer values (ASCII) of the characters that make up the string and return that number modulo the size of the hash table.

Although techniques have been discovered that allow very good hash functions to be developed, it is very difficult to create the ideal hash function. As such, consideration must be given to how to handle multiple elements hashing to the same value. Although there are many variations, there are basically two methods to handle *collisions*: chaining and open addressing.

Chaining

Chaining is the more versatile of the two techniques. With this method, the hash table is an array of n linked lists that are initially empty. As elements are added to the set, they are placed in the linked list to whose index value they hash. Elements hashing to the same index are placed in the same list. If the hash function is well chosen, the lists should be very short and the time for the basic set operations will be nearly constant.

The implementation of this type of set representation is straightforward. The basic set representation will include the hash table and a field indicating the size of the hash table:

```
typedef struct set {
    list *hashtable;
    int tablesize;
} set;
```

No space is actually allocated for the hash table through this definition. The space will be pointed to by **HashTable**, but the space must first be allocated. The initialization routine calls for this allocation.

```
status init_set(p_S, n)
set *p_S;
int n;
{
    /*
     *   Initialize a chained hash table of size n.
     */
    int i;

    if (n < 1)
        return ERROR;

    p_S->hashtable = (list *) malloc(n * sizeof(list));
    if (p_S->hashtable == NULL)
        return ERROR;
    p_S->tablesize = n;
    for (i = 0; i < p_S->tablesize; i++)
        if (init_list(&p_S->hashtable[i]) == ERROR)
            return ERROR;
    return OK;
}
```

The size of the hash table is passed as a parameter to **init_set()**. **Malloc()** is called to allocate that many lists. If successful, the lists are initiallized to empty using the basic list function **init_list()**.

Inserting an item into a chained hash table is done by inserting the item into the appropriate list.

```
status set_insert(p_S, data, p_cmp_f, p_hash_f)
set *p_S;
generic_ptr data;
int (*p_cmp_f)();
int (*p_hash_f)();
{
    /*
     *   Insert an element into the chained hash table.
     *   Use the application−supplied hash function p_hash_f()
     *   to locate the correct list and p_cmp_f() to determine
     *   if the element is already in the list.
     */
    int hash_value = (*p_hash_f)(data);

    if (set_member(p_S, data, p_cmp_f, p_hash_f) == TRUE)
        return OK;
    if (hash_value >= p_S->tablesize)
        return ERROR;
    return insert(&p_S->hashtable[hash_value], data);
}
```

Set_insert() has four arguments: a pointer to the set, the data to insert, a comparison function, and the hash function. Set_member() is used to determine whether the element is already in the hash table. The definition of set_member() is such that invalid hash functions will cause a 0 return value, indicating that the data is not in the table. If the data is not found in the table, the hash function is called to determine which list is to be updated. If the hash function returns an invalid value, **ERROR** is returned. Otherwise, the basic list function **insert()** is called to insert the item into the appropriate list.

The membership function returns a boolean value: **FALSE** if the item is not in the set or if an error in the hash function occurs, and **TRUE** if it is in the set.

```
bool set_member(p_S, data, p_cmp_f, p_hash_f)
set *p_S;
generic_ptr data;
int (*p_cmp_f)();
int (*p_hash_f)();
{
    /*
     *   Determine whether data is in the hash table.
     *   Use the application−supplied hash function p_hash_f() to
     *   locate the correct list and p_cmp_f() to locate the
     *   element within the list.
     */
```

```
        list L;
        int hash_value = (*p_hash_f)(data);

        if (hash_value < 0 || hash_value >= p_S->tablesize)
            return FALSE;
        for (L=p_S->hashtable[hash_value]; empty_list(L)==FALSE; L=NEXT(L))
            if ((*p_cmp_f)(DATA(L), data) == 0)
                return TRUE;
        return FALSE;
    }
```

As with **set_insert()**, **set_member()** has four arguments. The hash function is called to determine which entry of the table should contain the data item. If the hash function returns an invalid value, 0 is returned, indicating that the data is not in the set. Otherwise, the appropriate list is traversed with the comparison function called at each node. If the comparison function returns 0, the data has been found in the list and **set_member()** returns **TRUE**. If the entire list is traversed and the item has not been found, it cannot possibly be in the hash table and **FALSE** is returned.

Open Addressing

In contrast to chaining, which allows for any number of members, open-address hashing limits the number of elements of the set to at most n. This is done by setting the hash table to hold the actual data as opposed to lists of data. This change limits each element of the table to hold exactly one data item. If two data items hash to the same value, the collision is resolved by "rehashing" the new data item. The rehashing algorithm can be called as many times as necessary to find a free cell.

Rehashing algorithms can be as sophisticated as hashing algorithms or they can be very simple. Ideal rehashing algorithms, if called enough times, should eventually return the index of every element in the hash table. This guarantees that all items will be placed in the hash table even if they are placed far from the original hash location.

One simple rehashing algorithm has two parameters: the location returned by the previous call, h, and the size of the hash table, n. The rehashing algorithm returns $(h+1) \bmod n$. This algorithm guarantees that every element will eventually be returned. A slightly more sophisticated algorithm searches the hash table and finds the next available location. This latter algorithm would only have to be called once, whereas the former may have to be called multiple times to find an empty cell. An implementation of open-address hashing is left as an exercise.

8.3   Sorting

Sorting is one of the most common tasks computers perform. It has been widely researched, and many different algorithms have been developed. These algorithms fall into two distinct categories: external sorting algorithms, and internal sorting algorithms. External sorting algorithms are applied to data sets that are too large to fit in memory. For example, if a 10-million-record file has to be sorted, it will not be possible to read the entire file into memory to perform the operation. Instead, the data set is analyzed in pieces with the unused portions kept on (sequential) external storage devices, such as disk drives or tapes. A feature of external sorting algorithms is that they attempt to minimize the amount of input and output, since that will be the slowest part of any implementation.

Internal sorting algorithms deal with data sets that can fit entirely within memory. Since any part of the data can be accessed directly, there is no need to restrict the algorithm to work with only one part of the data at a time, and, as such, there are many diffcrent internal sorting algorithms.

This section examines some of the more commonly used internal sorting algorithms. Each algorithm is described in pseudocode, followed by an analysis and a C implementation.

8.3.1   Selection Sort

Suppose there is an array of data to be sorted. The array can be viewed as two parts: the sorted part, and the unsorted part. Initially, the sorted part of the array contains no elements. A selection sort scans the unsorted part of the array for the smallest element and placcs it at the end of the sorted part of the array. Each time the selection process is performed, the sorted part of the array grows and the unsorted part shrinks by one element. The algorithm is applied until the unsorted part of the array contains no elements.

Algorithm

The selection sort algorithm sorts the data in place by using an index into the array to divide it into two parts. Let i be the dividing line between the two parts of the array. The algorithm will proceed by ensuring that the data in positions that are less than i is always sorted. This means that data in positions greater than or equal to i constitute the unsorted section of the array.

```
set i to 0
```

```
while i < n-1
    set CurrentMinimum to i
    set j to i+1
    while j < n
        if value(CurrentMinimum) > value(j)
            set CurrentMinimum to j
        increment j
    swap the data at i with CurrentMinimum
    increment i
```

Note that the outer loop is entered only $n - 1$ times. Each time through the loop, a new data item is placed in **array[i]**. $n - 1$ passes are needed rather than n because if the first $n - 1$ elements are in their correct positions, the final element must be as well.

Analysis

Examining the pseudocode for the selection sort, it is clear that the time-consuming portion of the algorithm must be in the inner loop. During pass i of the outer loop, $n - i$ elements must be examined to find the smallest remaining element. This requires $n - i - 1$ comparisons. To determine the complexity of the algorithm, the number of comparisons for all passes must be calculated.

$$\sum_{i=0}^{n-2}(n - i - 1)$$

This summation can be simplified by letting $j = n - i - 1$. The control variable i can be removed from the summation by substituting in 0 and $n - 2$ for i and using the corresponding value for j. This yields

$$\sum_{j=n-1}^{1} j = \sum_{j=1}^{n-1} j = \frac{n \times (n - 1)}{2}$$

Thus, selection sort is an $O(n^2)$ algorithm.

C Implementation

An implementation of this algorithm uses the **generic_ptr** data type and requires that a comparison function be passed as an argument.

```
void selection_sort(data, n, p_cmp_f)
```

```
generic_ptr data[];
int n;
int (*p_cmp_f)();
{
    /*
     *  Sort an array of generic_ptrs using the selection sort.
     */
    generic_ptr *p_minimum, *p_i, *p_j, tmp;
    generic_ptr *p_lastelement = data + n - 1;

    for (p_i = data; p_i < p_lastelement; p_i++) {
        p_minimum = p_i;
        for (p_j = p_i + 1; p_j <= p_lastelement; p_j++)
            if ((*p_cmp_f)(*p_minimum, *p_j) > 0)
                p_minimum = p_j;
        tmp = *p_i;
        *p_i = *p_minimum;
        *p_minimum = tmp;
    }
}
```

Selection_sort() makes extensive use of pointers in sorting the array. By using pointers, the extra (machine language) code generated when array references are used is avoided and, hence, the efficiency of the implementation is improved. Instead of using **i** and **j** as subscripts into the array, **p_i** and **p_j** are set to point to the corresponding elements. Similarly, instead of using $n - 1$ for the end of the array, a pointer to the last element is used (**p_lastelement**). This variable is set to the address of **data[n−1]** (given by **data + n − 1**) because the array is indexed from 0 to $n - 1$.

With the "sorted" section of the array shaded, "snapshots" (at the bottom of the outer **for** loop) show the progress of the function.

A simple driver illustrates how this function would be called to sort an array of strings.

```
main()
{
```

```
    int i;
    char *data[] = { "foo", "bar", "hello", "goodbye" };

    selection_sort(data, 4, strcmp);
    for (i = 0; i < 4; i++)
        printf("%s\n", data[i]);
}
```

Similar Sorting Techniques

Two sorting techniques exist that are quite similar to selection sorting: insertion sorting, and bubble sorting. Insertion sorting adds elements to the sorted part of the array by taking the first item in the unsorted part and inserting it in its correct position in the sorted part. This algorithm requires that the sorted part of the array be searched and the items shifted so as to make room for the new element. The start of an implementation of this algorithm was given in Section 8.2.3.

The bubble sort has a loop structure similar to the selection sort. However, rather than searching for the smallest element contained in the entire array and doing a single swap at each pass, adjacent elements are compared and swapped as necessary. By reversing the direction of the inner loop so that the end of the array is examined first, each pass through the outer loop will shift the smallest remaining element to the beginning of the subarray.

8.3.2   Mergesort

Mergesort is a sorting method that is popular for both its speed and ease of coding. The general idea behind mergesort is to divide the input in half and sort each half independently. The two halves can then merge and a single sorted array is the result.

Algorithm

When the input array is divided in half, each of the halves can be considered independently. Since each has to be sorted, the mergesort algorithm can be applied recursively. The input to this algorithm is the array to be sorted and the size of the array.

```
if the size of the array is 1 or 0
    return, the array is already sorted
divide the array into array1 and an array2
let i = n / 2 and let array1 contain i elements
```

```
mergesort(array1, i) •
mergesort(array2, n - i)
/* merge the two halves */
let buffer be a temporary buffer of size n
while there are still items in array1 and array2
    if value(array1) < value(array2)
        put value(array1) in buffer
        increment array1 index
    else
        put value(array2) in buffer
        increment array2 index
put remaining items in array1 in buffer
put remaining items in array2 in buffer
copy the buffer to array
```

Clearly, the sorting is actually performed as halves of the array are being merged.

Analysis

The merge routine steps along the elements in both halves, comparing the elements. When either list becomes empty, the other list is copied to the buffer. For n elements, this operation performs n assignments, using at most $n - 1$ comparisons, and hence is $O(n)$. The question, therefore, is how many merge operations are performed?

Mergesort divides the number of elements in half and recursively invokes itself on the smaller set. This process can be viewed as creating a tree of calls, where each level of recursion is a level in the tree:

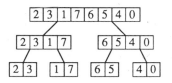

Effectively, all n elements are processed by the merge routine the same number of times as there are levels in the recursion tree. Since the number of elements is divided in half each time, the tree is a balanced binary tree. A balanced binary tree with n leaves has height $\log(n)$, hence, $\log(n)$ $O(n)$-time merges are performed. This makes the mergesort algorithm an $O(n * \log(n))$ algorithm.

The same result can be achieved more formally using the method of recursive expansion. The time it takes to perform the mergesort algorithm on n elements is equal to the time it takes to perform the algorithm on two sets of $n/2$ elements and the time it takes to merge the n elements. Calling this time $T(n)$ yields the following equation:

$$T(n) = 2 * T(n/2) + cn$$

for some constant c. Making a substitution for $T(n/2)$:

$$T(n/2) = 2 * T(n/4) + c(n/2)$$

$$T(n) = 2 * (2 * T(n/4) + c(n/2)) + cn = 4 * T(n/4) + 2cn$$

Making one more substitution (in an attempt to find a pattern) yields:

$$T(n) = 8 * T(n/8) + 3cn$$

The general equation is

$$T(n) = 2^k * T(n/2^k) + kcn$$

Letting $n = 2^k$, yields

$$T(n) = n * T(1) + \log(n) * cn$$

Since T(1) is 1, $T(n) = (1 + c * \log(n)) * n = O(n * \log(n))$.

A minor drawback of mergesort is that an external buffer of size n is required. "In-place" merging routines do exist, but they are relatively complex.

C Implementation

The routines developed thus far manipulate **generic_ptrs**. This was done to maintain data independence. Suppose, however, that a program was using an array that contained integers and that array has to be sorted. It would be inconvenient to convert that array to use **generic_ptrs**, call a sorting routine, and then convert the results back into the integer array. What is desired, in this case, is a routine that will sort an array of integers. Developing sort routines that operate only on integers violates the goal of maintaining data independence, however.

The ideal sorting implementation would take arrays of any type (including arrays of structures) and sort it correctly. This can be done by noting that there are only two places in which a sorting algorithm cares about the type of data being sorted. Obviously, performing comparisons can only be done when the type of data being compared is known. The other operation is copying elements. Due to the flexibility of the C language, these operations can be parameterized.

It has already been shown that functions can be passed for performing the comparisons. The only difficulty in developing the sorting algorithm lies then in the copying of elements. Note that no matter what an array contains, the elements are simply a sequence of bytes. To copy an element value requires copying the appropriate number of bytes. Therefore, by passing the size of the elements in the array, the array elements can be accessed, and copied, correctly. To determine the size of an element, the C **sizeof** operator can be used. If an array called **DataArray** is declared, the number of bytes in the elements of that array (regardless of the type of elements) can be determined using the expression

$$\textbf{sizeof(DataArray[0])}$$

Many, but not all, C libraries already include a routine to copy bytes from one location in memory to another. Since it is a simple routine to code, it is included here for completeness.

```
typedef char byte;
memcpy(to, from, count)
byte *to, *from;
int count;
{
    while (count-- > 0)
        *to++ = *from++;
}
```

The type **byte** is defined as before as a character, since it is of unit length.

With this auxiliary function, **mergesort()** can be developed in a data-independent fashion.

```
void mergesort(data, n, elementsize, p_cmp_f)
byte data[];
int n, elementsize;
int (*p_cmp_f)();
{
    /*
     *   Sort an array using mergesort.
     */
    byte *firsthalf;
    byte *endoffirsthalf;
```

```
    byte *secondhalf;
    byte *endofsecondhalf;
    byte *resultbuffer, *p_result;
    int halfsize;

    if (n <= 1)
        return;

    halfsize = n / 2;
    firsthalf = data;
    secondhalf = data + halfsize * elementsize;

    mergesort(firsthalf, halfsize, elementsize, p_cmp_f);
    mergesort(secondhalf, n - halfsize, elementsize, p_cmp_f);

    endoffirsthalf = secondhalf;
    endofsecondhalf = data + n * elementsize;
    resultbuffer = (byte *) malloc(n * elementsize);
    p_result = resultbuffer;

    while (firsthalf < endoffirsthalf && secondhalf < endofsecondhalf) {
        if ((*p_cmp_f)(firsthalf, secondhalf) < 0) {
            memcpy(p_result, firsthalf, elementsize);
            firsthalf += elementsize;
        } else {
            memcpy(p_result, secondhalf, elementsize);
            secondhalf += elementsize;
        }
        p_result += elementsize;
    }
    while (firsthalf < endoffirsthalf) {
        memcpy(p_result, firsthalf, elementsize);
        firsthalf += elementsize;
        p_result += elementsize;
    }
    while (secondhalf < endofsecondhalf) {
        memcpy(p_result, secondhalf, elementsize);
        secondhalf += elementsize;
        p_result += elementsize;
    }
    memcpy(data, resultbuffer, n * elementsize);
    free(resultbuffer);
}
```

Mergesort() first determines if the array passed is already sorted. By definition, an array containing 0 or 1 elements is already sorted. An array containing
more elements is assumed to be unsorted, so the middle of the array is found.

Firsthalf is set to point to the start of the first half of the array, and **second-half** is set to point to the start of the second half of the array. Note that in locating the second half of the array, the size of the elements must be explicitly included in the address calculation.

When **mergesort()** is called recursively, the number of elements in the array must be set appropriately. There will be exactly **halfsize** elements in the first half of the array. The number of elements in the second half of the array may be different if **n** is odd, so this value **n – halfsize** is calculated in the function call.

As expected, the merge step is somewhat more complicated. First, the ends of each half is located and a temporary buffer is allocated. The first **while** loop is entered when both halves of the array contain data. It compares an element in the first half with one in the second half and copies the smaller of the two elements into the temporary buffer. Then, the appropriate pointer is updated to point to the next element.

When all of the elements in either half have been copied, no more comparisons are needed. The next two **while** loops will copy the remaining elements into the temporary buffer. Of course, only one of the remaining **while** loops will be entered in any given invocation of **mergesort()**. At the bottom of the function, the data is copied out of the temporary buffer back into the data array and the buffer space is deallocated.

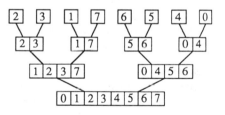

8.3.3 Quicksort

Hoare's quicksort is among the most popular sorting methods in use today. The principle is somewhat similar to mergesort: an element is chosen as a "pivot," and the array is partitioned into two parts. One part contains elements less than the pivot, and the other contains elements greater than or equal to the pivot. Each of the two parts is recursively sorted. When the recursion terminates, the array is sorted.

Algorithm

One of the major differences between this algorithm and the mergesort algorithm is that while mergesort can be viewed as "mergesort, mergesort, merge," this algorithm is "partition, quicksort, quicksort." With mergesort, the work is done in the merging, whereas with quicksort, the work is done in the partitioning.

```
select a pivot element
set left to the left end of the array
set right to the right end of the array
/* partition */
while left and right are not equal
    while value(left) < value(pivot)
        increment left
    while value(right) >= value(pivot)
        decrement right
    if (left < right)
    swap the elements at left and right
        increment left

quicksort the array from the base up to, but not including, right
quicksort the array from right to the end
```

As the array is being partitioned, the left and right pointers move in from either side. First, by searching from the left, the element whose value is greater than (or equal to) the pivot value is found. Then, by searching from the right, the element whose value is less than the pivot is found. Since these two values are in the wrong position with respect to each other, they can be swapped. This continues until the right and left pointers are equal.

When the right and left pointers become equal, all the values to the left are less than the pivot and all the values to the right are greater than or equal to the pivot. These two parts can then be sorted recursively.

Analysis

The partition process involves n comparisons with the pivot, with at most $n/2$ swaps, and, hence, is $O(n)$. The question, then, is how many partitionings are performed? If the pivot is such that the array is divided into two subarrays of the same size, then the situation is similar to mergesort. In this case, the algorithm is $O(n * \log(n))$. However, in the worst case, each partitioning will divide the array into parts of size 1 and $n - 1$. Partition would then be called n times, with array sizes ranging from 1 to n. As was shown before, this yields a run time of $O(n^2)$. Note the similarity between this degradation and that seen for imbalanced binary search trees. However, given random data, the average-case performance for quicksort is $O(n * \log(n))$. This figure is presented without proof as the derivation involves somewhat more advanced analysis techniques.

The constant factors associated with the $O(n*\log(n))$ run time of quicksort are very favorable. In order to ensure good performance over a wide range of possible inputs, it is usually wise to select the pivot with a little care. For example, worst-case performance can often be avoided by choosing the median of the first three elements as the pivot value. Note that since the partitioning process is $O(n)$, as much as $O(n)$ time could be spent selecting the pivot without changing the overall order of the algorithm. Of course, a slow pivot selection method will affect the constant factors.

C Implementation

The implementation of quicksort is not quite as straightforward as it may seem. Although the algorithm seems quite simple, two (related) special cases have been ignored. When performing the partitioning, the pivot value must not change. Therefore, either the value cannot refer to a location within the array or it must be guaranteed that the pivot value will not change locations within the array. Furthermore, after the data has been partitioned, it is quite possible that one subarray could be empty.

Suppose, for example, the data to be sorted is **8 4 5 10 5 7 4** and the pivot value is 4. If the algorithm as described before is followed blindly, then infinite recursion will occur as quicksort will be repeatedly called with arrays of size 0 and size n. The infinite recursion can be avoided by swapping the first element with the pivot element. This creates arrays of size 1 and size $n - 1$.

```
void quicksort(data, n, elementsize, p_cmp_f)
byte data[];
int n, elementsize;
int (*p_cmp_f)();
{
    /*
     *  Sort an array using Hoare's quicksort.
     */
    byte *p_left, *p_right, *p_pivot;
    int leftsize;

    if (n <= 1)
        return;

    p_left = data;
```

```
    p_right = data + (n − 1) * elementsize;

    /*
     *   Choose the pivot and move it to the right end
     */
    p_pivot = select_pivot(data, n, elementsize, p_cmp_f);
    memswap(p_pivot, p_right, elementsize);
    p_pivot = p_right;

    /*
     *   Partition.
     */
    while (p_left < p_right) {
        while ( (*p_cmp_f)(p_left, p_pivot) < 0 && p_left < p_right)
            p_left += elementsize;
        while ( (*p_cmp_f)(p_right, p_pivot) >= 0 && p_left < p_right)
            p_right −= elementsize;
        if (p_left < p_right) {
            memswap(p_left, p_right, elementsize);
            p_left += elementsize;
        }
    }
    if (p_right == data) {
        memswap(p_right, p_pivot, elementsize);
        p_right += elementsize;
    }
    leftsize = (p_right − data) / elementsize;
    quicksort(data, leftsize, elementsize, p_cmp_f);
    quicksort(p_right, n − leftsize, elementsize, p_cmp_f);
}

byte *select_pivot(data, n, elementsize, p_cmp_f)
byte data[];
int n, elementsize;
int (*p_cmp_f)();
{
    return data;
}

void memswap(s, t, count)
byte *s, *t;
int count;
{
    byte tmp;

    while (count−− > 0) {
        tmp = *s;
        *s++ = *t;
```

```
        *t++ = tmp;
    }
}
```

Quicksort() uses four local variables. **P_left** and **p_right** are used to traverse the array from either end. **P_pivot** is a pointer to the actual array element that contains the pivot value, and **leftsize** is used in the recursive calls to indicate the number of elements that are less than the pivot.

If the array contains at most one element, it is already sorted, so **quicksort()** returns. Otherwise, **p_pivot**, a pointer to the pivot element, is determined via a call to **select_pivot()**. In order to assure that the location to which **p_pivot** points always contains the pivot value, the pivot is swapped with the last element of the array and **p_pivot** is appropriately modified. Since the implementation shifts **p_right** when the value pointed to is less than *or equal to* the pivot value, it is guaranteed that this new last element of the array will not be shifted. The left and right pointers are set up, and the partitioning is performed as described in the algorithm. Note that the inner loops must also check to ensure that the left and right pointers do not cross.

At the bottom of the loop, the special case described before is considered. If the right pointer points to the left end of the array, then all the elements in the array are greater than or equal to the pivot. In this case, the actual array pivot element is swapped with this first element. Since the pivot element must be the smallest value in the array, this is its correct location. The size of this "left-hand" array is determined, and **quicksort()** is called recursively for the two subarrays.

Select_pivot() is used to return an element of the array that is to be used as a pivot. The algorithm used here is to simply return the first element. As mentioned before, this is not the only possibility.

The last function, **memswap()**, is used by **quicksort()** to swap values of the array. This function is similar in principle to **memcpy()**. Since all types of data can be referenced at the byte level, **memswap()** simply swaps the desired number of bytes.

In the following example, the elements corresponding to **p_left** and **p_right** are shaded.

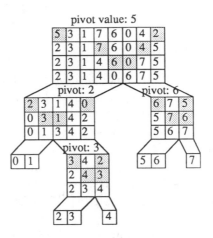

8.3.4   Heapsort

Another effective sorting technique uses the heap data structure developed in
Section 7.4. Recall that a heap is a balanced binary tree with the property
that the value of the node at the root of any subtree is less than the value
of either of its children. By reversing the sense of comparisons, an arbitrary
array can be converted into a heap, with the value at the root of any subtree
greater than its children. Although this relationship is not the desired one, the
array can be sorted by successively deleting the first item in the heap (which
will be the largest value in the array) and placing it in its correct position.

Algorithm

The algorithms presented here for inserting and deleting from a heap are the
same algorithms presented in Section 7.4. Consider the array to be in two
parts: the part that makes up the heap, and the part that is the unsorted
array. Initially, the heap is empty and the unsorted part contains all the
elements of the array. The first stage of the algorithm removes an item from
the unsorted part of the array and adds it to the heap. The heap is developed
so that the larger elements are at the top of the heap. In the second stage
of the algorithm, the array is also in two parts, but this time, a heap and a
sorted part. Items are deleted from the heap and added to the sorted part of
the array:

```
/* Stage 1 */
/* unsorted part goes from i to n */
set i to 0
```

```
loop:
    if i is equal n then exit the loop
    call procedure siftup from position i
    increment i
endloop:
/* Stage 2 */
/* the sorted part goes from sorted to n */
set sorted to n
loop:
    decrement sorted
    if sorted is equal to 0 then exit the loop
    let array[largest] equal heap[0]
    set heap[0] to heap[sorted]
    call procedure siftdown from position 0
endloop:

procedure SIFTUP from position i

set parent to (i - 1) / 2
if heap[i] > heap[parent]
    swap heap[i] and heap[parent]
    siftup from parent

procedure SIFTDOWN from position i

set leftchild to 2*i + 1
set rightchild to leftchild+1
if no children
    return
if 1 child
    if heap[i] < heap[leftchild]
        swap heap[i] and heap[leftchild]
    return
if 2 children
    if heap[i] < (heap[leftchild] or heap[rightchild])
        swap heap[i] with the largest of its children
        siftdown from (what was) the largest child
```

Note that the heap can be placed in the array, because as the heap grows, the other part of the array will shrink. Note further that when deleting elements from the heap, the last element need not be deleted. Since all the elements except for one are in their correct position, the last item must also be in the correct position.

It is beneficial to see how this algorithm manipulates an array as it is sorted. Let the array consist of eight elements ($n = 8$; the shaded cells represent the heap):

2	3	1	7	6	5	4	0
3	2	1	7	6	5	4	0
3	2	1	7	6	5	4	0
7	3	1	2	6	5	4	0
7	6	1	2	3	5	4	0
7	6	5	2	3	1	4	0
7	6	5	2	3	1	4	0
7	6	5	2	3	1	4	0

6	3	5	2	0	1	4	7
5	3	4	2	0	1	6	7
4	3	1	2	0	5	6	7
3	2	1	0	4	5	6	7
2	0	1	3	4	5	6	7
1	0	2	3	4	5	6	7
0	1	2	3	4	5	6	7

Analysis

By examining the main part of the algorithm, it can be seen that procedure siftup is executed n times and procedure siftdown is executed $n - 1$ times. Therefore, the time required by this algorithm, $T(n)$ is

$$T(n) = n * T(siftup) + (n - 1) * T(siftdown)$$

A balanced binary tree with n nodes has depth $\log(n)$. Since both the siftup and siftdown procedures traverse at most the entire tree once, the times for those procedures are $O(\log(n))$. Hence

$$T(n) = n * O(\log(n)) + (n - 1) * O(\log(n)) = O(n \log(n))$$

Like quicksort, heapsort runs in $O(n * \log(n))$ time. The advantage to heapsort, however, is that since the data is preprocessed into a heap, the worst-case running time is also $O(\log(n))$.

C Implementation

The implementation of heapsort can be developed directly from the routines given in Chapter 7. Those routines, however, use an array of **generic_ptr**'s as

opposed to an array of data items. Therefore, new routines will be developed
that operate directly on arrays containing the actual data.

```
void heapsort(data, n, elementsize, p_cmp_f)
byte data[];
int n, elementsize;
int (*p_cmp_f)();
{
    /*
     *   Sort an array using heapsort.
     */
    int i;
    int sorted;
    byte *p_sorted;

    for (i = 0; i < n; i++)
        siftup(data, i, elementsize, p_cmp_f);

    p_sorted = data + n * elementsize;
    for (sorted = n - 1; sorted != 0; sorted--) {
        p_sorted -= elementsize;
        memswap(p_sorted, data, elementsize);
        siftdown(data, sorted, elementsize, p_cmp_f);
    }
}

void siftup(data, element, elementsize, p_cmp_f)
byte data[];
int element;
int elementsize;
int (*p_cmp_f)();
{
    /*
     *   Find the correct position for data[element] by
     *   swapping it with its parent if necessary.
     */
    byte *p_parent, *p_element;
    int parent;
    int cmp_value;

    if (element == 0)
        return;

    p_element = data + element * elementsize;
    do {
        parent = (element - 1) / 2;
        p_parent = data + parent * elementsize;
        cmp_value = (*p_cmp_f)(p_element, p_parent);
```

```
            if (cmp_value > 0) {
                memswap(p_element, p_parent, elementsize);
                element = parent;
                p_element = p_parent;
            }
        } while (element != 0 && cmp_value > 0) ;
    }

void siftdown(data, n, elementsize, p_cmp_f)
byte data[];
int n;
int elementsize;
int (*p_cmp_f)();
{
    /*
     *  Find the correct position for data[0] by swapping with
     *  a child if necessary.  Continuing swapping that element
     *  with children until it is in the correct position.
     */
    int parent, leftchild, rightchild;
    int lastinterior;
    byte *p_parent, *p_left, *p_right;
    int right_cmp, left_cmp, lr_cmp;

    if (n == 1)
        return;

    lastinterior = (n / 2) - 1;
    parent = 0;
    do {
        leftchild = 2 * parent + 1;
        rightchild = leftchild + 1;
        p_parent = data + parent * elementsize;
        p_left = data + leftchild * elementsize;
        p_right = data + rightchild * elementsize;
        right_cmp = 0;
        left_cmp = (*p_cmp_f)(p_parent, p_left);
        if (rightchild >= n) {
            if (left_cmp < 0) {
                memswap(p_parent, p_left, elementsize);
                parent = leftchild;
            }
        } else {
            right_cmp = (*p_cmp_f)(p_parent, p_right);
            lr_cmp = (*p_cmp_f)(p_left, p_right);
            if (left_cmp < 0 || right_cmp < 0) {
                if (lr_cmp > 0) {
                    memswap(p_parent, p_left, elementsize);
```

```
                              parent = leftchild;
                       } else {
                           memswap(p_parent, p_right, elementsize);
                           parent = rightchild;
                       }


               }
           }
       } while (parent <= lastinterior && (left_cmp < 0 || right_cmp < 0)) ;
   }
```

As with all the sorting routines that operate on arrays of arbitrary type, **heap-sort()** has four arguments: the array, the number of elements in the array, the size of each element, and a function to perform comparisons. **Heapsort()** is very short since the work is done in **siftup()** and **siftdown()**.

In this implementation, **siftup()** has been implemented using a **do** loop. The element to be sifted up is compared with its parent, and, if necessary, the data is swapped. If no swap occurs, or the top of the heap is reached, the loop is exited. Either of these conditions indicates that the heap has been rebuilt.

Siftdown() has also been implemented using a **do** loop. It takes the first element in the data array and finds its correct position by comparing it with its children. This implementation is slightly longer than that in Section 7.4, since both the index and a pointer to the data are maintained for the parent and its children. The loop is exited when no swap is performed or when the node that is to be parent on the next pass through the loop has no children. This latter condition is checked by first determining the last possible interior node in the heap. The last interior node must be the parent of the last node in the heap. Since the last node is at position $n - 1$, the last interior node must be at position $(n/2) - 1$.

8.3.5   A Lower Bound for Comparison Sorting

The generalized sorting problem can be modeled as a decision tree. At each node in the tree is a comparison of two elements in the array. The leaves represent all of the possible permutations of the array, one of which is the sorted array. When two elements are compared, their relative order is determined (although their absolute positions are not). Each comparison thus eliminates half the possible permutations, because it enables one to distinguish those that have the compared elements in the correct relative position from those that do not. This can be viewed as proceeding down one branch of a binary search tree. For example, the minimum number of comparisons for sorting an array of three integers can be shown using the following binary search tree. The numbers

in the tree represent an index into the array. That is, when comparing **0** <
1, the values at **array[0]** and **array[1]** are being compared. The permutation
at the leaves represents the final order in which the values should be placed.
Note that the left branch indicates elements in correct relative order.

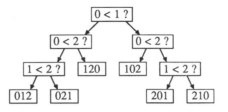

Viewed in this way, the sorting process involves pursuing a path down a
binary search tree with $n!$ leaves. Furthermore, the decision tree will always be
balanced, so the length of the path (depth of the tree) is $\log(n!)$. The problem,
then, is to find a lower bound on $\log(n!)$.

Since $n!$ is somewhat hard to analyze the first step is to find a similar
expression that is a lower bound on $n!$. $n!$ is a product of n terms, ranging
from n to 1. The $n/2$ largest terms range from n to $n/2$. Since $n!$ contains $n/2$
terms, each of which is greater than or equal to $n/2$, $n! > (n/2)^{(n/2)}$. Hence
$(n/2)^{(n/2)}$ is a lower bound on $n!$.

More formally,

$$n! = \prod_{i=1}^{n} i > \prod_{i=n/2}^{n} i > \prod_{i=n/2}^{n} n/2$$

Now the expression $\log((n/2)^{(n/2)})$ is analyzed.

$$
\begin{aligned}
\log((n/2)^{(n/2)}) &= n/2 * \log(n/2) \\
&= n/2 * (\log(n) - log(2)) \\
&= n/2 * (log(n) - 1) \\
&= (n * log(n) - n)/2 \\
&= O(n * \log(n))
\end{aligned}
$$

Therefore, there can be no general method for sorting by comparisons that
is faster than O(n*log(n)).

There are many important problems for which no such lower bounds exist.
For example, matrix multiplication has a trivial lower bound of $O(n^2)$, because
this much time is required merely to read the input. However the "true" lower
bound is an undetermined value between $O(n^2)$ and $O(n^3)$. Similarly, there

is an important set of computationally equivalent problems known as NP-complete, for which neither a polynomial algorithm nor a proof of the absence of a polynomial algorithm exists.

8.3.6 Radix Sorting

In practice, something is almost always known about the nature of the data to be sorted. This knowledge can be used to implement algorithms that are faster than traditional sorting by comparison. For example, suppose an array of n distinct elements with key values from 0 to $n - 1$ is to be sorted. The array could be traversed, with each element being copied to the cell position of an auxiliary array corresponding to the key value. This procedure can be done in place as well and clearly is $O(n)$.

To allow for multiple elements with the same value, an array of n circular linked lists could be used. Instead of simply copying data to the auxiliary array, items are inserted into the appropriate circular list. After all the elements have been placed in lists, the lists can be concatenated. While this entails more overhead than the previous procedure, it is still $O(n)$.

More generally, if the element values range from 0 to c^k, a k-pass procedure is performed using an array of c lists. On the first pass, elements are appended to the list with index **ElementValue mod c**. The lists are then concatenated and the procedure repeated. This time, however, elements are appended to the list at index **(ElementValue / c) mod c**. This procedure is followed for k passes, after which all parts of the elements will have been examined and the list will be sorted. More formally, the algorithm is

```
set pass to 0
while pass < k
    for each element in the array
        set location to (value(element) / (c^pass)) mod c
        insert the element in the list at aux[location]
    concatenate all the lists in aux
    increment pass
```

When applied to integers, c can be 10; for character strings, c can be 128. The implementation and analysis of radix sort is left as an exercise.

8.4 Exercises

1. How would you apply the selection sort function presented in the text

to sort an array of integers?

2. Implement selection sort for linked lists. What is its complexity?

3. Implement bubble sort for

   (a) arrays

   (b) linked lists

   (c) What is the time complexity of parts (a) and (b)?

4. Implement insertion sort for

   (a) arrays

   (b) linked lists

   (c) What is the time complexity of parts (a) and (b)?

5. Rewrite the polynomial addition program of Chapter 4 so that it allows you to enter the polynomial terms in any order. Which sorting technique(s) is (are) most appropriate?

6. Write bit-vector set functions for deletion, union, and intersection (C has bit-wise and operators & and &=).

7. What is the complexity of the various bit-vector set functions that access bits within bytes?

8. Write insertion, deletion, member, intersection, and union functions for sets represented as linked lists. What is the time complexity of these functions?

9. Write deletion, intersection, and union functions for sets represented as dynamically allocated arrays. What is the time complexity of these functions? Rewrite the insertion function to use **realloc()** as necessary.

10. Write insertion, deletion, member, intersection, and union functions for sets represented as sorted arrays. What is the time complexity of these functions?

11. Does the use of the variable **cmp_result** change the complexity of the set functions for binary trees? If not, is it worth using?

12. Write intersection and union functions for sets represented as binary trees. What is the time complexity of these functions?

13. Write deletion, intersection, and union functions for sets represented using open hashing. What is the time complexity of these functions?

14. Write insertion, deletion, member, intersection, and union functions for sets represented using open-address hashing. What is the time complexity of these functions?

15. Modify your open-address hashing insert routine to **realloc()** an array twice as large if the array fills.

16. How do the performance of chaining and open-address hashing compare?

17. Write quicksort for doubly-linked lists. How does its performance compare to quicksort for arrays and quicksort for singly-linked lists?

18. Why is it impractical to represent arbitrary binary trees in arrays?

19. Rate the performance of the sorting algorithms presented in the chapter on your computer for a variety of reasonably large data sets. Do the differing results reflect the nature of your computer, the way you coded the algorithm, or the algorithm itself?

20. **Mergesort()** allocates and frees a buffer for each recursive call. Analyze the function to determine approximately how many recursive calls are made and how large the buffer must be if a single buffer were allocated for all the recursive calls.

21. Compare the performance of the recursive versions of **siftup()** and **siftdown()** presented in Chapter 7 with those presented in this chapter. Which is a better implementation along this metric? Why?

22. Can you state a lower bound for searching by comparisons?

23. Would you say that hashing and radix sorting are analogous techniques? Why?

24. Implement a radix-sorting algorithm that sorts an array of n cells with values 0 to $n - 1$ in place.

25. Implement a general radix-sorting algorithm for linked lists. You should prompt the user for c and k, and dynamically allocate the array of lists. You should take input in the form of integers.

26. What is the time complexity of the generalized radix-sorting routine for integers developed in Exercise 25?

27. Write a general radix sorting algorithm for strings.

BIBLIOGRAPHY AND
SUGGESTED READING

Aho, A., J. Hopcroft, and J. Ullman, *Data Structures and Algorithms.* Reading, MA: Addison-Wesley, 1983.

Aho, A., J. Hopcroft, and J. Ullman, *The Design and Analysis of Computer Algorithms.* Reading, MA: Addison-Wesley, 1974.

Annevelink, J. and P. Dewilde, "Object-oriented Data Management Based on Abstract Data Types," *Software Practice and Experience,* 17:11 (Nov. 1987), 757-81.

Baeza-Yates, R., "Some Average Measures in M-ary Search Trees," *Information Processing Letters,* 25:6 (July 1987), 375-81.

Bastani, F. and S. Iyengar, "The Effect of Data Structures on the Logical Complexity of Programs," *Communications of the ACM,* 30:3 (Mar. 1987), 250-59.

Bender, E., C. Praeger, and N. Wormald, "Optimal Worst Case Trees," *Acta Informatica,* 24:4 (Aug. 1987), 475-89.

Bentley, J. "Programming Pearls: Thanks, Heaps," *Communications of the ACM,* 28:3 (Mar. 1985), 245-50.

Bentley, J., "Programming Pearls: How to Sort," *Communications of the ACM,* 27:4 (Apr. 1984), 287-91.

Bentley, J., *Writing Efficient Programs.* Englewood Cliffs, NJ: Prentice-Hall, 1982.

Berry, R. and B. Meekings, "A Style Analysis of C Programs," *Communications of the ACM,* 28:1 (Jan. 1985), 80-88.

Bird, R., "Improving Programs by the Introduction of Recursion," *Communications of the ACM,* 20:11 (Nov. 1977), 434-39.

Brooks, F. Jr., "No Silver Bullets," *Unix Review,* 5:11 (Nov. 1987), 39-48.

Brooks, F. Jr., *The Mythical Man-Month.* Reading, MA: Addison-Wesley, 1975.

Cardelli, L. and P. Wegner, "On Understanding Types, Data Abstraction, and Polymorphism," *ACM Computing Surveys,* 17:4 (Dec. 1985), 471-522.

Carlsson, S., "A Variant of Heapsort with Almost Optimal Number of Comparisons," *Information Processing Letters,* 24:4 (Mar. 1987), 247-50.

Chang, C. and R. Lee, "Letter-oriented minimal perfect hashing scheme," *Computer Journal,* 29:3 (June 1986), 277-81.

Chang, H., and S. Iyengar, "Efficient Algorithms to Globally Balance a Binary Search Tree," *Communications of the ACM,* 27:7 (July 1984), 695-702.

Cheriton, D., and R. Tarjan, "Finding Minimum Spanning Trees," *SIAM Journal on Computing,* 5:4 (Dec. 1976), 724-42.

Cichelli, R., "Minimal Perfect Hash Functions Made Simple," *Communications of the ACM,* 23:1 (Jan. 1980), 17-19.

Cunto, W. and J. Gascon, "Improving Time and Space Efficiency in Generalized Binary Search Trees," *Acta Informatica,* 24:5 (Sep. 1987), 583-94.

Dijkstra, E., "A Note on Two Problems in Connexion with Graphs," *Numerische Mathematik,* 1:5 (Oct. 1959), 269-71.

Dobosiewicz, W., "Optimal Binary Search Trees," *International Journal of Computer Mathematics,* 19:2 (1986), 135-51.

Earley, J., "Toward an Understanding of Data Structures," *Communications of the ACM,* 14:10 (Oct. 1971), 617-27.

Er, M., "Efficient Generation of Binary Trees from Inorder-postorder Sequences," *Information Sciences,* 40:2 (1986), 175-81.

Evans, J., "Experiments with Trees for the Storage and Retrieval of Future Events," *Information Processing Letters,* 22:5 (Apr. 1986), 237-42.

Even, S., *Graph Algorithms.* Rockville, MD: Computer Science Press, 1979.

Flajolet, P. and H. Prodinger, "Level Number Sequences for Trees," *Discrete Mathematics,* 65:2 (June 1987), 149-56.

Floyd, R., "Algorithm 97: Shortest Path," *Communications of the ACM,* 5:6 (June 1962), 345.

Foster, J. and I. Currie, "Remote Capabilities," *Computer Journal,* 30:5 (Oct. 1987), 451-57.

Frederickson, G., "Data Structures for On-line Updating of Minimum Spanning Trees, with Applications," *SIAM Journal on Computing,* 14:4 (Nov. 1985), 781-98.

Frederickson, G., "Fast Algorithms for Shortest Paths in Planar Graphs with Applications," *SIAM Journal on Computing,* 16:6 (Dec. 1987), 1004-22.

Frederickson, G., "Implicit Data Structures for Weighted Elements," *Information and Control,* 66:1-2 (July-Aug. 1985), 61-82.

Fuckick, J. and J. Kral, "Hierarchy of Program Control Structures," *Computer Journal,* 29:1 (Feb. 1986), 24-32.

Gajewska, H. and R. Tarjan, "Deques with Heap Order," *Information Processing Letters,* 22:4 (Apr. 1986), 197-200.

Gannon, J., R. Hamlet, and H. Mills, "Theory of Modules," *IEEE Transactions on Software Engineering,* SE-13:7 (July 1987), 820-29.

Gerasch, T., "An Insertion Algorithm for a Minimal Internal Path Length Binary Search Tree," *Communications of the ACM,* 31:5 (May 1988), 579-85.

Glaser, H., "Lazy Garbage Collection," *Software Practice and Experience,* 17:1 (Jan. 1987), 1-4.

Goller, N., "Hybrid Data Structure Defined by Indirection," *Computer Journal,* 28:1 (Feb. 1985), 44-53.

Gonnet, G., and J. Munro, "Heaps on Heaps," *SIAM Journal on Computing,* 15:4 (Nov. 1986), 964-71.

Gotlieb, C., and L. Gotlieb, *Data Types and Data Structures.* Englewood Cliffs, NJ: Prentice-Hall, 1978.

Harbison, S. and G. Steele, *C: A Reference Manual (2nd ed.).* Englewood Cliffs, NJ: Prentice-Hall, 1987.

Herlihy, M. "Quorum-consensus Replication Method for Abstract Data Types," *ACM Transactions on Computer Systems,* 4:1 (Feb 1986), 32-53.

Hofri, M. and A. Konheim, "Padded Lists Revisited," *SIAM Journal on Computing,* 16:6 (Nov. 1987), 135-43.

Hopcroft, J., and R. Tarjan, Efficient Algorithms for Graph Manipulation," *Communications of the ACM,* 16:6 (June 1973), 372-78.

Huang, B. and M. Langston, "Practical In-place Merging," *Communications of the ACM,* 31:3 (Mar. 1988), 348-52.

Iyengar, S. and H. Chang, "Efficient Algorithms to Create and Maintain Balanced and Threaded Binary Search Trees," *Software Practice and Experience,* 15:10 (Oct. 1985), 925-42.

Jalote P., "Synthesizing Implementations of Abstract Data Types from Axiomatic Specifications," *Software Practice and Experience,* 17:11 (Nov. 1987), 847-58.

Kempf, M., R. Bayer, and U. Guentzer, "Time Optimal Left to Right Construction of Position Trees," *Acta Informatica,* 24:4 (Aug. 1987), 461-74.

Kernighan, B., and D. Ritchie, *The C Programming Language (2nd ed.).* Englewood Cliffs, NJ: Prentice-Hall, 1988.

Kernighan, B., and R. Plauger, *Software Tools.* Reading, MA: Addison-Wesley, 1976.

Kernighan, B., and R. Plauger, *The Elements of Programming Style (2nd ed.).* New York, NY: McGraw-Hill, 1978.

Knuth, D., *The Art of Computer Programming, Volume I: Fundamental Algorithms (2nd ed.).* Reading, MA: Addison-Wesley, 1973.

Knuth, D., *The Art of Computer Programming, Volume III: Sorting and Searching.* Reading, MA: Addison-Wesley, 1973.

Kruse, R., *Data Structures and Program Design (2nd ed.).* Englewood Cliffs, NJ: Prentice-Hall, 1987.

Lamb, D., "IDL: Sharing Intermediate Representations," *ACM Transactions on Programming Languages and Systems,* 9:3 (July 1987), 297-318.

Larson, P., "Dynamic Hash Tables," *Communications of the ACM,* 31:4 (Apr. 1988), 446-57.

Ledgard, H., with J. Tauer, *C with Excellence.* Indianapolis, IN: Hayden Books, 1987.

Lodi, E., and F. Luccio, "Split Sequence Hash Search," *Information Processing Letters,* 20:3, (Apr. 1985), 131-36.

Maekinen, E., "On the Rotation Distance of Binary Trees," *Information Processing Letters,* 26:5 (Jan. 1988), 271-72.

Mannila, H., and E. Ukkonen, "A Simple Linear-time Algorithm for *in situ* Merging," *Information Processing Letters,* 18:4 (May 1984), 203-8.

Martin, J., *Data Types and Data Structures.* Englewood Cliffs, NJ: Prentice-Hall, 1986.

Merritt, S., "An Inverted Taxonomy of Sorting Algorithms," *Communications of the ACM,* 28:1 (Jan. 1985), 96-99.

Mills, H. and R. Linger, "Data Structured Programming: Program Design Without Arrays and Pointers," *IEEE Transactions on Software Engineering,* SE-12:2 (Feb. 1986), 192-97.

Ming-Hua, Z., "A Second Order Theory of Data Types," *Acta Informatica,* 25:3 (Apr. 1988), 283-304.

Moffat, A. and T. Takaoka, "An All-pairs Shortest Path Algorithm with Expected Time $O(n^2 \log n)$," *SIAM Journal on Computing,* 16:6 (Dec. 1987), 1023-31.

Morgan, C., "Data Refinement by Miracles," *Information Processing Letters,* 26:5 (Jan. 1988), 243-46.

Motzkin, D., "Meansort," *Communications of the ACM,* 26:4 (Apr. 1983), 250-51.

Nipkow, T., "Non-deterministic Data Types: Models and Implementations," *Acta Informatica,* 22:6 (Mar. 1986), 629-61.

Pagli, L., "Self-adjusting Hash Tables," *Information Processing Letters,* 21:1 (July 1985), 23-25.

Powell, M., "Strongly Typed User Interfaces in an Abtract Data Store," *Software Practice and Experience,* 17:4 (Apr. 1987), 241-66.

Prim, R., "Shortest Connection Networks and Some Generalizations," *Bell System Technical Journal,* 36 (1957), 1389-1401.

Sager, T., "A Polynomial Time Generator for Minimal Perfect Hash Functions," *Communications of the ACM,* 28:5 (May 1985), 523-32.

Sajeev, A. and J. Olszewski, "Manipulation of Data Structure Without Pointers," *Information Processing Letters,* 25:6 (July 1987), 135-43.

Sleater, D. and R. Tarjan, "Biased Search Trees," *SIAM Journal on Computing,* 14:3 (Aug. 1985), 545-68.

Sleator, D. and R. Tarjan, "Self-adjusting Heaps," *SIAM Journal on Computing,* 15:1 (Feb. 1986), 52-69.

Stout, Q. and B. Warren, "Tree Rebalancing in Optimal Time and Space," *Communications of the ACM,* 29:9 (Sep. 86), 902-8.

Strassen, V., "Gaussian Elimination is not Optimal," *Numerische Mathematik,* 13:4 (Aug. 1969), 354-56.

Stroustrup, B., *The C++ Programming Language.* Reading, MA: Addison-Wesley, 1986.

Tarjan, R., "Algorithm Design," *Communications of the ACM,* 30:3 (Mar. 1987), 204-12.

Tarjan, R., "Depth First Search and Linear Graph Algorithms," *SIAM Journal of Computing,* 1:2 (June 1972), 146-60.

Taylor, D. and J. Black, "Experimenting with Data Structures," *Software Practice and Experience,* 16:5 (May 1986), 443-56.

Tenenbaum, A. and M. Augenstein, *Data Structures Using Pascal (2nd ed.).* Englewood Cliffs, NJ: Prentice-Hall, 1986.

Tsakalidis, A., "AVL Trees for Localized Search," *Information and Control,* 67:1-3 (Oct.-Dec. 1985), 173-94.

Tucker, A., *Applied Combinatorics.* New York, NY: Wiley, 1980.

Van Tassel, D., *Program Style, Design, Efficiency, Debugging, and Testing (2nd ed.).* Englewood Cliffs, NJ: Prentice-Hall, 1978.

Vuillemin, J., "A Unifying Look at Data Structures," *Communications of the ACM,* 23:4 (Apr. 1980), 229-39.

Weinberg, G., *The Psychology of Computer Programming.* New York, NY: Van Nostrand, 1971.

Williams, J., "Algorithm 232 (Heapsort)," *Communications of the ACM,* 7:6 (June 1964), 347-48.

Wirth, N., "Program Development by Stepwise Refinement," *Communications of the ACM,* 14:4 (Apr. 1971), 221-27.

Wirth, N., *Algorithms + Data Structures = Programs.* Englewood Cliffs, NJ: Prentice-Hall, 1976.

Wood, D., "The Towers of Brahma and Hanoi Revisited," *Journal of Recreational Mathematics,* 14 (1981-2), 17-24.

Yourdon, E., *Techniques of Program Structure and Design.* Englewood Cliffs, NJ: Prentice-Hall, 1975.

INDEX